T0220106

# Mapping the Enterprise

## Modeling the Enterprise as Services with Enterprise Canvas

Tom Graves

Apress®

*Mapping the Enterprise: Modeling the Enterprise as Services with Enterprise Canvas*

Tom Graves
Sailors Gully, VIC, Australia

ISBN-13 (pbk): 978-1-4842-9835-0    ISBN-13 (electronic): 978-1-4842-9836-7
https://doi.org/10.1007/978-1-4842-9836-7

## Copyright © 2023 by Tom Graves

Managing Director, Apress Media LLC: Welmoed Spahr
Acquisitions Editor: Aditee Mirashi
Development Editor: James Markham
Coordinating Editor: Aditee Mirashi

Cover designed by eStudioCalamar

Cover image by Freepik (https://www.freepik.com)

Distributed to the book trade worldwide by Apress Media, LLC, 1 New York Plaza, New York, NY 10004, U.S.A. Phone 1-800-SPRINGER, fax (201) 348-4505, e-mail orders-ny@springer-sbm.com, or visit www.springeronline.com. Apress Media, LLC is a California LLC and the sole member (owner) is Springer Science + Business Media Finance Inc (SSBM Finance Inc). SSBM Finance Inc is a **Delaware** corporation.

For information on translations, please e-mail booktranslations@springernature.com; for reprint, paperback, or audio rights, please e-mail bookpermissions@springernature.com.

Apress titles may be purchased in bulk for academic, corporate, or promotional use. eBook versions and licenses are also available for most titles. For more information, reference our Print and eBook Bulk Sales web page at http://www.apress.com/bulk-sales.

Any source code or other supplementary material referenced by the author in this book is available to readers on GitHub (https://github.com/Apress). For more detailed information, please visit https://www.apress.com/gp/services/source-code.

Paper in this product is recyclable

# Table of Contents

# About the Author

**Tom Graves** has been an independent consultant for more than four decades, in systems development, business transformation, enterprise architecture and knowledge management. His clients in Europe, Australasia and the Americas cover a broad range of industries including small-business, banking, utilities, manufacturing, logistics, engineering, media, telecoms, research, defense and government. He has a special interest in whole-enterprise architectures for non-profit, social, government and commercial enterprises.

# About the Technical Reviewer

**Slade Beard** is an ICT Architect and Program Manager with extensive experience in the design and implementation of ICT infrastructure environments, including integration with large construction projects. He has knowledge and experience in major IT infrastructure rollouts in the Defense, National Security, Emergency Services, Health and Secure Systems environments.

He has proven experience in supporting the effective design, implementation and commissioning of complex ICT systems in high-risk environments where considerations such as avoiding disruption of existing operations are crucial to project success. In addition, as result of his extensive construction design and build experience, he is able to frame and articulate the integration of complex ICT systems within the service elements of facility build considerations and act as an effective advocate for ICT requirements within construction teams.

# Acknowledgments

Amongst others, the following people kindly provided comments and feedback on themes in the various drafts of this book: Jose Antonio Alvarez (MX), Sally Bean (GB), Shawn Callahan (AU), Adrian Campbell (GB), Pat Ferdinandi (US), Ian Glossop (GB), Nigel Green (GB), Anders Jensen (DK), Cynthia Kurtz (US), Nick Malik (US), Alex Matthews (GB), Alex Osterwalder (CH), Kim Parker (AU), Ron Segal (NZ), Kevin Smith (GB), Michael Smith (GT), Peter Tseglakof (AU), Peter Ward (GB), John Wu (US), Alex Yakovlev (GB).

Please note that, to preserve commercial and personal confidentiality, the stories and examples in this book will usually have been adapted, combined and in part fictionalized from experiences in a variety of contexts, and do not and are not intended to represent any specific individual or organization.

Registered trademarks such as Zachman, TOGAF, ITIL, Business Model Canvas etc are acknowledged as the intellectual property of the respective owners.

# Introduction

How can we describe the enterprise? More specifically, how do we describe what happens there, how, when, where, why, by whom, with what?

For architects and others tasked with creating conversations and connections across the enterprise, these are not trivial questions: they strike right to the core of the work that we do. The usual answer is 'models' – data-sets, drawings, diagrams – that illustrate specific aspects of the respective issues. But the catch is that there are so many different model-types in use in enterprise-architectures and elsewhere, all different, all applying at different levels, all applying only to specific subsets of the context, and all with weak connection at best to any other type of model. It's a huge problem – though one that's not easy to see until we try to link everything together across the whole of the enterprise.

Hence the Enterprise Canvas: a new model-template and checklist for service-design that can be used to describe just about anything in any part and at any level of the enterprise, and that also acts as a consistent frame for all the other types of models that we need in our architectures.

The Canvas can take several different forms, such in the example shown in Figure I-1, but the same basic frame provides a consistent anchor in how to view everything else in the enterprise. It doesn't really *replace* any other model: but within that frame, all those other models start to work together, and start to make practical sense.

That's the role of the Enterprise Canvas: not "one model to rule them all", perhaps, but "one model to bind them". Consistency at last; consistency that makes sense; that's the aim here. Interested?

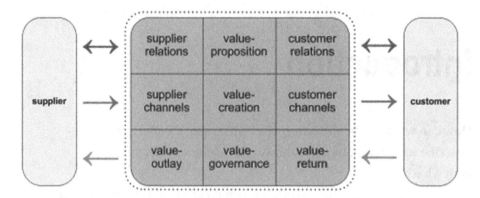

***Figure 1.*** *Enterprise Canvas: a basic example*

# Who should read this book?

The book is intended for enterprise architects, business-architects, IT-architects, process-designers, service-designers and others who deal with the practical implications of whole-of-enterprise issues.

It should also be useful for strategists and service-managers, and for anyone else who works with other enterprise-wide themes such as supply-chains, value-webs, quality, security, knowledge-sharing, sustainability, business ethics and social responsibility, or health, safety and environment.

# What's in this book?

The text is divided into two main sections:

- a step-by-step introduction to each of the components in the Enterprise Canvas model, and their function and use in modelling the overall enterprise

- a variety of patterns, practical examples and business usages for the model and its associated tools and techniques

Each chapter builds on the previous descriptions, introduces another core concept or component for Enterprise Canvas, and provides a set of ideas and methods to apply straight away in your day-to-day work. Although there's a fair amount of theory behind the Canvas, the emphasis is always on *practice* – something that you can *use* – so each chapter includes examples and stories to place the ideas into a real-life context. Most chapters also include an Into Practice section, with sets of questions to help you apply the material within your own context.

There's also a set of appendices at the end of the book, providing a visual-summary, additional notes on converting to and from the popular Business Model Canvas, notes on using the Enterprise Canvas in computer-based modelling-tools and as a service-viability checklist, and pointers to other sources for further information.

But what *is* the Enterprise Canvas, anyway? Let's start with a brief overview.

# CHAPTER 1

# What Is the Enterprise Canvas?

The Enterprise Canvas is a quick, easy way to describe just about anything in an enterprise. It's a visual checklist that's simple enough to scribble on the back of a napkin, yet it can also carry enough detail to link in with formal modeling tools for project management, system design, strategy simulation, and the rest.

The role of Enterprise Canvas is that it's a way to support conversations about ensuring that everything connects together properly across the whole enterprise. And the reason we'd want to do that would be to support better *effectiveness* across the enterprise, because *things work better when they work together, on purpose.*

The way we do that with Enterprise Canvas is to describe everything in the enterprise in terms of *services* – that everything in the enterprise either is, represents, or implies a service. We'll explore that idea in more detail in Chapter 2, "The Nature of Service."

A key part of the value of Enterprise Canvas is that it's *context neutral*: it works the same way with every type of content or context, at every scope and scale, for every level of the organization from big-picture strategy to frontline operations, and with every stage of the change process from initial idea to design, implementation, and deployment. It also works with every type of enterprise and organization and the connections to market and more. We'll go into more detail on that in Chapter 3, "Service Context and Market."

© Tom Graves 2023
T. Graves, *Mapping the Enterprise*, https://doi.org/10.1007/978-1-4842-9836-7_1

The worked example we'll use throughout this book is a fictitious shoe manufacturer and retailer called Las Zapaterias de México – usually abbreviated to ZapaMex. For our purposes here, we assume that they are currently selling only to physical shoe-shops in the local market, but they also want to start selling online and to expand out elsewhere into Latin America over the next few years.

---

A colleague and I invented the imaginary ZapaMex company a few years ago while we were working together on enterprise-scale issues for several banks in Guatemala and Mexico. It was hard to get them to focus on anything other than their IT and information flows, so we realized we needed a nonbank example to illustrate some of the broader aspects of services, particularly those about people and about physical equipment and the like. We'll see more on that later on in this book, particularly in Chapter 6, "Service Actors and Other Entities"; Chapter 7, "Service Roles and Relationships"; Chapter 9, "Service Flows"; and Chapter 13, "Service Content."

---

As mentioned above, we can use Enterprise Canvas in either a back-of-the-napkin sketch format or in a more formal style for use in Powerpoint or modeling tools. We'll do a quick overview of both of those styles here. But it's probably easier to understand what's going on in services, and how the Canvas represents that, if we start first with the sketch format.

# On the Back of a Napkin

Imagine that you're in a cafe with some colleagues, or in a breakout room at the office, and you want to describe some service that you need to analyze or to build. You have a notepad on the cafe table or a whiteboard in front of you. Pen in hand, you're about to start drawing, and the thought comes to you: What *is* a service? How do services *really* work? What do they actually *do*? What's the relationship between services and products – and in what ways are they different, anyway? So let's look at how we can describe all of this in sketch format with the Enterprise Canvas – though there are a couple of things that we need to explore first before we get there.

To start, we go all the way back to absolute first principles for services and service design. The service always exists in the context of a shared enterprise, and we assert that there's always one key idea that in effect *defines* that enterprise. Everything that happens in the enterprise revolves around this one overarching idea or "*vision*," which in turn tells us the *values* that guide that shared enterprise. (We'll see more on this in Chapter 2, "The Nature of Service," and explore how to define an enterprise vision in Chapter 4, "Service Vision and Values.") For example, everyone involved in the shared enterprise that ZapaMex belongs to will connect in their own way with an enterprise vision of "make your feet healthy and happy." This single idea defines what that enterprise *is*: everything else is some means to help make that vision happen and share it among the players in the enterprise.

Everything that happens in the enterprise is driven in some way by the tension between what we currently have – the "realized ends" – and what we strive toward, the "desired ends," represented by the vision. As shown in Figure 1-1, we show that tension as a vertical arrow between what we have now and the vision that we reach toward.

**Figure 1-1.** *Serving the enterprise vision*

In turn, everything in the enterprise is a *service* that contributes toward that vision. (Or it should do – hence, the need for conversations, to find out what's going on at each point and what we could do to make it more effective at contributing toward the vision.)

The purpose of a service is that it serves something: it adds value. We bring in something from elsewhere in the shared enterprise; we create or add value; and we pass it on to some other player in the enterprise, often in the form of a product. (Products exist only between services and connect services together: we'll see more on this in Chapter 9, "Service Flows.")

This flow of value around the enterprise is a supply chain, a value chain, and a value web: the name we use doesn't matter that much, but what does matter is this flow of value. In our back-of-the-napkin sketch, as shown in Figure 1-2, we can show this flow as a horizontal line, connecting to the vision via the service.

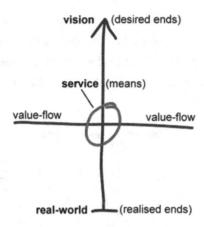

**Figure 1-2.** *Each service connects the value web to the vision*

That gives us the simplest version of the Enterprise Canvas, with the service as a *means* to *add value* to the overall enterprise, at an intersection of *value* and *values*. That simple sketch would be enough to identify what the service is and does and guide an initial conversation with service stakeholders.

For example, we might ask about what's moving around in this value web, or about who else is involved in the value flow. The questions we could ask at this stage might include:

- Who are the *suppliers* for this service – its *providers*? What services do they provide, and in what form?

- Who are the *customers* for this service – its *clients*? What services do they consume, and in what form?

- What connection do those suppliers and customers each have with the desired ends – the vision – for this overall service?

- And what relationships does this service have with each of its suppliers and customers?

5

Given the answers to questions such as these, we might add to the sketch diagram a supplier-side and a customer-side, to document what comes in, what goes out, what is shared with whom, and the reasons and choices for that flow of value. The sketch would then look something like that shown in Figure 1-3.

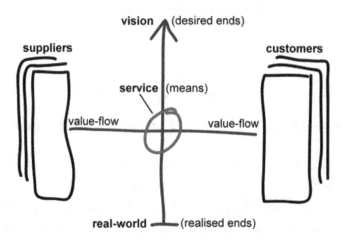

***Figure 1-3.*** *Service, suppliers, and customers*

As we'll see later, it's useful to split each flow into and out of our services into three distinct phases: what happens *before*, *during*, and *after* the main transactions of a service. As shown in Figure 1-4, this gives us a simple pattern for our sketch diagram that can help us gather more detail about the service flows.

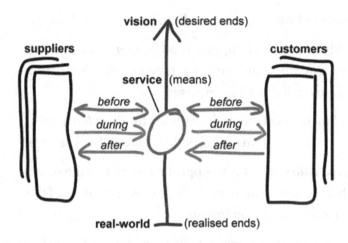

**Figure 1-4.** *Flows before, during, and after transactions*

We might ask our stakeholders some further questions to elicit a bit more detail about the structure and operation of the service itself. For this, we would expand our view of the service to add another dimension: the core of the service itself and the parts that face either toward suppliers or toward customers. As shown in Figure 1-5, this gives us a kind of three-by-three pattern, with each of the cells representing a smaller service that serves the respective needs and flows for that part of the overall service.

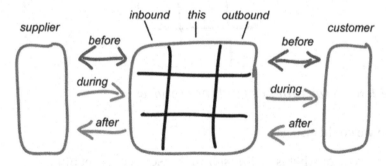

**Figure 1-5.** *Service, suppliers, customers, and flows*

We could ask further questions about what guides this service:

- Who or what will support *coordination* of this service with others in the same organization, or value web, or the overall shared enterprise?

- Who or what takes responsibility for *direction* of the service and for mapping out the future of this service?

- And who or what will support *validation* of the service, help to keep it on track to the vision and values of the broader shared enterprise?

As shown in Figure 1-6, we can add placeholders for each of these on our sketch diagram, where we can link our stakeholders' answers for the service that's currently in focus on the Canvas.

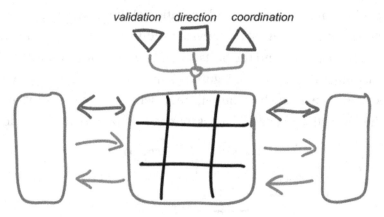

***Figure 1-6.*** *Service and its guidance services*

And we could also ask:

- Who or what is an *investor* in this service, to get things started?

- Who or what extracts value from the overall flow, as a *beneficiary* of the service, rather than a customer?

Again, as shown in Figure 1-7, we can add placeholders on our sketch diagram for the answers to those questions.

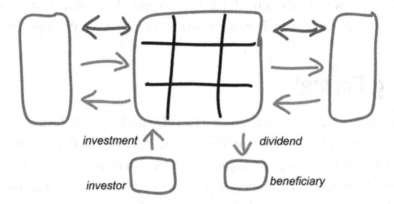

***Figure 1-7.*** *Service investors and beneficiaries*

We can mix-and-match between all these various views and add-ons as we need. The same Canvas – and the same service in focus – could be shown as anything from a simple cross, as we saw back in Figure 1-2, to an all-the-extras "kitchen sink" view as shown in Figure 1-8, depending on the amount of detail that we need in our back-of-the-napkin scrawl.

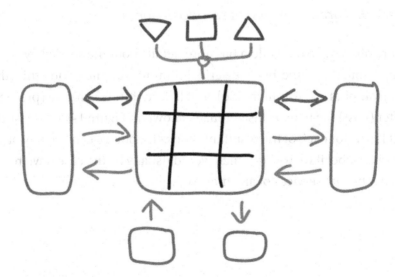

***Figure 1-8.*** *"Kitchen sink" back-of-the-napkin Canvas (service)*

And we then can link in any other models we might want, too: for example, that might include a Zachman matrix or Porter Five Forces or a SWOT or a BPMN process model. The Canvas provides a frame that can link them all together and help them to make more sense as a unified whole.

# Going Formal

Going beyond the sketch diagram, we can also make it more formal – the kind of boxes-and-lines diagram that we would show on a Powerpoint slide rather than the back of a napkin. As shown in Figure 1-9, the simplest version is a depiction of the service on its own, as a means to act on the value flow in alignment with the desired aims of the overall enterprise.

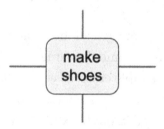

*Figure 1-9. Formal version: the service in focus*

More often, we would add a bit more detail about the service by splitting it into that three-by-three grid: inbound (supplier-side); this (this service); outbound (customer-side); and before (future), during (present), and after (past) the main transaction. As shown in Figure 1-10, there are default labels for each of the resultant nine cells, but we can use any other appropriate label if we wish – which would usually be the case if we're modeling the real services of an enterprise.

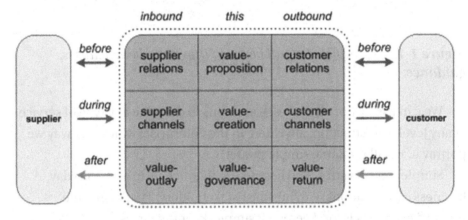

**Figure 1-10.** *Formal version: standard nine-cell grid*

As with that back-of-the-napkin sketch, we might add further detail about other services that connect with this service and about the flows that make up the value web between all these services, as shown in Figure 1-11.

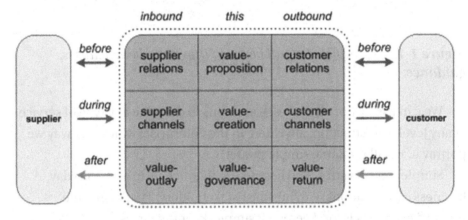

**Figure 1-11.** *Formal version: supplier, customer, and value web*

And as shown in Figure 1-12, we might also want to add the investors and beneficiaries, or links to the various guidance services.

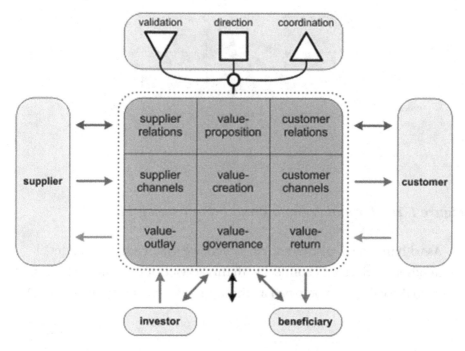

**Figure 1-12.** *Complete formal version: investors, beneficiaries, guidance*

We can use any or all of these variations to describe any type of service, at any level of abstraction, anywhere in the enterprise: whichever way we portray it, it's all the same simple model.

Simple, yet powerful. And easy to use in practice, in real everyday business conversations with business stakeholders. That's what the Enterprise Canvas is for: keeping it simple, keeping it real.

# Into Practice

Imagine that you're an enterprise architect, a service designer, or in a similar role, tasked with leading a major business transformation. You need your senior stakeholders to understand that this transformation must connect everything together across the whole enterprise and that you and they will need a consistent way to describe this, to get everyone on board. Use the ideas in this chapter and the following questions to help you guide that conversation:

- What models and model types do you use in your work on service design and the like? To what domains and levels of abstraction does each of those models apply?

- How and why do you link the various models together? If you can't link the models together, what difficulties does this present in practice?

- Do you develop or work with business models? If so, in what ways do you need to extend that model to broaden its scope, or to link it to other types of models? How do you implement a business model in practice?

## Summary

In this chapter we've seen a brief overview of the Enterprise Canvas model, both in its sketch-diagram form and in the more formal structure that would be used in presentations and modeling tools.

In the next chapter, we'll explore more detail about the core ideas behind the Enterprise Canvas model and how it can be used to describe almost everything that happens in an enterprise.

# CHAPTER 2

# The Nature of Service

Within any organization, we need to keep track of how everything connects with everything else, all the way up to the big-picture view, all the way down to everyday process and practice, and all the way across every aspect of the enterprise, end-to-end through all of the different silos and business domains. One picture of the enterprise, as a whole, in all of its richness, all of its complexity, all of its detail, all of it changing dynamically over time – yet also all of it easy for anyone to understand.

That's the requirement: yet up until now, it's often seemed an impossible challenge. There's been no straightforward means to cover the whole of that range, in any consistent way, or even at all; at one end of that spectrum, we can lose our way in the clouds, while at the other end there's a real danger of drowning in all of the detail. Each type of model or method will be optimized to describe just one part of the puzzle, so we end up trying to translate from one model to another, jumping back and forth from abstract to concrete – and there's a lot that can get lost in the translation. There's an almost desperate need for consistency here.

Yet there *is* one way to make it all work: assert that **everything is a service**, then build the models outward from there. And that's where the Enterprise Canvas comes into the story. As we'll see later, there's a lot of richness and nuances to Enterprise Canvas, which is why and how we *can* use it to model almost everything in the enterprise. Yet at its core, it's actually very simple – and its real power comes from that simplicity, in how it links together a handful of key ideas:

© Tom Graves 2023
T. Graves, *Mapping the Enterprise*, https://doi.org/10.1007/978-1-4842-9836-7_2

- The enterprise exists to create and share value – in whatever way "value" may be defined in that enterprise.

- An enterprise is a *dynamic* structure – a "value network" – in which value is continually created, transformed, and transferred in a continuous process of flow and change.

- Everything in the enterprise is or delivers a service of some kind that adds value to the enterprise, and that passes value on to other services in the overall enterprise.

- The enterprise consists of services that connect with and support each other in creating value for that enterprise.

For Enterprise Canvas, **everything is a service**, each helping to create value as it flows around the overall enterprise. Products sit *between* services, are inputs and outputs for services; in some cases they're also "proto-services," perhaps, in that they provide people with part of the means to self-deliver a desired service via the use of that product. Each of the actors in the enterprise – as suppliers, customers, competitors, regulators, or whatever other roles – provides those services to the overall enterprise. Even the enterprise itself is a service: it exists to serve a vision of some kind, in accordance with some set of values, even if only implied and unacknowledged. So the Enterprise Canvas is a generic map to describe any service, anywhere in the enterprise, together with its interdependencies and flows.

To give a bit more detail, to make this more usable in practice, we can assert the following:

- Everything exists within one infinite ecosystem, which we might label "the universe" or "the everything."

- For practical reasons, and for sanity's sake, we'll usually restrict our view to a much smaller subset of that "the everything." We can choose whatever view we like – an infinite array of possible sets, all overlapping and enclosing and intersecting with each other – though we do always need to remember that whatever view we choose, it will always be some part of and connected to that overall "the everything."

- One useful option, especially for organizations, is to select the subset that describes the part of that "the everything" within which the organization operates – the organization's *context*. This is what we call the "enterprise," or "shared enterprise," where the enterprise itself is a kind of ecosystem bounded by a shared purpose, and must always be broader in scope than the organization itself. (We'll see more on that in Chapter 3, "Service Context and Market.") As we saw in the previous chapter, an enterprise coalesces around a single idea or descriptor, usually referred to as the "vision" for the enterprise.

- Within that enterprise, we assert that *every entity either is, represents, or implies a service.* Every entity delivers services, provides services, consumes other services, and passes products between services. The ecosystem – the business ecosystem, in this case – is made viable by this constant interchange between services.

- This interchange occurs at every level. Everything is a service, from whole organizations to the faucet in the bathroom or a single line of program code.

*Everything* in the enterprise is a service, provides a service, implies a service, can be described in terms of services and flows between services; there are no apparent exceptions to this. And **every service serves** – it serves something else, someone else; it serves the unifying "vision" that defines the extended enterprise.

We also note that, over the ecosystem as a whole, **all relations are symmetrical**. Everything is a service; hence, everything is also a "supplier" to at least one other service, and a "customer" of at least one or more others – otherwise, the service literally has no valid purpose within the enterprise as a whole. Within the overall flows of value in the enterprise, **everyone is both "supplier" and "customer"**: those types of roles arise from the relationships between the players rather than from the enterprise itself, and increasingly – such as in Agile-development techniques and crowdsourcing – the old boundaries between these roles will often become blurred. Overall, everything needs to balance out somehow, yet also keep creating value for every player. If some of the players set out to "win" by trying to make everyone else lose, eventually the enterprise as a whole will die – in which case *everyone* loses.

Another key theme is about **layers of abstraction**. At the top-most layer, there is only the enterprise itself, and the vision and values that define it; at the lowest layer, there are the myriad of activities and details where the aims of the enterprise come into contact with the real world. Between those two extremes are other distinct layers: strategy, tactics, action plans, and so on. The same patterns of services and relationships will recur at each layer – hence, we can use those patterns to describe how strategies and tactics will be put into practice, and how ideas and experiences from the real world can influence those tactics and strategies.

There's a strong underlying **emphasis on effectiveness**: finding the right dynamic balance between efficiency, reliability, human factors, the overall business purpose, and the processes that link all of these together.

Finally, some other key points that we'll also need to consider would include:

- Service relationships and structures are often fractal and recursive, with services clustered together to provide broader or more abstract services.

- Affordances – "unexpected services" – arise from the ways in which the capabilities that underpin services may be reused in or for other services.

- A platform is a cluster of related services used as a base for affordance of other services

- What services act on, and deliver, may take many forms, including physical "things," virtual information, relational links between people, or an aspirational sense of meaning or purpose.

- To make sense of a service, we also need to explore themes such as service contract, service policy, service level, service guarantee, service status, and service completeness.

- Without adequate verification of service completeness, a service may fail or deliver a "disservice" or "anti-service," destroying value rather than creating value.

We'll see more on all of these themes as we explore the Enterprise Canvas in depth.

# A Matter of Metaphor

Two specific metaphors will be of real value here. The first is that of **enterprise as organism**, rather than enterprise as machine.

For the past century and more, the dominant organizational metaphor, built upon notions of "scientific management," or "Taylorism," has been that of "organization as machine" – a machine for command and control, a predictable machine for making money, and so on. This machine is focused on making product: and being a machine, it has no concept of service as such.

An enterprise, though, is a *social* construct: it's bounded by *human* values and shared commitments. This goes all the way back to the 18th-century economist Adam Smith, who described enterprise as "a bold endeavor; the animal spirits of the entrepreneur" – emotions and feelings that are far beyond the capability of any present-day machine. And while it's hard to get machines to emulate real people, it's relatively simple to force people to emulate machines. Yet so many subtle and maybe essential nuances can be lost in that translation that "command and control" is little more than an illusion – and one that can be very dangerous indeed to the overall enterprise.

Hence, the value of viewing the enterprise as an *organism*, a living entity in its own right. Where a machine is made up of engineered *components*, a living system consists of *services*, each interweaving and interacting with all the other services in the overall ecosystem.

An enterprise is defined by shared commitment to a shared vision. The purpose of a machine is always *extrinsic*, defined from outside of itself; but for a human enterprise, its purpose is *intrinsic*, an essential part of its definition of itself. Since the enterprise is a *social* structure rather than a machine, this warns us that we can't actually "engineer" an enterprise: to get it to work to its greatest effectiveness, we have to start with purpose and people and build outward from there.

In line with that metaphor of enterprise-as-organism, the core idea behind Enterprise Canvas is that everything can be described in terms of services. So while we can perhaps interpret each element and service in an Enterprise Canvas model as a kind of component – and this certainly does make more sense as we get closer to real-world action – we do need to take care not to fall back into the Taylorist trap of thinking of it only as a machine. No matter how machine-like something may seem, it's still delivering a *service* within a larger "life-like" ecosystem.

The second metaphor is that of **model as holograph**, rather than model-as-photograph.

A *photograph* depicts a scene from a single viewpoint and is usually quite easy to decipher. If we cut up a photograph, we'll have a pile of tiny jigsaw-puzzle pieces, each in full detail, yet often with nothing to link those pieces together.

A *holograph*, as its name suggests, depicts a scene from every possible viewpoint, all at once. If we cut up a holograph, each of those fragments still depicts the *whole* scene, though in less detail than the complete holograph.

Most existing model types in business contexts are more like the photograph: they depict one part of the context from a single point of view. That's often essential at the detail level; but if that's all we have, it's often very hard to link them all together. The usual solution is to try to build some kind of frame that describes "life, the universe, everything," all of it in "excruciating detail" (to quote John Zachman). But that's often hopelessly impractical, because it could literally take forever – and in the meantime the world will have moved on anyway, so the whole approach is doomed to failure even before it starts.

With the Enterprise Canvas, though, each view or module is more like a fragment of a holograph. Each view carries its own small collection of detail, just like any other conventional model: but that model is *always* linked to everything else, is always part of a greater whole, in an *identifiable* way.

In practice, the Canvas is sometimes more of a hybrid, combining the advantages of both metaphors – photograph *and* holograph, detail *and* scope – in ways that still make simple, straightforward, practical sense. Yet when we look at the amount of detail that can be carried in a single Enterprise Canvas model, it's sometimes easy to forget that it *is* still connected to everything else; so it's useful to remember that holograph metaphor, and always keep it in mind while we work.

# Into Practice

For your business-transformation project, you now need your senior stakeholders to understand and agree on using an "everything is a service" approach, as a way to keep the focus always on overall effectiveness. You also want them to understand the importance of using the right metaphors to describe any change. Use the ideas in this chapter and the following questions to help you guide that conversation.

# On Services

- If everything in the enterprise is a service, what or whom does each service serve? How would you model those relationships of service?

- If everything in the enterprise is a service, how does that change your perception of the enterprise itself? Whom does the enterprise serve, and why, and how?

- In what other ways could you describe the functioning of the whole enterprise? How does each of these views change your perception of the enterprise and how it works?

- In your architecture, how do you describe the different layers of abstraction – from vision to strategy to tactics to operations, and back again? How do you describe and govern the various transitions between these layers of abstraction? How do you depict the same nominal service at different layers of abstraction?

# On Metaphor

- In what ways do you describe the enterprise as a machine? How is this reflected in everyday language, such as "operations," "functions," "business units," and the like? What impact does this metaphor have on the operation of the enterprise as a whole?

- In what ways do you describe the enterprise as some kind of living organism? How is this reflected in everyday language, such as "culture," "health," "taking the pulse," or even the term "corporation"? What impact does this metaphor have on the operation of the enterprise as a whole?

- What other metaphors do you use to describe the enterprise? How are these reflected in everyday language, such as "getting a green light" (a roads metaphor), "taking a bet" (finance as gambling), or "cooking up a new project"? What impacts do these metaphors have on the operation of the enterprise as a whole?

# Summary

In this chapter, we introduced the core ideas beneath the Enterprise Canvas, and in particular, the notion that everything in the enterprise can be described as a service – an entity that creates and delivers value in terms of a desired aim or "vision" that is shared across the entire extended enterprise.

In the next chapter, we'll explore more about how to identify the context for a service and how the organization's business models and more must connect with that broader context.

# CHAPTER 3

# Service Context and Market

No service exists in isolation: it always exists within a context or "ecosystem" of other services with which it interacts.

This occurs at every level, with every service, from an operations-layer web service or the services of a customer-service desk or an entire organization. It's simplest, though, to describe this first at the whole-organization level.

To make sense of the relationships between services within the overall context, we need a clear distinction between "organization" and "enterprise." Although these two elements can coincide, and many people often seem to think they're one and the same, for enterprise architecture and the like we do need to treat them as separate. For our purposes here, an organization is an entity that delivers services within an enterprise.

An **organization** is bounded by rules, roles, and responsibilities. There's an explicit boundary of protocol and contract, an explicit boundary of responsibility for revenue, taxes, legal liability, and so on. (In this sense, an individual person is an organization of one.) Boundaries are explicit and "logical," and much of the structure and purpose and identity of the organization revolves around command and control.

© Tom Graves 2023
T. Graves, *Mapping the Enterprise*, https://doi.org/10.1007/978-1-4842-9836-7_3

An **enterprise** is bounded by vision, values and (shared) commitment. The "vision" for an enterprise identifies its emotional drivers, "that which gets me out of bed in the morning." (An individual is technically an intersection point of an almost infinite number of enterprises.) Boundaries are often blurry and "non-rational"; and much of the structure and identity and purpose of the enterprise revolves around engagement and trust.

Or to put it in its simplest terms

- The enterprise *is*; the organization *does*.

- The enterprise provides *motivation*; the organization provides *action*.

The boundaries of organization and enterprise *may* sometimes coincide – hence, the notion of the organization as "the enterprise." But in effect that's only a special case, and a potentially dangerous one at that, because it can lead us into a kind of narcissistic self-centrism or a combative "us versus them" relationship with the business ecosystem. (Mutual interlocking responsibilities are important, too, not just within an organization, but also across the shared enterprise – though we'll see more on that later in Chapter 13, "Service Content.")

The enterprise creates the connections that the organization needs between itself and its ecosystem: in enterprise architectures, we'll usually define an architecture *for* an organization, but *about* an appropriate enterprise in relation to that organization. The same applies to when we assess any other kind of service: our aim is to describe the service (the "organization"), but we must always do so in context of its ecosystem (the "enterprise").

For most practical purposes, the enterprise that we need in scope should be at least two to three steps larger than the boundaries of the organization in scope: first the suppliers and customers in its immediate transaction space; then its broader market; and the overall shared enterprise beyond. For example, if we view an IT-service unit as "the organization" in its own right, its immediate transaction space would be other business units within the parent company, but it needs to be aware of potential impacts on the company's suppliers and customers (its broader "market") and the regulators and the like (the wider ecosystem and "shared enterprise" for the company as a whole).

## Service and Market

To make sense of this, we would typically model the service's market and ecosystem in a series of stages. As shown in Figure 3-1, one place to start is with the common self-referential notion of the service itself as both "the organization" *and* its own enterprise, where all meaning and value is defined in terms of the organization itself – as in the old railway joke that "the trains would run perfectly on time if it wasn't for the passengers!"

***Figure 3-1.*** *The organization as enterprise*

A disturbing number of organizational units and even of whole organizations do tend to think this way – that the world not only revolves around them but that it begins and ends with them alone, that there is nothing of any value beyond them. A few moments of thought, though, would indicate that we can't make sense of services this way: a service has to serve *something*. So the next step outward is the basic business model: as shown in Figure 3-2, we receive goods or services from a supplier, add some form of value, and deliver the amended goods or services to a customer. There's a two-way flow of value here – typically goods and services one way, and some form of payment or "value return" the other way.

**Figure 3-2.**  *The basic business model as enterprise*

There's not much opportunity for change and enhancement in that view, though, and we have no way to see what might affect our enterprise from outside, impacting on our direct suppliers and customers. One option here, as shown in Figure 3-3, is to expand our view of the supply chain – such as in the SCOR (Supply-Chain Operations Reference) standard, which extends from supplier's supplier to customer's customer.

**Figure 3-3.**  *The supply chain as enterprise*

This gives us a good tactical view of our market, but not a good strategic one, because there's more to a market than just our own supply chain. Thinking strategically, we also need to be aware of all the prospective customers and suppliers, our competitors and other market players, industry standards bodies, analysts, government regulators, and many more besides, as we can see in Figure 3-4.

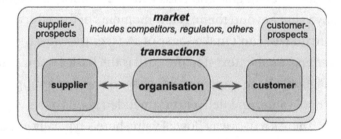

**Figure 3-4.**  *The market as enterprise*

This would seem to make sense as long as we only think in terms of the most visible transactions of goods and services. Yet as shown in Figure 3-5, there's much more to an overall enterprise than that, because there are many people who may not engage in direct exchange of products or services with us, but who are still affected by what we do – and who can affect us in return, too.

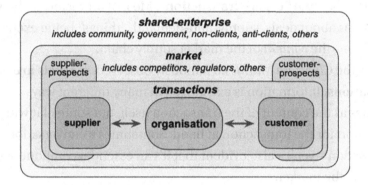

*Figure 3-5.*  *The shared story as enterprise*

This shared enterprise includes government in the broader sense – such as general taxes, rather than industry regulation.

It includes the families of our employees, the towns and municipalities where they live, the broader economic and social communities in which we operate and that determine our social "license to operate," as business writer Charles Handy puts it.

It includes non-clients – people who are not and will probably never be customers of ours, such as people who live in a different country than the one we serve.

And it also includes our anti-clients, people who don't trade with us in the normal sense but who don't like us or what we do – of whom we now need to be much more aware, because social media and other new technologies provide them with much more leverage than they may have had in previous times.

The ways in which we interact with this enterprise ecosystem do differ from the simple exchanges of goods and services in our main market: but we ignore them at our peril, because they're the most common cause of "unexpected" business problems and even business failure. To make sense of this, we need to understand the real nature of the broader "market" of the enterprise.

It's true that **markets are transactions**. Most of the visible activity of the market is about deals, supply-and-demand, "things" being exchanged and paid for – the *content* of the market supply chain.

Yet as the *Cluetrain Manifesto* famously observed, **markets are conversations**. Information is exchanged in many different ways – sometimes as the content of the transaction itself, but some of it with little direct import for the transaction at hand. Sometimes a conversation is just a conversation – yet it's also evident that it's an essential component of the workings of the market.

And **markets are relationships** too. In every market, relationship has an enormous bearing on the way the market works – though that fact is perhaps more obvious in a street market than in the sanitized "market" of a seemingly soulless shopping mall.

Finally, **markets are purpose**. In effect, a market is *defined* by the shared purpose of its enterprise vision, the overall descriptor for its "common set of missions or goals."

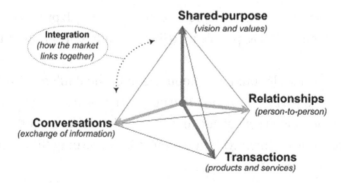

**Figure 3-6.** *Four-dimension tetradian of activity in the market*

When we summarize this, it's clear that, as shown in Figure 3-6, there are four distinct strands or dimensions here, each in rough correspondence to one of the four core categories of activities and assets:

- *Physical*: Alienable "things" – if I give it to you, I no longer have it.

- *Virtual*: Non-alienable items such as information – if I give it to you, I still have it.

- *Relational*: A person-to-person connection that cannot be directly exchanged with or transferred to anyone else.

- *Aspirational*: A personal commitment to an idea or belief such as a brand or enterprise vision – again, cannot be *directly* exchanged with or transferred to anyone else.

The usual view of the market is about transaction: the transfer of "exchangeable goods" via the *main channel* of the supply chain and, separately and in return, payment or its equivalent, through a *return channel*. And in its simplest form, profit is the difference between the *value return* that comes in from the return channel from the customer-side, compared to the *value outlay* that goes out on the return channel on the supplier-side. Once we also subtract the value outlay for internal costs of running the service itself, the result is the "bottom-line" net profit that is the near-obsessive focus of so many business folk.

Yet those transactions of "exchangeable items" are only one part of the overall activities of the market; and all of those transactions – and the resultant profit – occur only at the tail end of what we might call the *market cycle*, as shown in Figure 3-7.

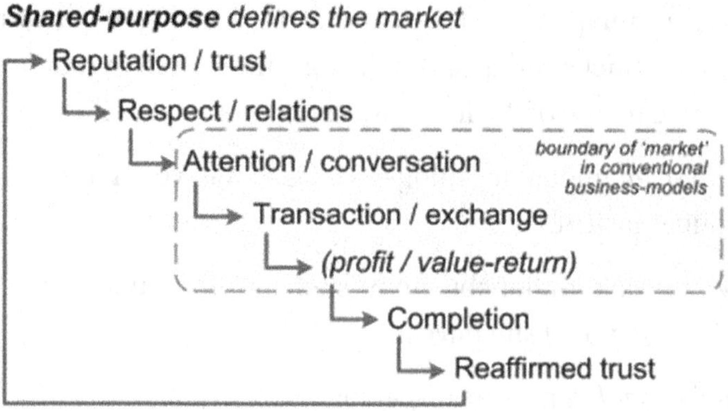

**Shared-purpose** *defines the market*

Reputation / trust

Respect / relations

Attention / conversation    *boundary of 'market' in conventional business-models*

Transaction / exchange

*(profit / value-return)*

Completion

Reaffirmed trust

***Figure 3-7.*** *The market cycle*

---

The *market cycle* is a whole-of-organization variant of the more generic *service cycle*. We'll see more on that in Chapter 9, "Service Flows."

---

The whole structure of the cycle is a complex feedback loop. For example, reputation – which itself is a kind of third-party precursor to trust – depends in part on whether the transactions are perceived overall as "fair exchange." Hence, *before* any transactions can take place, the relationships need to exist: and those relationships – and conversations too – are strongly linked to and dependent on the service's value proposition. Likewise, *after* the transaction, there not only needs to be the return-channel exchange that completes the "fair exchange" of the transaction, but that too also needs to link back to the value proposition and the relationships, tying everything together in terms of the various definitions of what "value" actually *is* within the overall enterprise.

All of this needs to be symmetrical, in that – in terms of the overall market – this service that is our current focus is both a customer of other services and a provider to other services; hence, all of the above will apply in similar ways on both "supply side" and "customer side." We need "supplier relationship management," for example, just as much as we need "customer relationship management."

And the value transfers and follow-up need to be in terms of *all* forms of "value" defined by the overall enterprise – and *not* measured solely in monetary terms, for example, no matter what the shareholders may demand.

## Vision, Values, and the Enterprise

The actual core of an enterprise is its *vision*, which we'll explore more in the next chapter, "Service Vision and Values." The key point for here is that the vision is a stable, permanent, shared reference point for *all* players in the enterprise – including the organization for whom we're building an enterprise architecture.

---

By the way, note that there's an important distinction we need to note here, because there are two quite different meanings of the term "vision."

For our purposes with Enterprise Canvas, we use the meaning from the ISO-9000:2000 quality-system standard, with "vision" as an anchor for the overall quality system for the entire shared enterprise.

The other meaning, which we don't use here, is the one used in the Business Motivation Model standard, with "vision" as a description of some kind of goal or desired outcome.

Both meanings are valid in their own way, but it's very important not to mix them up, because doing so can cause a lot of confusion.

---

We can summarize all of this in terms of the structure "vision, role, mission, goal," as shown in Figure 3-8.

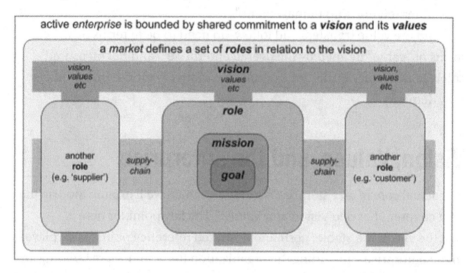

**Figure 3-8.** *Organization and enterprise: vision, role, mission, goal*

The vision expands out to a set of values, which determine what is value in the enterprise. The values are expressed in practice as principles, which – to use the ISO9000 quality-system terminology – act as the guides for policies, which in turn expand out to procedures, and thence to the fine detail of work instructions. Yet all of these will anchor back to the core vision and values, which determine what value *is* within the enterprise, what we mean when we use the term "value." And that specific combination of "value" and values is unique to each enterprise.

The enterprise vision and values are shared in some way by all of the players in that specific enterprise, which in turn is *why* they are players in that shared enterprise. As shown in Figure 3-9, each of those players presents some kind of "value proposition" that aligns with the vision, and that then links them with other players in the enterprise.

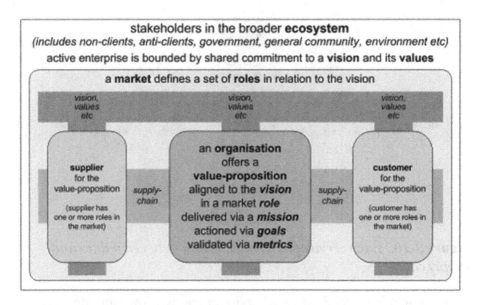

***Figure 3-9.*** *Every player presents a value proposition*

Later we'll explore more of this question of "what is an enterprise," but the key point here is that, as we saw in that rough sketch diagram back in Figure 1-2 in Chapter 1, "What Is the Enterprise Canvas?" the vision and values traverse *vertically* through each player – each organization – whereas the supply chain or value web provides a *horizontal* link between them.

Each player thus exists at an intersection in the value web of the overall shared enterprise, at a point where organization brings the vision and values of the enterprise in touch with its respective roles in the supply chain or value web. Every organization within the enterprise provides a service within that chosen enterprise. In turn, each organization can be subdivided into sub-organizations, and sub-sub-organizations, and so on, almost ad infinitum; and each of these "units" provides a *service* that delivers *value* to the overall enterprise.

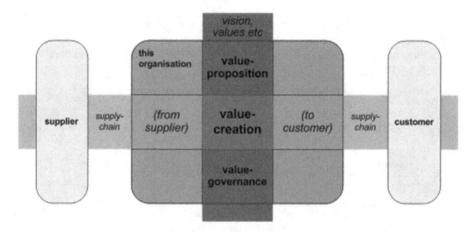

**Figure 3-10.**  *Each service sits at intersection between values and supply chain*

As shown in Figure 3-10, each service provides its own unique emphases on value:

- *Value proposition*: What the organization commits to be responsible for (what value it will add to the enterprise)

- *Value creation*: How, where, and by what means the organization will add value to the enterprise

- *Value governance*: How the organization will ensure that it can, has, and will continue to add value to the enterprise

This set of emphases also links back to those three distinct transaction stages that we saw earlier:

- What happens *before* transactions of "exchangeable items" – an emphasis on *relations*, which link most strongly to the service's *value proposition*

- What happens *during* (and with) transactions of "exchangeable items" – an emphasis on *actions*, which link most strongly to the service's *value creation*

- What happens *after* transactions of "exchangeable items" – an emphasis on *value transfers* (payments and receipts, etc., as "value outlay" and "value return") and other follow-up and overall integration, which link most strongly to the service's *value governance*

In a "service-oriented architecture" of this kind, *everything* is a service – so we'll see these value themes recur in *every* part and aspect of the organization and enterprise. This provides the basis for our Enterprise Canvas – a model we can use in a consistent way to model anything in the enterprise.

# Into Action

For your next session with those senior stakeholders for your business-transformation project, you'll want them to think about the world beyond the organization itself: Not just about customers, suppliers, and the more immediate realm of the market, but also the broader business context. Use the ideas in this chapter and the following questions to help you guide that conversation.

## Organization and Enterprise

- What to you is an organization? What to you is an enterprise? Are they the same? If not, how would you distinguish between them, and why? How would you explain these differences to others, and for what purposes? What are the practical implications of treating them as the same, or as separate?

- If we view any specific service as "the organization," what is its encompassing "enterprise"? How do you make sense of the ways in which all these different "enterprises" intersect?

# Service and Market

- What is the market and industry – or industries – in which your organization operates? What is it that defines the respective market and industry? What belongs in each? What does *not* belong in each, and why? What defines the boundaries?

- Who are your organization's market – the people provide services to your organization, or who use your organization's services?

- In what ways do you distinguish between roles such as "supplier" and "customer"? In what ways and for what reasons may the boundaries between these roles become blurred?

- What are the transactions in that market? What is exchanged, by whom, how, and why?

- What are the conversations that take place in that market? How do these conversations underpin the transactions? In what ways are they distinct from the "exchange" transactions – in effect, separate transactions in their own right?

- What are the relationships in the market? What creates those relationships? How are those relationships maintained? What actions, inactions, or events place those relationships at risk, or cause damage to those relationships? How, and why? And what can be done to mitigate those risks?

- What is the purpose of the market – its shared purpose? How is this purpose conveyed to and shared by every player in that market? What mechanisms exist to keep everyone on track to that purpose of the market? What happens if a player – whether by accident or intent – goes against that shared purpose?

- How do the relationships between players balance out across the enterprise? What happens when one player tries to take control of the enterprise for their own benefit alone, trying to force everyone else into a subservient relationship to them? How are those strains expressed in practice in the enterprise?

# Vision, Values, and the Enterprise

- What are the boundaries of the extended enterprise in which your organization operates? What vision and values *define* that shared enterprise? How does your organization connect with that vision and its values?

- Who are the various players in that extended enterprise? What vision or reason links together *all* the players in this enterprise?

- In what ways do the chosen visions of each player differ from each other? In what ways are they the same? What are the common threads that link the players together, and keep them apart?

- What transactions take place in the market and enterprise? What conversations? What relationships? For what overall purpose? And how and why and to whom are each of these of value?

- What value proposition does your organization present to the shared enterprise? What services underpin that value proposition?

- For each service that delivers anything, who or what manages that service? Who or what coordinates that service with other services? Who or what ensures compliance with enterprise vision and values? What links all of these subsidiary services together?

## Summary

In this chapter, we explored the context for a service within a shared enterprise or shared story that usually extends well beyond not just the respective organization, but even beyond the nominal market of that organization. The service's overall "business model" must encompass every aspect of that shared enterprise.

In the next chapter, we'll go into more detail on the vision and values for an enterprise and how to identify these and use them within our services and service designs.

# CHAPTER 4

# Service Vision and Values

The vision is the ultimate anchor for the entire enterprise – perhaps the one point on which everyone involved in that enterprise would agree. A functional vision for an enterprise is not centered around a single organization, and, crucially, it's *not* a marketing pitch – although marketing may well be derived from it later. Instead, it's a much simpler phrase or "mantra" that summarizes that enterprise's "reason to be." Good examples of valid visions include the Open Group's vision about supporting "*boundaryless information flow*," or the vision for the TED conferences, "*ideas worth spreading*." We'll see later here how we can derive a working vision for our ZapaMex worked example.

A vision is literally emotive: in a very real sense, it needs to be powerful enough to drive everyone involved out of bed in the morning, helping them to *want* to get to work for the enterprise. (This is also a key reason why "maximizing returns for our shareholders" rarely works as an enterprise vision.)

© Tom Graves 2023
T. Graves, *Mapping the Enterprise*, https://doi.org/10.1007/978-1-4842-9836-7_4

It's perhaps important to emphasize here that this vision is not imposed on the organization from outside by some unspecified "the enterprise." In reality, the organization decides which enterprise to "belong" to. The organization *chooses* a vision to work to, but when the choosing is done properly, it will instead feel like the enterprise vision has chosen *it*.

The vision is a statement of *the* core requirement – the "desired ends" – for all players in that overall enterprise. Everything else in the entire enterprise devolves from that: everything provides a service as a means that contributes toward realizing those desired ends represented by the vision of the shared enterprise. Figure 4-1 shows how this works, using the TED vision of "ideas worth spreading" as a basic example.

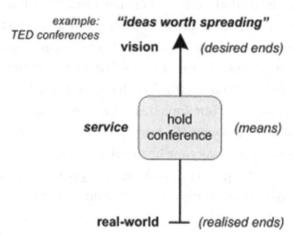

**Figure 4-1.** *Service as a means to realize desired ends*

Another way to describe this, as mentioned in the last chapter, is in terms of *vision, role, mission, goal,* and *outcomes*:

- The **vision** and associated values define the aims of the enterprise as shared by all its players – in essence, an *aspiration* or idea.

- The organization identifies its **role** within this enterprise, the part it chooses to play in achieving those desired ends – a role which also indicates points of connection with other players who choose other parts or roles within the overall enterprise.

- The organization's **mission** is the set of capabilities or services via which it will deliver its overall *value proposition* that will contribute toward achieving the vision of the enterprise.

- Each activity within the organization will typically contribute toward some bounded **goal** within the organization's mission and role.

- Every goal in the organization needs an identifiable **outcome** – the *realized ends* of the service – and that outcome needs *metrics* that link it back to the original vision of the enterprise, to indicate achievement in terms of those desired ends.

- The outcome's **metrics** help to verify the *effectiveness* of the role, mission, goals, and activities in relation to the overarching vision.

Figure 4-2 provides a visual summary of how all these elements link together, connecting back and forth between ends and means.

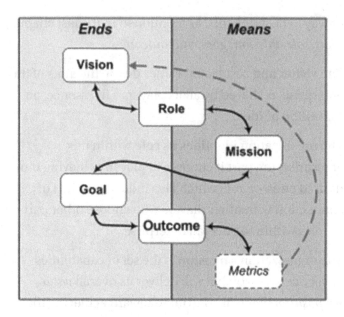

**Figure 4-2.** *Linking ends and means*

The anchor for the whole of this "stack" is the enterprise vision – hence, that is what we need to identify first.

# Identifying the Vision

In setting out to identify a usable enterprise vision, remember the two key criteria here: that it must be *emotive* and it must apply to *all* players in the shared enterprise, not just to the organization alone. Before we start, then, it's worthwhile to look at some real-world examples of "visions" that will *not* work for this purpose, and see *why* they will not work here:

- *Role as "vision"* (brewer example: "providers of brewed products to the Australia/New Zealand market"): This blurs the ends and the means, and tends to invite a "so what?" response.

- *Mission as "vision"* (retailer example: "achieve and maintain 20% of market share"): This is self-referential, leaving no room for customers, suppliers, and other players in the shared enterprise.

- *Goal as "vision"* (car-manufacturer example: "beat our biggest competitor!"): This kills all motivation stone-dead when the goal is achieved.

- *Desired future condition as "vision"* (IT-unit example: blueprint for "to-be" IT-systems estate): The "future state" is effectively mission-as-vision.

- *Success criterion as "vision"* (police-department example: "taking a lead in the security of this county"): This blurs the activities of the role and the metrics for the mission; the success criterion may also be spurious or unmeasurable – such as, in this example, no clear means for a legally mandated monopoly to measure "taking a lead."

- *Marketing slogan as "vision"* (bakery example: "to be the best bakers of the century!"): This combines every error above – role-based, self-referential, goal-driven, and success criterion without a testable metric.

An enterprise vision that *does* work will usually consist of a very brief phrase with a distinctive three-part content and structure:

- Something that identifies the *content* or *focus* for this enterprise

- Some kind of *action* on that content or focus

- A *qualifier* that validates and bridges between content and action

These components may occur in any order, but all of them need to be present in a vision descriptor. Ideally the phrase would be just three words long – one word for each element – but will usually be around four to five words, and should certainly be no longer than ten.

For example, take "ideas worth spreading," the vision for the TED conferences. It's clear, succinct, and emotive – and it conforms exactly to that preceding structure:

- "Ideas" [*content*]

- "Worth" [*qualifier*]

- "Spreading" [*action*]

Note too that none of these elements describe the organization at such: but they *do* describe the main content or focus of the overall shared enterprise ("ideas"); the area of action ("spreading"); and the key value descriptor ("worth") that defines the meaning of "success," around which meaningful metrics could be built. That's what we need to look for at this stage.

The *content* part of the descriptor should be a noun that identifies and summarizes the "things" of the enterprise as a whole. These will usually *not* be products or services as such, because that's just what the players in the enterprise deliver to each other in order to create value in the enterprise. Instead, it's more about what those products or services *act on* and are of interest to *every* player in the enterprise.

The *action* part should be a verb, summarizing the *overall* activity of the shared enterprise. If possible, it should be explicit and distinct, rather than a generic such as "supporting" or "making" or "creating" – though such generics can be useful to give something to work with while searching for a more distinctive vision.

The *qualifier* part should be an adjective or suchlike that is both emotive and implies some value or valuation – for example, the adjective "worth" in the TED vision of "ideas worth spreading" would imply some means and value criteria to identify which ideas are worth spreading, and which are not.

To identify the vision, look around both within and outside the organization for anything that engages or excites people in their work and in their relations with others in the shared enterprise. And excitement or engagement *is* the key here – though note that it can often take somewhat strange forms.

---

There's a nice example I saw once on a large billboard beside a freeway in Melbourne, Australia. The poster shows a football game at night: all the spectators in the floodlit stadium are intent on the action that's happening on the pitch, just out of shot from the billboard. All spectators except one, that is: there's a man in yellow rain-slickers, standing up, facing the other way to everyone else, gazing up at the huge floodlights. The caption? "We're excited about electricity, even if you're not."

The billboard was for an electricity company, of course, but makes the point very well: you may not be interested in electricity right now, but when you *are*, we're the kind of people you'd probably want to meet.

Remember that enterprises are *dynamic*, not static: people in "customer"-type roles especially will wander into and out of a shared enterprise according to their needs of the time. It's up to those who are most committed to an enterprise to make it of interest to others to choose to join in. This is where good marketing will often come into the picture, but a better approach is to focus on vision as a way to draw people in when they need to connect, and *also* allow them to disconnect cleanly when their needs no longer align with that vision.

---

Given all of that, let's apply this to our ZapaMex worked example.

First, the *content* or focus. ZapaMex is a shoemaker, so the seemingly obvious choice would be to make it about shoes. But as we talk with the ZapaMex team, it becomes clear that they want to broaden this a bit to make room for others in the enterprise, and instead shift the focus from just the shoes themselves, to the feet that would wear them. We could maybe suggest to the team to make this less abstract, more human and personal, and say *"your feet"* as the content that everyone in the enterprise is focused on.

Next, the *qualifier*, the theme that gives this enterprise its real reason to exist. There's a kind of double theme here: shoes that look good may make us feel happy in that sense, but might not be comfortable or healthy; and conversely, shoes that are comfortable may not look all that good. ZapaMex wants to be known for shoes that both look good *and* are healthy and comfortable to wear, so we end up here with the phrasing *"feel happy and healthy."*

Finally, the *action* that everyone is doing about "your feet" and "feel happy and healthy." The team first try "making," for "making your feet feel happy and healthy," but as a phrase it feels somewhat flat. The team go round the loop a few times, and eventually settle on *"helping,"* because that would bring into the enterprise others that work in that space, such as podiatrists and so on.

If we bring those three elements together, this gives ZapaMex an enterprise vision of *"helping your feet feel happy and healthy."*

---

Expect to take several tries at this before you get it right: our experience has been that for most business folk there's an almost automatic reflex to go for marketing "puffery," and it can take a while to find a way past that habit. But when you *do* get it right, you'll recognize it immediately – it'll engage everyone straight away, both outside and inside the organization, and have an *aliveness* to it that just isn't there in the usual marketing slogans.

---

There are many other possible vision descriptors that ZapaMex could have chosen, of course: for example, if they had focused on shoes rather than feet, they might have ended up with a vision such as *"celebrating the beauty of shoes"* or *"making sturdy, reliable footwear."* The vision descriptor is *always* a choice. Note, though, that each of those vision descriptors will denote a *different* enterprise, with different values, guiding principles, and success criteria, and often also a different set of players in that overall enterprise. Whatever we choose as the vision descriptor will have real consequences throughout the organization and the broader shared enterprise within which it operates – so we do need to choose it with care.

# Values, Principles, and Success Criteria

The vision itself should suggest distinct **values**, either direct from the "qualifier" part of the vision descriptor or by implication. The values that we need to identify here are those values that are needed to realize the desired ends indicated by the vision, and hence values that we actually want and need in the organization.

To identify the values that are required for an enterprise, assess what "effectiveness" would look like within the enterprise. Some values, such as fairness, trust, and financial probity, would all be required in any functional enterprise. Other values, though, will arise from the specific enterprise and its vision, and we can usually derive those just from the feelings that arise during some quiet contemplation on the vision descriptor and its implications in practice across the various aspects of the enterprise. To illustrate this with our ZapaMex worked example, its vision descriptor of "helping your feet feel happy and healthy" tells us two values straight away: *"happy"* and *"healthy."* It also implies some other values such as comfort, support, satisfaction, "looking good, feeling good," and so on. For each of these values, we'll need to include metrics in our architectures and service designs to monitor how well our organization is performing relative to the respective value.

Note, though, that those enterprise-level values must by definition apply *everywhere* across the entire shared enterprise. For example, ZapaMex's values of "happy and healthy" would not just be about shoes, or for the people who wear those shoes, but also for everyone who makes them, everyone who finds or grows and manufactures the materials to make them, everyone who sells them, or advertises them, or provides podiatry or healthcare or is involved in sports that would use them, and so on and so on – every player and stakeholder across the entire shared enterprise. And in turn, it's in ZapaMex's *business interest* to ensure that those values *do* apply in all those perhaps-unexpected places across that shared enterprise within which it operates. That's the real meaning of the enterprise vision descriptor and the values that arise from it.

---

When we start to expand on these, we should also note that there's often a large difference between *required* values, *espoused* values, and *enacted* values – and we need to be clear which is which!

*Required values* are the values we need to make the enterprise work. *Espoused values* are the values that the organization claims that it holds to, and to which it expects to be held accountable. *Enacted values* are the values that the organization *actually* lives by – which in some cases may be *very* different even from the espoused values, let alone the required values.

To identify actual enacted values, explore the behaviors or phrases actually used within the organization, or as indicated in social media and the like. Stafford Beer's somewhat cynical yet often painfully accurate dictum POSIWID – "the purpose of the system is [expressed in] what it does" – can also be a useful guideline here. Note, though, that these actual values will often vary at different levels or in different parts of the organization, and differ again as seen from inside or outside.

---

From values we move to **principles**, because the organization's principles describe how its values should be expressed in practice. In themselves, values are somewhat abstract, whereas principles are – or should be – concrete, actionable, and verifiable. (Values on their own are just a "nice idea": it's only when they're expressed as principles that they become meaningful in practice *as* values.)

Principles represent core reasons and decisions for the organization, pervading the values throughout every layer and function, downward into the fine detail of systems designs and individual actions. We typically document each principle in a four-part structure:

- *Name*: A succinct summary of the principle itself

- *Statement*: An unambiguous description of the rule and its intent

- *Rationale*: The practical benefits from following the principle

- *Implications*: Summary of probable impacts and gains from following the principle, and costs, risks, or losses from *not* following it

If we take the Zapamex value of "*happy and healthy*" as an example, one principle that would devolve from that value might be defined as follows:

- *Name*: Protect and preserve health of employees.

- *Statement*: ZapaMex shall take action to support the health of all employees, by subsidizing healthcare costs, by providing health and safety training to all employees, by providing safety equipment and safety systems as needed throughout all ZapaMex sites, by continually assessing and taking action on all health-related risks, and by monitoring health metrics in order to guide such action.

51

- *Rationale*: Employee health is directly related to productivity and to risk reduction and risk mitigation; protecting employee health therefore protects productivity and reduces business risk.

- *Implications*: By protecting employee health, productivity will be maintained; failing to protect employee health will negatively impact productivity, and is likely to increase a wide variety of different types of risk.

The same value of "*healthy and happy*" might well lead ZapaMex to want to extend the same concerns to the employees and others at their suppliers – but that would need to be expressed as a different principle, because ZapaMex can only influence what happens at their suppliers, and does not have the same choices that they have about what to do within the ZapaMex organization itself.

---

One obvious complication is that principles will often compete or conflict: transparency versus privacy, for example, or innovation versus the safety of "the known." We'll return to this later in Chapter 10, "Service Guidance"; for now, just document any such clashes you can see, and move on.

---

Finally, we need to identify key **success criteria** and potential fail criteria, and also their matching metrics, that would apply across the entire shared enterprise and hence also for and within our own organization.

In many cases, we can derive these from the "*Implications*" section of the documentation for the respective principles, as above. In the ZapaMex example of that principle of "Protect and preserve health of employees," a matching success criterion might be that health metrics in a given year have been maintained or improved relative to the previous year, while a matching fail criterion would be that health metrics have worsened by a statistically significant amount.

# Into Action

In this next session for your business-transformation project, your stakeholders will be the executive team and strategy team, as these decisions about vision, values, governance, and the quality system can only be made at that level. Use the ideas in this chapter and the following questions to help you guide that conversation.

## Identifying the Vision

- What are the *"things" or context* that are the main focus for everyone in the shared enterprise?

- What is the main *activity* on those "things" or context that concerns everyone in the shared enterprise?

- What adjective best describes people's engagement in those "things" and activities – the *qualifier* that provides the driving "why" for the shared enterprise?

- Linking the above answers together, what *vision* is common to all stakeholders in the enterprise? What single phrase *describes* the overall enterprise?

## Vision, Role, Mission, Goal, Outcome

- Given the vision mentioned previously, what *role* or roles does the organization play within the enterprise, to contribute toward the vision? What roles does it *not* play – hence, leaving open for other stakeholders? Who are these other stakeholders, and what roles do *they* play within the overall enterprise? How would you verify that each role – especially the organization's own chosen role or roles – does support the enterprise vision?

- What *mission* or missions – ongoing services and capabilities – would be needed to support each role undertaken by the organization in that enterprise? What metrics would you need to confirm that each mission is "on purpose" and *effective* in supporting the respective role?

- What short-, medium-, and longer-term *goals* and objectives underpin each mission? What are the timescales and deliverables for each goal?

- By what means – what *outcomes* – would you verify that each goal is achievable, and has been achieved? How would you verify that each goal does support the respective mission in an appropriate and effective way?

## Values, Principles, and Success Criteria

- What is value? What do *you* value? What is considered to be "value" in your organization, or in other organizations that you know?

- How do you *describe* value? How do you depict it? How do you model it, in your own work, and in the enterprise?

- How is value created, changed, destroyed, shared? How does this differ from one type of value to another? How would you model these changes in value, and for what reasons?

- How do you measure value? In what ways are these metrics different for different forms of value? Are there any forms of value that you cannot measure? If so, why or how?

- What values devolve from the enterprise vision? What shared values are required from *every* player in the overall enterprise, in order for that enterprise to achieve success within the terms of its vision?

- What do these values imply for your organization in terms of requirements for quality, in all its various forms? In what ways can you express these values in terms of principles to guide decision-making within your organization and its relations with the broader enterprise?

- What individual and collective values – either implicit or explicit – are required to support the organization's role within the enterprise?

- What values does the organization espouse, both in its relationships with others and its relationships within and to itself? What actual values does the organization express in its actions and relations with others and within itself? If there are misalignments between required, espoused, and actual values, what impacts do these differences have on the effectiveness of the shared enterprise and the organization? What could you do to correct these misalignments?

- What principles devolve from and between each of these values? How are – or should – these principles be expressed in practice in the organization and the broader enterprise?

- What to you is effectiveness? How does your organization define effectiveness? How would this differ from efficiency alone – the usual focus of most business-change efforts? How does effectiveness link to value? What impact does effectiveness have on value? Why does effectiveness matter, and to whom?

- What success criteria devolve from what your organization identifies as its vision, values, and effectiveness? In what ways do these align, or not align, to those of the broader shared enterprise? How does your organization monitor its performance relative to those success criteria, and alignment to those of the shared enterprise as a whole?

# Summary

In this chapter, we saw how the shared enterprise is defined by its vision and values. Every service within the enterprise needs to align with the vision and values, and assist in making them real via appropriate principles, metrics, and matching success criteria – and demonstrate that it does so, through meaningful metrics. A simple checklist of "vision, role, mission, goal, outcomes" can help our stakeholders make sense of this in practice; further checklists help the process of identifying the values, principles, and success criteria that arise from the vision.

In the next chapter, we will explore the key architectural concept of layers of abstraction and see how this applies to services and service design.

# CHAPTER 5

# Service Layers

One of the core concepts for the Enterprise Canvas is the notion of *layering*. We need to be clear, though, as to what type of layering we mean, and what we don't, because there are at least four different types of layers that are in common use in the business context:

- Layers of *separation* (often as "distance-from-self")

- Layers of *reporting* relationships (management hierarchy)

- Layers of *decomposition* (fractal structure of services, sub-units, etc.)

- Layers of *realization* (from abstract to concrete)

Layers of separation are always relative to a single focus point that is chosen as "the center," and all relationships are mapped outward from there. This is often useful in service design, as we'll see in Chapter 6, "Service Actors and Other Entities," and even more in Chapter 7, "Service Roles and Relationships."

© Tom Graves 2023

T. Graves, *Mapping the Enterprise*, https://doi.org/10.1007/978-1-4842-9836-7_5

That kind of layering can be problematic, though, if the focus theme becomes hardwired and cannot be changed. One common example of this is the "BDAT stack" of business, data, applications, and technology infrastructure, as used in many IT architectures, and in which the IT itself is regarded as the fixed "the center" around which everything else revolves. In general, we should avoid using that kind of hardwired content-based layering with Enterprise Canvas and service design.

Reporting relationships are important, of course, but any apparent layering of those relationships depends on management hierarchies that could be changed at any moment. Instead, we need to focus more on the information flows and guidance roles for service management and then allow any layering of reporting relationships and the like to arise dynamically from that. We'll see more on this in the section "Information Flows for Service Management" in Chapter 9, "Service Flows," and the section "Direction Services" in Chapter 10, "Service Guidance."

Layers of decomposition provide a way to describe how services are composed of sub-services, units are composed of sub-units, and so on. This is a core aspect of Enterprise Canvas, as we'll see later in Chapter 12, "Service Decomposition."

Layers of abstraction and realization are fundamental to the Enterprise Canvas, because they describe how to connect abstract ideas to concrete reality, and also because each service may need to be described in different ways dependent on the current layer of abstraction. That core concern is the focus of this chapter.

# Layers of Abstraction and Realization

For our purposes with Enterprise Canvas and service design, we use seven distinct layers of abstraction. The numbering for these layers starts at "0" (zero) rather than "1," for compatibility with the commonly used Zachman framework.

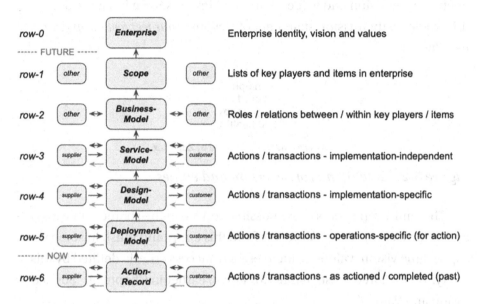

***Figure 5-1.*** *Layers of abstraction for Enterprise Canvas*

As shown in Figure 5-1, these layers are distinct from each other because they each add something more at each transition "downward" in the stack. Row-0 is essentially timeless; Rows 1–5 – as in Zachman – describe views of what we intend to happen in the future, moving downward from big picture to fine detail; the "Now," the moment of real-time action, sits at the boundary between Row-5 and Row-6; and Row-6 is about the past, a record of what *has* happened, which we can use to guide us to keep on track to the desired ends of the vision.

As a general rule, we will need a different Enterprise Canvas model for each layer of abstraction, to show the respective level of detail for that layer. The only routine exception to this rule is where we want to show how one layer devolves or translates into another.

In *Row-0* **Enterprise**, this topmost layer usually consists of just one item – the descriptor for the broader shared enterprise as a whole, as defined by its vision and values. For ZapaMex, as shown in Figure 5-2, this would be their vision statement of "*helping your feet feel happy and healthy.*"

> **"helping your feet feel happy and healthy"**
>
> enterprise-vision as identified by ZapaMex

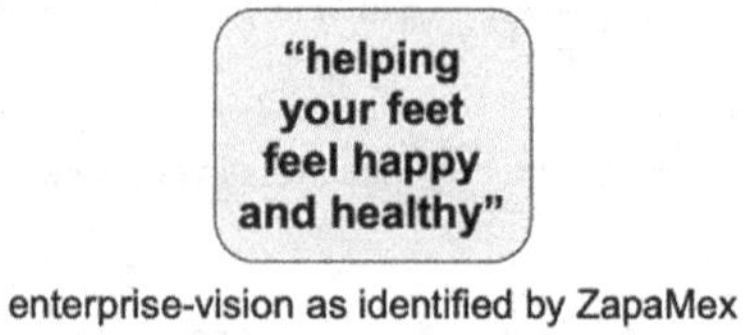

**Figure 5-2.** *Row-0 Enterprise: vision and values*

This entity represents every possible service in the shared enterprise; and in turn, every service devolves from this entity and must, in some way, support the vision, values, principles, and success criteria defined by this entity. We explored these themes for Row-0 earlier in Chapter 4, "Service Vision and Values."

In *Row-1* **Scope**, the layer consists of lists of key elements for the shared enterprise, without any relationships or attributes as such. For ZapaMex, these will be the key elements that make up its shared enterprise of "*helping your feet feel happy and healthy.*" Note, though, that this is about the *whole* shared enterprise, not solely the part of that enterprise that ZapaMex will address. Ultimately, the enterprise as a whole will only work if at least one player in the story will address each element – and if ZapaMex itself doesn't want to work with some element of the enterprise, then it's in its business interest to ensure that there *is* someone else who will do so.

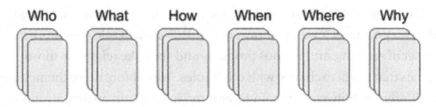

**Figure 5-3.** *Row-1 Scope: lists of entities*

We do need to keep things simple at this level: each list should usually consist of no more than around ten items of that respective type. As shown in Figure 5-3, one common way to populate these lists is by using the interrogatives Who, What, How, Where, When, and Why in relation to the shared enterprise as a whole. For example, the "Who" list would identify relevant player roles in the enterprise, including the role that the organization itself will choose. We'll explore these themes about the "Who" of the enterprise in more detail in Chapter 6, "Service Actors and Other Entities."

In *Row-2* **Business Model**, we add relationships between the roles and other elements – in other words, we start to add the horizontal value network to the vertical dimension of shared value, to identify the types of *services* to be presented by each role or other entity. These relationships are determined in part by the respective *value propositions* offered by and to each of the players. Given this level of detail, ZapaMex can select one of the roles as its chosen strategic positioning within the overall shared enterprise.

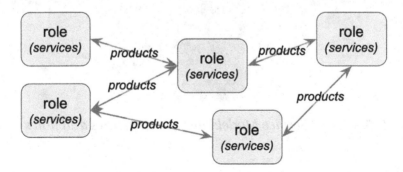

**Figure 5-4.** *Row-2 Business Model: roles and relationships*

61

This is the first layer at which we start to see services as such, though only a very abstract level. As shown in Figure 5-4, each role presents its own set of services, and various products and suchlike related to those services that it will exchange with other roles. We explore these themes and the differences between a whole-of-enterprise view and an organization-specific view of the services, in more depth in Chapter 7, "Service Roles and Relationships."

In *Row-3* **Service Model** (also known as the *system model* or *logical model* layer), we start to include more details of attributes alongside the relationships, describing the internals of each high-level service and the flows between them. At this level, these are always abstract and generic: they define one or more classes of possible implementations, but do *not* specify any particular technology or method. For ZapaMex, it would use descriptions at this layer not only to describe the services it presents to other players in the shared enterprise, but also its own internal services, of any type and at any level.

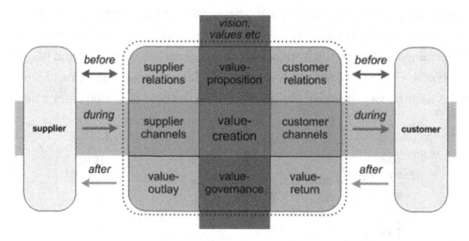

***Figure 5-5.*** *Row-3 Service Model: abstract structures and flows*

As shown in Figure 5-5, this is the first layer in which we would use the full Enterprise Canvas to describe the internal structure of each service, along with high-level overviews of its interactions with other services. We'll explore the various aspects of these themes within the series of chapters from Chapter 8, "Service Structure," onward to Chapter 14, "Services As Systems."

In *Row-4* **Design Model** (also known as the *physical model* layer), we move into more detailed design, building complete specifications for technologies, processes, interfaces, flows, protocols, skillsets, and the like, translating the abstract system models into requirements and project plans for detailed implementation, all the way down to final deployment. For ZapaMex, this is where it would choose how to implement each of its services, with the right mix of people, machines, and IT in each case.

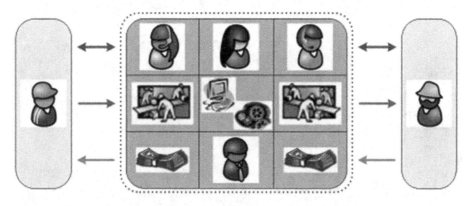

***Figure 5-6.*** *Row-4 Design Model: specifications for implementation*

On the surface, this type of model would look much the same as for the Row–3 *Service Model*: the difference, as shown in Figure 5-6, is that in this layer we describe an *actual* intended solution rather than a whole class of possible implementations. We would need to go into more specific implementation detail here and would be likely to do much more service decomposition to describe that detail. Much as we did for Row-3, we'll explore the respective themes in each of that set of chapters from Chapter 8, "Service Structure," onward to Chapter 14, "Services As Systems."

In *Row-5* **Deployment Model** (also known as the *operations model* or *action plan*), we add the extra details needed to specify a service configuration to be used and/or enacted on a specific day at a specific location for a specific purpose with specific staff, and so on. For example, where the Row-4 design model might specify a database server, here we need to know the exact identifiers, types, configurations, physical locations, and virtual addresses of the production servers, fallback servers, development servers, test servers, and all the related support equipment and switchgear. For ZapaMex, this would include down-to-the-ground details such as the staff-roster for the morning shift on February 24th for the shoe-assembly section of the factory floor.

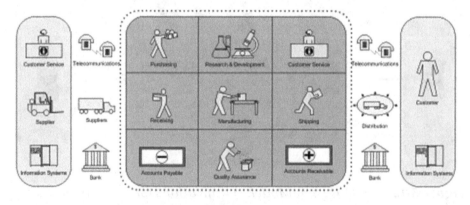

***Figure 5-7.*** *Row-5 Deployment Model: run-time action plan*

We could describe this layer with the Enterprise Canvas in the same way as for Row-3 and Row-4, but as shown in Figure 5-7, there would be a *lot* more detail embedded in the model. This is below where most architecture and change teams would work, though they would occasionally dive down into this level of detail to gain a better understanding of qualitative concerns such as availability, adaptability, variance in loads, and so on.

In *Row-6* **Action Record**, we gather all of the information collected during any kind of operations or other actions. Unlike the other layers, this layer is not a model of an intended future, but a record of actions in the past. For ZapaMex, this would include the reports for managers and the like, but also the records that would be used by external auditors and regulators, by the organization's own change teams looking to improve business capabilities and processes, and by the procurement teams needing to make sure that all the materials needed for next week's production run will be available whenever they're needed.

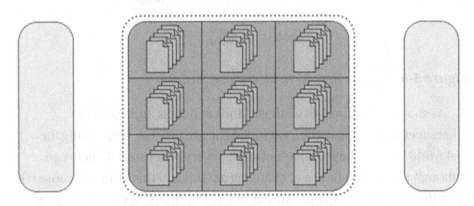

**Figure 5-8.**  *Row-6 Action Record: detailed metrics*

As shown in Figure 5-8, these metrics would describe the same level of detail as in the Row-5 action plan. In principle, the core of it *should* be exactly the same as in that action plan, but in practice it will often be different in various ways: for example, rostered staff might have been absent for any number of reasons; a machine or server broke down; people got switched around onto different machines; half of the expected customers were at home watching the football match; a traffic-hold-up forced a change of the delivery schedule; and so on.

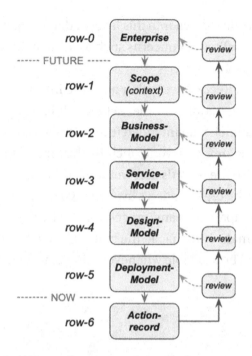

**Figure 5-9.** *Action Record metrics close the loop*

As shown in Figure 5-9, all those kinds of details and everyday differences help to close the loop in the change process, connecting the real world back to the initial intent and to every other stage in between. Although there's no chance of changing anything in this layer – because it's all in the past – these records are extremely important to process designers, to organizational-learning specialists, and to others who do extensive system design (Row-3 and Row-4) in order to enhance effectiveness at the operational level (Row-5). Whenever we do any work with the Enterprise Canvas, at any layer, we should always aim to identify Row-5/Row-6 metrics that could help us to keep on track to the initial Row-0 enterprise vision, values, and principles.

In summary:

- *Row-0 Enterprise* shows vision, values, and principles only.

- *Row-1 Scope* adds lists of actors and other items in scope in the enterprise.

- *Row-2 Business Model* adds relationships between actors and other items, describing roles and responsibilities.

- *Row-3 Service Model* specifies generic (implementation-independent) content within services and in flows between services.

- *Row-4 Design Model* identifies implementation-specific content (technology, assets, locations, skillsets, etc.) within and between services.

- *Row-5 Deployment Model* identifies specific configuration details for run-time operations.

- *Row-6 Action Record* identifies what has actually happened and supports continual learning and continual innovation.

*Strategy* will focus primarily on Rows 0-2, with some emphasis on Row-3.

*Tactics* will focus primarily on Rows 3-4, with some emphasis on Row-5.

*Operations* will focus primarily on Rows 5-6.

# Into Action

With the organization's big picture "Why" for your business-transformation project established in the previous session, you now need the conversations to move more toward the "How." For this session, your stakeholders will be team leads and key players from project management. You want to introduce them to the need for consistency in the way things are described in models, designs and plans for change, and the value of a consistent model of "layers of abstraction and realization." Use the ideas in this chapter and the following questions to help you guide that conversation:

- Does what you're looking at describe anything other than vision, values, or principles? (If so, the layer must be Row-1 or below.)

- Is it simply a list of items, without relationships between those items? (If so, it will be in Row-1, or Row-3 if internal details and attributes of those items are also described.)

- Does it describe relationships between items? (If so, it must be in Row-2 or below.)

- Does it describe detailed attributes of items, or flows between items? (If so, it must be in Row-3 or below.)

- Does it describe a specific implementation, technology, vendor, business process, or the like? (If so, it must be in Row-4 or below.)

- Does it specify explicit deployment details – a complete set of assets, functions, locations, capabilities, trigger events, and business rules? (If so, it must be in Row-5 or below.)

- Does it describe a record of something that has already happened in the past? (If so, it must be in Row-6.)

# Summary

In this chapter we discovered that a service may be usefully described in terms of a set of distinct layers of abstraction, extending from the idealized vision down to the concrete reality of what was actually achieved. As we move downward through the layers of abstraction from overall intent to real-world implementation, the same nominal service will need to be described in different ways, with different levels of detail.

In the next chapter, we start to move toward realizing the vision, identifying the key actors, assets, and other entities that would be required to make the vision happen in the real world.

# CHAPTER 6

# Service Actors and Other Entities

One of the key functions of the Enterprise Canvas is to help us to think wider, to understand more about the ecosystem in which our organization operates. Among other advantages, doing this will also help us to identify "unexpected" opportunities and risks.

To do this exploration, we need to go right back to the roots, beyond the nominally "known" of our organization. Given that we've already seen how to identify the core vision and values of the shared enterprise for Row-0, back in Chapter 4, "Service Vision and Values," what we aim to do here in Row-1 is to identify all of the key items or "elements" that are needed to make this enterprise happen.

At this level, we always look at the *whole* shared enterprise – *not* solely the view as seen from our own organization's perspective. Later, in Row-2, and especially in Row-3 and below, we'll identify the parts of the enterprise that our organization will choose to do or not do, for its own business model and the like; but for this part of the work, we will need a complete picture of the shared enterprise, so that we can also identify the roles and activities that others will play.

© Tom Graves 2023
T. Graves, *Mapping the Enterprise*, https://doi.org/10.1007/978-1-4842-9836-7_6

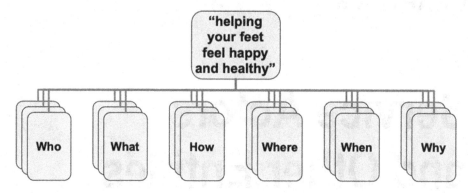

**Figure 6-1.** *Every element in each list links back to enterprise vision*

As shown in Figure 6-1, we do this here by circling around six simple interrogatives: Who, What, How, Where, When, and Why. The answers we derive for any one of those queries will often trigger off a review of one or more of the others, and so on, round and round, until we have every key element or element type for the enterprise somewhere in our lists. We do need to remember to include not just our basic supply chain, but extend outward to the industry and market, all the way out to the entirety of the shared enterprise, as in the "shared-story-as-enterprise" model that we saw in "Service and Market" in Chapter 3, "Service Context and Market").

---

Note that we do need to keep some sense of focus here, because in many cases the answers could run almost to infinity. The idea is to gather "just enough detail" to guide subsequent development and enquiry: aim to gather perhaps ten to twenty elements for each of the interrogatives, but probably not much more than that.

---

For simplicity, it's best to focus on element types rather than specific elements at this stage: we'll assign names and other more specific details later in Row-2 and below, as we'll see in Chapter 7, "Service Roles and Relationships."

The "**Who?**" question asks us who is likely to be involved, is likely to feel engaged in and motivated by the vision and its values. For ZapaMex's vision of "helping your feet feel happy and healthy," this list would, of course, include ZapaMex itself, but it would also include anyone who's interested in footwear for any reason: the general buying public, fashionistas, sports facilities and trainers, schools, general health and footcare specialists, industrial health and safety, and so on. It includes people on the supply side: manufacturers of materials, or, further back, the farmers and others who supply those materials. There are marketers, advertisers, and event organizers. On the distribution side, there would be retailers, wholesalers, warehouses, and logistics providers. There are local or national government, the communities, employees' families, and others. And there are standards bodies, testers, market analysts, and other industry-level players.

---

Note that we *don't* use role labels such as "supplier" or "customer" or "competitor" here: we only describe the type of player or "actor" *relative to the enterprise as a whole*, not relative to ourselves as an organization. We'll come back to that role analysis later, in Row-2: see Chapter 7, "Service Roles and Relationships."

---

The "**What?**" question asks for a list of assets or resources that would be needed within the shared enterprise. (For this purpose, there's no need to distinguish between assets and resources; the distinction we'll use later is that assets are resources for which the organization is directly responsible.) We need here to include not just physical assets, but also information and other virtual assets, relational assets that provide links to real people, and aspirational assets such as brands. For ZapaMex's enterprise, this includes complete shoes, shoe components, and shoe-making equipment and facilities; it includes buildings and physical and virtual (web) distribution channels; it includes customer records and customer relations; it includes brands, both for each organization and for the industry as a whole.

The "**How?**" question asks for functions, processes, and capabilities that would be needed to create value within the enterprise. (Often these may be bundled rather carelessly together with the "Who?" elements, but it's best to describe them separately because that often highlights other opportunities and risks later on in the model-development process.) For ZapaMex, this would include shoe design, shoe-making, shoe retail, assessment of footwear needs, marketing, materials manufacture, materials acquisition, logistics, testing, and so on.

---

Note that, for simplicity, we do bundle function, process, and capability together here as if they're the same. They're not, but the distinctions don't really matter at this level. They *do* matter when we go further down into the detail, but we can sort that out later: see Chapter 13, "Service Content."

---

The "**Where?**" question asks about locations of all types – physical, virtual, or otherwise. For ZapaMex's enterprise, the geographical locations are actually worldwide, even though ZapaMex itself only operates in Mexico. Note that there's also often a cross-over here between Where and What – or rather, that many What elements, such as warehouses and retail outlets, will each have a physical location as well. Include virtual locations such as phones, emails, and websites; include relational locations such as supplier or market networks; and note too that brands often have a kind of "location" relative to each other as well.

The "**When?**" question asks about events that are important in and to the shared enterprise. For ZapaMex's enterprise these would include physical events, such as materials arriving at a factory, or a parcel entering or leaving logistics. It would include virtual or information-related events, such as the accounting cycle or the tax cycle. It would include composite events such as the physical and relational event of a customer-prospect walking into a store. And it might also include aspirational events such as PR impacts on a brand. There are plenty of examples to choose from there, anyway.

The "**Why?**" question is the one that is most strongly linked to the enterprise vision – because the vision *is* the core "why" for the entire enterprise – but it also asks about other types of decisions that are required for the proper functioning of the shared enterprise. For ZapaMex, these would include decisions to launch or close a product; to expand or contract market positioning, in any sense of the term; or to place orders for materials or to purchase products.

Each question cross-links with other questions: Why leads to How leads to When, which leads back to Why; What may lead to How, and onward to Who, which again leads us to How. Anywhere may take us anywhere else, and often does – hence, this kind of exploration is often iterative, each question triggering off a review of the content previously provided via another question.

Note also that

- The What will link strongly to the "things" or context of the vision descriptor ("your feet," for ZapaMex's vision).

- The Why will link strongly to the qualifier of the vision descriptor ("feel happy and healthy," for ZapaMex).

- The "How" will link strongly to the action verb of the vision descriptor ("helping," for ZapaMex).

Once again, remember that the end result of this enquiry is a set of lists, without any explicit relationships between them; and it covers the whole of the shared enterprise, *not* solely the organization or service that is the main focus of our interest.

# Into Action

For the next session in your business-transformation project, you'll work with the same stakeholders, and perhaps some others at the executive level, to map out the big picture of the business context and all the "Row-1" elements that underpin that overall story. Use the ideas in this chapter and the following questions to help you guide that conversation:

- Who are the people and organizations needed to make the vision come to life in the real world? What links each of these actors to the vision and values of the shared enterprise?

- What types of assets and resources are needed to make the vision a reality? What links each of these elements to the vision and values of the shared enterprise?

- What functions, processes, and capabilities are needed to make the vision a reality? What links each of these elements to the vision and values of the shared enterprise?

- In what locations – physical, virtual, or otherwise – will the work of the shared enterprise take place? What types of locations will be needed to make the vision a reality? What links each of these locations to the vision and values of the shared enterprise?

- What events would drive the transactions and interactions of the various players and processes in the shared enterprise? What events will be needed to make the vision a reality? What links each of these events to the vision and values of the shared enterprise?

- What decisions will guide the choices and interactions in the shared enterprise? What decisions will be needed to make the vision a reality? What links each of these decisions to the vision and values of the enterprise?

## Summary

In this chapter, we explored how to identify all the key types of actors, assets, and other entities that would be required to make the vision happen in the real world. At this level, these are just lists of items or elements, though the list will include the organization or service that will be our main focus of attention.

In the next chapter, we will discover how to identify and map out the roles of the enterprise and the relationships between them.

# CHAPTER 7

# Service Roles and Relationships

In the brainstorming exercise for Row-1 Scope, in the previous chapter, we identified all the key elements needed to make the vision of the shared enterprise a reality – Who, What, How, Where, When, and Why. Here we'll do the same for the Row-2 Business Model layer: we now need to link all of those elements and items together into a complete picture of the enterprise and then establish our organization's proper place within that picture.

For this exercise, we carry through the lists we created in Row-1, ready to use as our source material for a new set of cross-maps of roles, responsibilities, and relationships.

---

For a whiteboard session, we might set out the elements in each list as individual sticky notes, using a different color sticky note for each of the lists.

---

We then pick one list to start with – typically "Who" – and build a map of the working enterprise from the content of that list. In effect, each "Who" presents one or more services to the overall enterprise: in which case, what *are* those services? Who consumes them? Who provides them? What will flow between those services in each interaction? This helps us

T. Graves, *Mapping the Enterprise*, https://doi.org/10.1007/978-1-4842-9836-7_7

to build an initial map of the players in the enterprise and the probable relationships between them. For example, we could map out the players and relationships in ZapaMex's shared enterprise of "*helping your feet feel happy and healthy*" in a layout such as that shown in Figure 7-1.

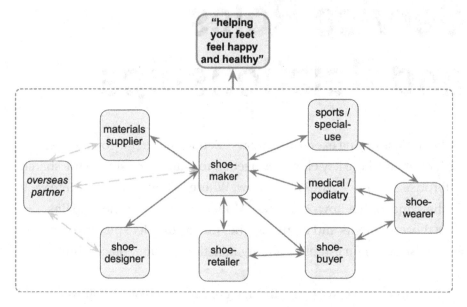

**Figure 7-1.** *Roles and relationships for the whole shared enterprise*

If we start from "Who" in this way, that review will automatically raise questions about what is used in each service, and transferred as products in each interaction with other players. We could explore what is done in each player's services, how it is done, where it takes place, the trigger events for each interaction, and the decisions needed in each case to keep the overall flow of value around the enterprise on track to the overall vision.

Note that it doesn't actually matter which list we start with: we can do the same kind of map by starting with "What," or "How," or any of the other lists. Whichever way we do it, the aim is to build up a picture of the overall flow of value around the enterprise, and who or what is responsible for each activity and decision in each case.

So far all of that has been relative *to the shared enterprise* – not to our own organization. To make sense of where we fit in that shared enterprise, we do another map in which we place our own organization at the center, assigning ourselves one or more roles from the "Who" list. We then select elements from each of the other lists that represent what our own organization does – or, for a "to-be" map, what our organization would choose to do – to play its part in this overall enterprise.

As can be seen in Figure 7-2, ZapaMex does this by placing itself in the role of a shoe manufacturer that sells direct to its client, without an intermediary shoe retailer run by a different organization. It does connect with podiatrists and other medical aspects of footwear, but it does not intend at present to make sportswear, so it doesn't need to connect with that aspect of the shared enterprise. We can also identify who its competitors would be: they're organizations that connect directly with the same types of players that ZapaMex does.

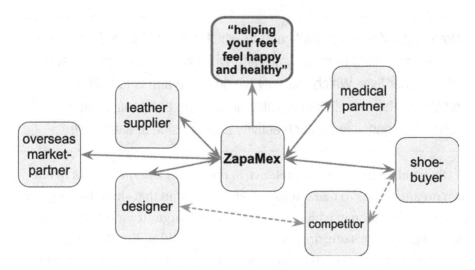

**Figure 7-2.** *Roles and relationships relative to the organization*

Every other element in the lists that is not referenced in our own organization's map is something that our organization would choose to not do, *yet needs to exist for the overall enterprise to work well*. In other words, we do need it to exist *somewhere* in the overall story, and be addressed by *someone* in that story, even if we ourselves don't do it or use it. Which, in turn, defines our relationships with all of those aspects of the enterprise that we (or our organization) will choose not to do.

Roles relative to our own organization will fall out automatically from the respective relationships and mutual responsibilities. For example, we can identify three classic supply-chain roles:

- Anyone who provides a service, or has responsibility for an item, that we need in playing our part in the enterprise has a potential *supplier* relationship with us.

- Anyone who, for their part in the enterprise, has need of a service or item for which we have responsibility, has a potential *customer* relationship with us.

- Anyone whose part in the enterprise suggests that they
  need a relationship with any potential "customer"
  or potential "supplier" of ours may have a potential
  *competitor* and/or *partner* relationship with us.

Note that other players may well have multiple roles relative to us
in terms of the whole enterprise: the same organization could well be
supplier, customer, competitor, *and* partner, all in distinct and separate
relationships relative to us.

We need to keep developing this map until *all* of the elements that we
identified in the Row-1 Scope exercise have been referenced at least once
somewhere in either of the models – the whole-enterprise map, or our own
organization's map. The reason for this is that we've already established
that each of these elements is needed for the effective operation of the
overall enterprise: so if there's no one doing that type of work, or we have
no direct or indirect relationship to it, then it represents either a risk to
us or to the whole enterprise. In either case, the apparent risk may well
represent a worthwhile business opportunity for someone – and it might
well be us. That point can often be useful indeed.

Remember that this is really only an idealized overview at this stage:
the real-world detail will come later, in Row-3 Service Model and below.
We need to develop a good sense of the overall flows – the nodes and links
of the value network that enacts the enterprise – but we also need at this
stage to keep the emphasis here on the abstract big-picture view, and not
allow ourselves to get dragged down too far into the depths of the detail.

# Into Action

In this session for your business-transformation project, you'll want that
same group of team leads, project-management group, strategy team, and
executives to map out the "Row-2" description of the roles, relationships,
and responsibilities across the big-picture business context and the

choices about how, where, and why the organization positions itself in that story. Use the ideas in this chapter and the following questions to help you guide that conversation.

- Starting from "*Who*," who are the players in this enterprise? What roles do they each take within the enterprise? What relationships and transactions are implied by these different roles within the enterprise? What assets and resources do they need to carry out these roles? Which assets and resources would they be responsible for? To which functions, processes, and capabilities would they apply? Where would they do this role? What events trigger activities and transactions for which these roles are responsible? What decisions do they need to take on behalf of the extended enterprise? And which real-world individuals or organizations would carry out these roles?

- Starting from "*What*," which assets and resources are used in this enterprise? What are their relationships to each other? In which transactions do these assets and resources play a part? Who is responsible for each of these assets and resources? What functions, process, and capabilities are used to create or change these assets and resources, and add value within the enterprise? Where are these assets and resources located, at each point in their lifecycle? What events trigger changes relative to these assets and resources? What decisions apply in each case?

- Starting from "*How*," what functions, processes, and capabilities apply in this enterprise? What are their relationships to each other? In which transactions and interactions do they play a part? Who is responsible for each of these functions, processes, and capabilities? On what assets and resources do they apply? In what locations are these functions, processes, and capabilities applied and used? What events trigger the use of these functions, processes, and capabilities? What decisions control or guide their use?

- Starting from "*Where*," what locations apply for this enterprise? What are their relationships to each other? In which transactions and interactions do they play a part? Which roles apply at each of these locations? Who is responsible for each of these locations? What assets and resources are found at or acted upon at these locations? What functions, processes, and capabilities are used at these locations? And what decisions apply to or at each location?

- Starting from "*When*," what events occur within this enterprise? What relationships exist between these events? Which transactions and interactions do they trigger, or are triggered by? To which roles do each of these events apply? Who is responsible for each event? What assets and resources are affected by each event? What functions, processes, and capabilities are required by each event? At what locations do each of these events take place, and which locations do they connect? What decisions trigger or guide each of these events?

- Starting from "*Why*," what decisions control or guide this enterprise? What are their relationships to each other? In what transactions and interactions would each of these decisions be involved? To which roles would each of these decisions apply, and who would be responsible for each? To what assets and resources would each decision apply? To which or in which functions, processes, and capabilities? In which functions, processes, and capabilities would each decision be enacted? Where would these decisions take place? Which events would trigger these decisions, or be triggered by them?

- Starting from your own organization as "Us," which role or roles within the enterprise would you choose? Why? Which assets and resources would you use in this role? With which functions, processes, and capabilities? At what locations? In response to or creating which events? And enacting which decisions?

- What aspects of the enterprise – who, what, how, where, when, why – would you *not* do, and why? What relationships does each of these decisions imply with other players in the enterprise? What transactions and interactions does each of these relationships imply?

- Which elements, if any, does *no one* appear to be doing or using within the enterprise? What risks or opportunities does this imply for the enterprise as a whole, and for your part within it?

# Summary

In this chapter, we discovered how to map out the roles and relationships across the whole shared enterprise, and also relative to our own organization's chosen position within that shared enterprise. This tells us how value moves around the shared enterprise and suggests the services that would be needed to support that overall flow of value.

In the next chapter, we start to explore the structure of services, using the core of the Enterprise Canvas model as a visual checklist and template.

# CHAPTER 8

# Service Structure

In Row-2 Business Model, in the previous chapter, we established a big-picture overview of the shared enterprise as a whole and of our organization's role and place within it. That overview provides an important anchor for strategy, but we also need to start to link that strategy down toward real-world action. To do this, we turn to the Enterprise Canvas template, as a systematic means to model the services of the enterprise. We'll divide this into six parts:

- The overall *structure* of services, in a generic sense – described in this chapter.

- The flows *between* services that create the value web of the enterprise – see Chapter 9, "Service Flows."

- The various related services that help to link this service with others and keep it on track to the aims of the overall enterprise – see Chapter 10, "Service Guidance."

- Relationships with the service's investors and beneficiaries, in various forms of value – see Chapter 11, "Service Investors and Beneficiaries."

- How to expand each of these descriptions out into detailed real-world services – see Chapter 12, "Service Decomposition."

© Tom Graves 2023
T. Graves, *Mapping the Enterprise*, https://doi.org/10.1007/978-1-4842-9836-7_8

- The fine detail of the structure and content of each
  of these services and flows – see Chapter 13, "Service
  Content."

For here, though, we'll summarize a structure that can be applied to
*any* type of service.

To start on this, we go back to the notion that a service is a means via
which the desired ends of the vision can be achieved in the real world.
The service does this in part by linking "vertically" to the enterprise vision
and adding to the value flow as it moves "horizontally" around the overall
shared enterprise, as shown in Figure 8-1.

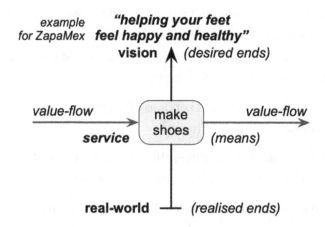

***Figure 8-1.*** *Service at intersection of vision and value flow*

Some while back, in Chapter 3, "Service Context and Market," we
saw that each service provides its own three distinct views on value –
value proposition, value creation, and value governance – and that
these, respectively, relate to what happens before, during, and after the
main transactions of "exchangeable value." That was about the internal
operation of the service itself; but we can also generalize that three-way
view to include the matching relations with services on the incoming
side of the supply chain, from suppliers or service providers, and on the
outgoing side, to customers or service consumers.

The relationships with other services are symmetrical in the sense that *every* service shares the same pattern: the only difference between "supplier-side" and "customer-side" is the main direction of service flow relative to the entity that is our current focus of attention:

- Future/before-oriented relationships are essentially peer-to-peer and will flow back and forth in both directions.

- Present/during-oriented relationships are mainly about supply-chain transfer of goods and services from supplier to self, or self to customer (i.e., left-to-right on the Canvas).

- Past/after-oriented relationships are mainly about balancing the supply-chain transfer via a "return channel" from customer to self, and self to supplier (i.e., right-to-left on the Canvas).

This gives us a three-by-three nine-cell matrix that summarizes clusters of "child" services within each service, all of which are necessary in some form for the proper operation of that service.

A service *serves* – and in every case, what it's really serving is the vision of the enterprise, via the mission that underpins its role in the enterprise. This nine-cell structure, as shown in Figure 8-2, gives a first glance at how it actually delivers its service, in relationship with other services.

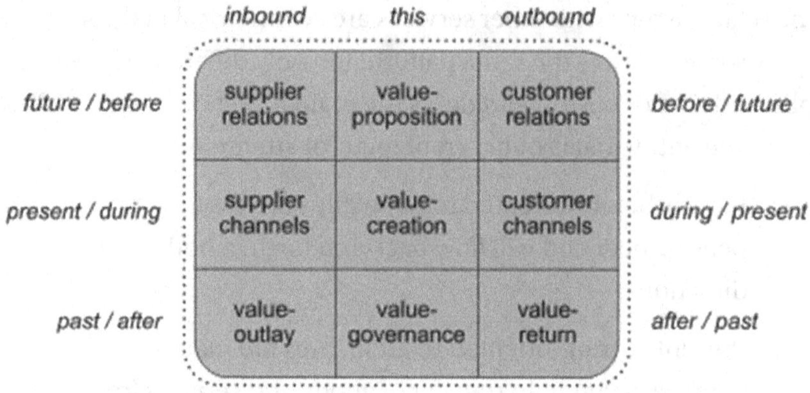

**Figure 8-2.** *Nine-cell service structure*

Let's explore each of these cells in a bit more detail:

**– Supplier-side** (inbound to this service):

- *Supplier relations (supplier-side/future)*: Build and maintain relationships with potential and/or actual "supplier" service-provider entities, about things that may or will need to happen in the future and to keep on track to the vision.

- *Supplier channels (supplier-side/present)*: Receive goods and/or services from "supplier" entities.

- *Value outlay (supplier-side/past)*: Provide balance or compensation to "supplier" entities (such as pay for goods).

**– Self** (what this service does):

- *Value proposition (self/future)*: Identify what this entity will do and deliver, aligned to the overall enterprise purpose and values.

- *Value creation (self/present)*: Take all actions necessary to create and deliver the goods and/or services specified in the value proposition.

- *Value governance (self/past)*: Ensure the appropriate functioning of the overall entity, balancing past, present, and future.

 – **Customer-side** (outbound from this service):

- *Customer relations (customer-side/future)*: Build and maintain relationships with potential and/or actual "customer" service-consumer entities, mainly about what may or should happen in the future, and to communicate the value proposition in relation to the enterprise vision.

- *Customer channels (customer-side/present)*: Deliver goods and/or services to "customer" entities.

- *Value return (customer-side/past)*: Receive balance or compensation from "customer" entities (e.g., payment for goods).

To guide consistency, we would initially assign the cells with those generic labels such as supplier relations. In practice, though, we would more usually translate those generic labels into those of other real-world services that respectively deliver the same kind of function. For example, ZapaMex has a simple manufacturing setup, so the more visible part of its main transactions – the "during" part – would look like this:

- *Supplier channels*: Warehouse inbound – materials and components come in through the warehouse.

- *Value creation*: Production floor – materials and components are made into shoes on the production line.

- *Customer channels*: Warehouse outbound – completed shoes are despatched as end products via the warehouse.

---

Note that although in that ZapaMex example, the inbound and outbound channels went through the same warehouse, the channels have different functions, and it's extremely important to keep those functions apart even if they share the same location.

One of my clients – an engineering research establishment – found this out the hard way. Everything came in and out through the one warehouse; and their method for deciding which way anything was going relied on a risk-prone mix of paperwork and guesswork. Eventually, as one might expect, the system failed spectacularly. A truck driver came by during a lunchbreak with a large aircraft part for testing. No one was around, so he dumped it in the middle of the warehouse bay. One of the laborers came back from his meal, saw the seemingly used-looking part lying on the floor, assumed that it was scrap, and dumped it in the trash metal bin, which was duly picked up a short while later. By the time the researcher called by to check whether his irreplaceable quarter-million-dollar aircraft part had arrived, it was long gone – and despite many frantic days of searching at every scrap merchant in the city, and even every rubbish tip, the part was never found. After that fiasco, the warehouse was provided with clearly marked "In" and "Out" sections on the floor.

---

Yet for any service, we also need to remember what has to happen before the main transactions can occur. For ZapaMex, that "before" part would look something like this:

- *Supplier relations*: Procurement – researching and acquiring new materials and components.

- *Value proposition*: Product development – develop and market new products, in line with the overall vision and values of the shared enterprise.

- *Customer relations*: Sales – point-of-sale activities and customer service.

And then there's also everything that needs to happen after the main transactions. For ZapaMex, that "after" part would look something like this:

- *Value outlay*: Accounts payable – paying suppliers for materials and components.

- *Value governance*: Line management – ensure accounts balance and keep everything on-track to enterprise and organizational success criteria.

- *Value return*: Accounts receivable – receive payment for shoes from customers.

When we bring all of that together, we could summarize the core services for ZapaMex in an Enterprise Canvas layout as shown in Figure 8-3.

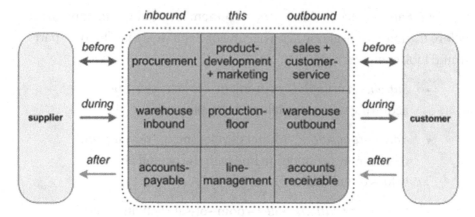

**Figure 8-3.** *Simplified example: ZapaMex shoe manufacturing*

Remember that this generic structure will apply to *any* service – every scope and scale, any type of content or context, and so on. In modeling at the Row-3 Service Model level, it's likely that the first service or "Self" that we'll work with will be the organization as a whole, or perhaps some specific department or business unit within the organization. But as we start to look in more detail – and especially as we work downward into Row-4 Design Model and Row-5 Deployment Model – we'll use this same structure to explore the services that make up the more visible "business services" that we see *as* services at the larger scale. In that sense, every service has the same overall pattern, even though every service is also different from any other. This structure gives us a consistent frame with which to compare every type of service at every level of decomposition.

We can also think of this nine-cell pattern as a kind of functional decomposition in its own right: each of these "cells" delivers its own services to the entity and could thus, recursively, be represented by and described on its own Enterprise Canvas.

And as we saw back in Chapter 5, "Service Layers," we can also describe each service entity in terms of a spectrum between most abstract (the enterprise as a whole) to most concrete (the detailed past). We design and implement a service by moving "down" the layers; we redesign and rethink by moving "up." As we move "down" toward the real world, we'll usually need to add more and more detail – but in essence it's still the same overall service, or rather a more specific *implementation* of that service. We'll explore this in more depth later, in Chapter 13, "Service Content."

# Into Action

With the big-picture context for your business-transformation project established through the work of your previous sessions, you now have a free rein to move deeper into the "How." You want to encourage your teams to use a consistent approach to how they model and describe services, and the relationships, responsibilities, products, exchanges, and flows that link between them. In these sessions with team leads and change teams, you'll recommend that they should use Enterprise Canvas everywhere as a template and checklist for that purpose. Use the ideas in this chapter and the following questions to help you guide those conversations:

- Who or what is responsible for the **Value Proposition** of this service – developing and defining what it can offer to create in terms of the enterprise definition of "value" and identifying the preparation needed to implement this in Value Creation? How does this part of the service do its work? What resources does it need to do this? In what locations does it do it? What events must it initiate or respond to? And what decisions will guide it in this work?

- What real-world services or business functions implement the Value Proposition work of this overall service?

- Who or what is responsible for **Value Creation** in this service – creating and adding value to the overall value web of the shared enterprise? How does this part of the service do its work? What resources does it need to do this? In what locations does it do it? What events must it initiate or respond to? And what decisions will guide it in this work?

- What real-world services or business functions implement the Value Creation work of this overall service?

- Who or what is responsible for **Value Governance** in this service – ensuring that everything is kept on track to the service's role, mission, goals, and outcomes? How does this part of the service do its work? What resources does it need to do this? In what locations does it do it? What events must it initiate or respond to? And what decisions will guide it in this work?

- What real-world services or business functions implement the Value Governance work of this overall service?

- Who or what is responsible for **Supplier Relations** in this service – ensuring that everything required for "inbound" transactions and interactions is properly set up? How does this part of the service do its work? What resources does it need to do this? In what locations does it do it? What events must it initiate or respond to? And what decisions will guide it in this work?

- What real-world services or business functions implement the Supplier Relations work of this overall service?

- Who or what is responsible for the **Supplier Channels** of this service – dealing with tangible (or sometimes intangible) inbound products and services required by this service for its operation? How does this part of the service do its work? What resources does it need to do this? In what locations does it do it? What events must it initiate or respond to? And what decisions will guide it in this work?

- What real-world services or business functions implement the Supplier Channels work of this overall service?

- Who or what is responsible for **Value Outlay** in this service – returning the required value to the service's suppliers and ensuring satisfaction in the terms of the enterprise? How does this part of the service do its work? What resources does it need to do this? In what locations does it do it? What events must it initiate or respond to? And what decisions will guide it in this work?

- What real-world services or business functions implement the Value Outlay work of this overall service?

- Who or what is responsible for **Customer Relations** in this service – ensuring that everything required for "outbound" transactions and interactions is properly set up? How does this part of the service do its work? What resources does it need to do this? In what

locations does it do it? What events must it initiate
or respond to? And what decisions will guide it in
this work?

- What real-world services or business functions
  implement the Customer Relations work of this overall
  service?

- Who or what is responsible for the **Customer Channels**
  of this service – dealing with outbound products and
  services being delivered by this service? How does
  this part of the service do its work? What resources
  does it need to do this? In what locations does it do it?
  What events must it initiate or respond to? And what
  decisions will guide it in this work?

- What real-world services or business functions
  implement the Customer Channels work of this overall
  service?

- Who or what is responsible for **Value Return** in this
  service – obtaining the required returned value from
  the service's customers and ensuring satisfaction in
  the terms of the enterprise? How does this part of the
  service do its work? What resources does it need to do
  this? In what locations does it do it? What events must
  it initiate or respond to? And what decisions will guide
  it in this work?

- What real-world services or business functions
  implement the Value Return work of this overall
  service?

- What real-world services or business functions appear to bridge two or more cells of the Enterprise Canvas? What does this show you in terms of the real-life partitioning of the work? What risks – if any – does this specific partitioning entail?

## Summary

In this chapter we saw how to make sense of what services need to do, by partitioning the service itself into a simple standardized pattern of a three-by-three matrix: a time-related axis of before, during, and after, and a direction-related axis of inbound, this service, and outbound. Each cell represents a distinct and discrete set of activities and viewpoints for the service as a whole.

In the next chapter, we explore the flows that connect between the various players and their respective services across the overall shared enterprise.

# CHAPTER 9

# Service Flows

To understand the value web that is the shared enterprise, we need to pay as much attention to the value flows between services as to the services themselves. Value *creation* takes place *inside* a service, whereas value *flow* bridges the gaps *between* services. As we'll see later, each flow consists of its own mix of products and other types of assets and resources, to be exchanged in various ways between the respective services.

This applies not just to whatever service that is our current focus of attention, but also to each cell within the respective Enterprise Canvas frame. Each of these has its own distinct set of flows, which we'll explore in four parts:

- Main transaction flows with other services – see this chapter.

- Information flows for service management – see later in this chapter.

- Guidance flows – see Chapter 10, "Service Guidance."

- Investor-management flows – see Chapter 11, "Service Investors and Beneficiaries."

We'll explore how to identify the detailed content for each of these flows in Chapter 13, "Service Content."

© Tom Graves 2023
T. Graves, *Mapping the Enterprise*, https://doi.org/10.1007/978-1-4842-9836-7_9

# Main Transaction Flows

These flows form the most visible transactions and interactions of the service. It's useful to separate these into the "before," "during," and "after" phases of transaction, because those phases are often handled by different groups of people or different sub-services within the overall service. And as we saw in the previous chapter, there are also some important differences in the emphasis of each of those types of flow:

- "*Before*" flows link primarily with supplier/customer relations and must *always* be regarded as bidirectional.

- "*During*" flows link primarily with supplier/customer channels; while there are always some bidirectional components, the main flow is along the supply chain – in other words, left to right in the Enterprise Canvas diagram.

- "*After*" flows link primarily with value outlay/return; while there are always some bidirectional components, the main flow is *opposite* to the supply chain – in other words, right to left in the Enterprise Canvas diagram – hence, "return channel."

We can summarize these differences visually as shown in Figure 9-1.

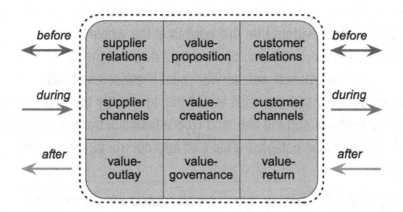

**Figure 9-1.** *Flows: pre-transaction, transaction, post-transaction*

We also need to view these flows in terms of the market model and market cycle that we explored in Chapter 3, "Service Context and Market." A transaction takes place within the context of a market, which itself takes place within the context of a shared enterprise. The market sets the rules for transactions; the shared enterprise provides the reasons and purpose for transactions.

Before the service can enact any *transaction*, it needs to establish that it's in the right market, following that market's rules. To do that, it needs to engage in *conversation* with a potential supplier or customer. But before it can do that, it needs to create a *relationship* with that prospect, to gain sufficient respect to bring them into the market; and to do that, it needs first to establish reputation and trust that the service shares the same overall *aspirations* – in other words, is in the same shared enterprise. Hence, there are many often-subtle interactions that need to take place before there's any chance of a profitable transaction.

It should be self-evident that this applies at the whole-organization scale, yet it also applies right down at the detail-level too. A cloud-based web service must likewise establish "conversation" with a potential transactor, to identify the appropriate interface protocol and the like; and where financial transactions are involved, must also establish trust that appropriate payments will be made.

Moving outward a level or two, firewalls, public-key encryption, and the like are used to establish boundaries of trust. And further out, there will be a real person somewhere who makes the design decisions that permit the web services to establish their automated versions of mutual respect and trust. These interactions are not just "overhead," because without them the transaction would not take place at all.

For the market and enterprise to succeed, the transactions and interactions also need to be profitable to *all* parties involved – not solely to the service in focus. (Note too that "profit" will be defined by the nature of "value" in the enterprise and will usually be much broader than monetary terms alone.) Hence, as shown in Figure 9-2, there will need to be closure at the end of each interaction or transaction, to ensure that that balance is achieved and trust overall is reaffirmed.

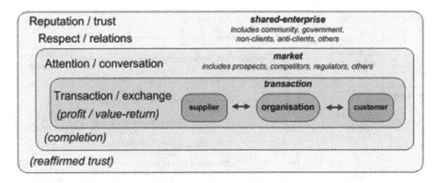

*Figure 9-2. Enterprise and market cycle*

The Supplier Channels and Customer Channels manage the main transaction flows of the supply chain, and the Value Return and Value Outlay cells deal with the main returned value coming back in the reverse direction along the same pathway. But we need to be aware that there's much more to the service flows than just those two out-and-back interactions, and we also need to take care that the other parts of the overall flows are not dismissed as unnecessary "overhead." The same applies to the Supplier Relations and Customer Relations cells that manage most of the "before-transaction" flows and to the Value Return and Value Outlay cells that deal with the remainder of the "after-transaction" flows – yet each of these also needs to work with all of the other cells on that side of the respective service in order to ensure correct closure of the market cycle.

To make it work, we need to expand the "completions" section at the end of the market cycle to make a distinct completion for each of those "before" steps, so that the activities and flows for each "before-action" step can be matched up with their own respective "after-action" completion. The resultant step-by-step, symmetric Service Cycle, as shown in Figure 9-3, will work not just at the market level, as in the market cycle, but for *every* type of interaction between services.

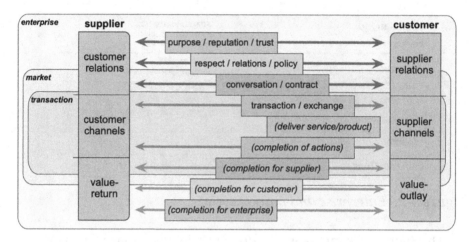

**Figure 9-3.** *Service Cycle – before, during, and after, step-by-step*

The Supplier Relations and Customer Relations cells establish connection with prospects by communicating the service's value proposition, which also links the service to its market (via the offer embedded in the value proposition) and to the shared enterprise (via vision and values). One of the key functions of these "before-transaction" flows is to establish that prospective suppliers and customers also align to the vision and values of the shared enterprise – because if they don't, problems will almost certainly ensue further down the line.

---

Note that for this purpose, it's often useful to have a published guide to business principles, to which the service asserts that it will adhere and to which it expects all players – *including itself* – will be held accountable. As Shell once put it in their "General Business Principles," "We are judged by how we act – our reputation is upheld by how we live up to our core values": an explicit published document about principles will help to provide clarity where it is often much needed!

---

For our fictitious company ZapaMex, it would no doubt be easy for its production team to think only in terms of the supply-chain transactions, and ignore everything else, as shown in Figure 9-4.

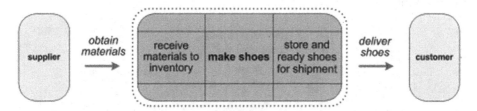

**Figure 9-4.** *Production view of service flows*

Line management, however, would insist that some attention should be paid to monetary flows; and sales, marketing, and procurement would all have their say as well – in other words, a *market* view, as shown in Figure 9-5.

**Figure 9-5.** *Market view of service flows*

Yet ZapaMex will need to think beyond just that basic transaction-oriented view of the market: it also needs to build trust and gain respect, within the market and beyond. A focus on values, for example, would guide any discussions with suppliers or customers about material quality, because the values define what "quality" *is* within the enterprise. In the same way, ZapaMex needs to ensure proper closure in terms of the Service

Cycle that underpins the market cycle – otherwise its reputation will be at risk, and the market with it. From that perspective, the full set of flows that ZapaMex will need to address will include all of those shown in Figure 9-6, and probably more.

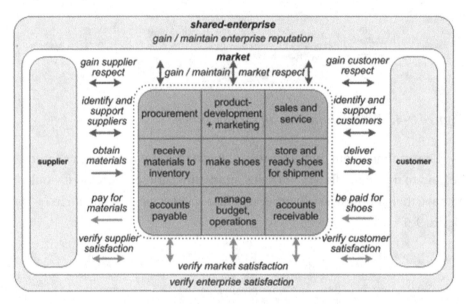

***Figure 9-6.*** *Enterprise view of service flows*

When we assess the flows of a service in an Enterprise Canvas, we need to be clear which kind of scope we're working with and to ensure the completeness of the picture in each case.

# Information Flows for Service Management

Another key type of flow we need to consider is the information flows between services in a service hierarchy. We can illustrate this with a simplified view of a service that creates a new account, shown in BPMN process-model notation in Figure 9-7.

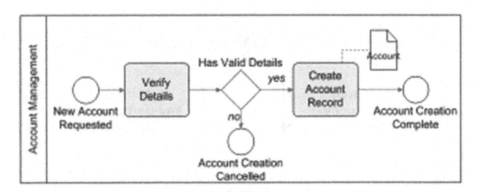

**Figure 9-7.** *Simplified account-creation service as BPMN process diagram*

These diagrams are common enough in solution architectures, but in essence they only describe the basic transaction flows and, if we're lucky, some aspects of the flows in the return channel. What these diagrams very rarely describe is the *context* of the service – especially its reporting relationships up and down the service hierarchy and its coordination with other services. To understand the service, we need to know not just its transactions, but also how it would be managed, what performance criteria it should report, and where those reports should be sent, as indicated in Figure 9-8.

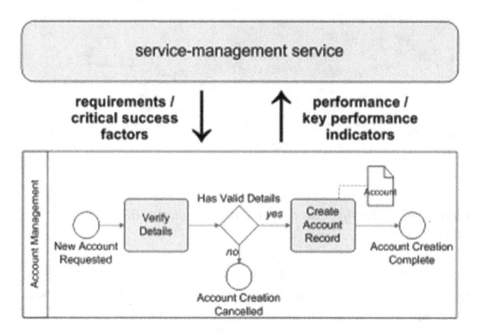

*Figure 9-8.* *Context for simplified account-creation service*

The same would be true of this service's links with its "child" services "Verify Details" and "Create Account Record": they too would need to share requirements and performance information with their "parent" service. In Enterprise Canvas, we show these flows as a vertical double arrow, as illustrated in Figure 9-9.

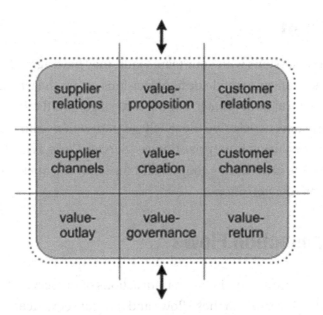

***Figure 9-9.*** *Service-management information flows*

In essence, these flows are usually the responsibility of the Value-Governance cell, so although the flows may move both "upward" and "downward" in the service hierarchy, often only the lower double arrow is shown.

---

Note that the space for the upper link may already be occupied anyway if links to guidance services are also shown on the Enterprise Canvas – see Chapter 10, "Service Guidance."

---

We'll explore the methods for assessment of detailed content for all of these flows in more depth in Chapter 13, "Service Content."

# Into Action

In the previous sessions with your team leads, they have agreed that they'll use Enterprise Canvas to guide design decisions across the whole of your business-transformation project. For the next stage, you'll want them to go deeper into how to describe the details of transactions and interactions between services, using Enterprise Canvas' Service Cycle as a template and checklist. Use the ideas in this chapter and the following questions to help you guide those conversations.

## Main Transaction Flows

- What flows form the main transactions of the service? What is carried in these flows and in what sequence? What value is added to the overall transaction flow by this service? From which supplier does each incoming flow derive? To which customer is each outgoing flow directed, and how? Who is responsible for each of these flows, both incoming and outgoing?

- What flows form the return channel for each main transaction? What is carried in these flows and in what sequence? From which customer does each incoming return flow derive? To which supplier is each outgoing return flow directed, and how? Who is responsible for each of these flows, both incoming and outgoing?

- What return value is captured from the return channel by this service for its own use? What governance is applied to this value capture? What measures are taken to ensure that this capture is aligned with the values of the overall shared enterprise?

- What methods are used to ensure and verify satisfaction of all parties in a supply-chain relationship?

- What flows are required before any transactions may take place, either with suppliers or with customers? What is carried in each of these flows, and in what sequence? What values are implied, expressed, and referenced within each of these interactions? With which customer, supplier, or other non-transaction stakeholder is each interaction linked and by what means? Who is responsible for each of these flows?

- What methods are used to monitor and verify reputation and respect of the service within its market and its broader shared enterprise? What methods are used to monitor the impact of each flow on such reputation and respect?

# Information Flow for Service Management

- What flows form the "upward" linkage between this service and any "parent" service in the service hierarchy or management hierarchy? What is carried in these flows and in what sequence? What methods are used to ensure that each flow is directed to the appropriate "parent"? What value is added to the organization, the market, and the overall enterprise by each flow? Who is responsible for each of these flows?

- What flows form the "downward" linkage between this service and any "child" service in the service hierarchy or management hierarchy? What is carried in these flows and in what sequence? What methods are used to ensure that each flow is directed to the appropriate "child"? What value is added to the organization, the market, and the overall enterprise by each flow? Who is responsible for each of these flows?

# Summary

In this chapter, we applied the same kind of structure review to the flows that make up the relationships between services, to establish what needs to pass back and forth with each provider or client, before, during, and after each of their main transactions. We also reviewed the information and other assets that need to pass up and down the service-management hierarchy.

In the next chapter, we explore the key support services that provide guidance to the service in focus, for direction on strategy, tactics, operation, and change, for coordination with other services, and for maintaining and improving the quality of service.

# CHAPTER 10

# Service Guidance

So far, we've explored how each service identifies its purpose within a broader shared enterprise and how it structures its tasks and its relationships with others in the overall flow of value around the enterprise. Yet each service will also need some form of *guidance* to connect with that wider world, and in practice – certainly in any organization much larger than a one-man band – each service will depend on other more-specialized services to provide that guidance.

To make sense of this, it's useful to come back to that notion of the organization as a "living system" rather than as a machine. For that living system to be "viable," as a whole, within its broader context – a "Viable System," as Stafford Beer described it – each of its services will need not just the ability to do its own tasks, but also must have some means to *decide* what it needs to do at each moment; to *coordinate* its activities with other services; to *plan* its future activities, its tactics, and strategy; to *remember* what it has done; and to use the knowledge to help it *adapt* to and *improve* its relationship with its own environment. Much of this needs to be done in coordination with others, to ensure that everything works together as a unified whole – and all of it "on purpose," both on its own terms and in relationship with that broader enterprise. Few services will be able to do all of this on their own – and that's where the *guidance services* come into the picture.

© Tom Graves 2023
T. Graves, *Mapping the Enterprise*, https://doi.org/10.1007/978-1-4842-9836-7_10

If we describe the service itself as a "doing" service or *delivery service* – because each service does or delivers *something* – then we can partition all of those other requirements into roles for three distinct categories of support services:

- *Direction services* that support decision-making, planning, and change and also provide links to other whole-of-system services such as finance, HR, and infrastructure.

- *Coordination services* that link both within and beyond the organization, to enable the smooth flow of service and supply chains and also guide the coordination of change.

- *Validation services* that monitor and maintain quality throughout the organization, support continuous improvement, and also help the development of skills, competence, and capabilities.

Figure 10-1 provides a visual summary of the relationships between these different types of services and how some of them necessarily extend beyond classic notions of "management."

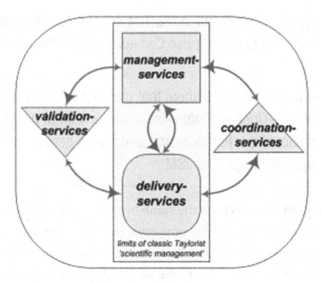

**Figure 10-1.** *Four categories of services*

As a side note, those symbols used in Figure 10-1 are intended to match up with their equivalents in Stafford Beer's "Viable System Model" or VSM, as mentioned earlier above: the circle or rounded-corner box for delivery services, which aligns with the role of VSM's "system-1"; the upward-pointing triangle for coordination services, which sort-of aligns with the role of VSM's "system-2"; the square for management services, which aligns with the roles of VSM's "system-3," "system-4," and "system-5," and the downward-pointing triangle for validation services, which sort-of aligns with VSM's "system-3*."

That point is not important here, though: for our purposes, they're just symbols that we can use to identify those different service roles. For what it's worth, VSM does actually provide some of the core theory behind Enterprise Canvas, but in practice we don't really need to know any of that to *use* Enterprise Canvas, which is the main focus of this book.

If you *do* want to know more about that underlying theory, see my book *The Service-Oriented Enterprise* – there's a lot of detail in there about the relationships, parallels, and crossmaps between service modeling, service design, and VSM.

---

Ultimately, all services have the same overall structure, because all of them deliver a service: whichever way we might label or categorize them, in the end *every* service is a "delivery service." In effect, the only key differences between services are in the value proposition for each specific service, the content that each service delivers, and perhaps in how it delivers that service and content; but the *patterns* of relationships within and between services always remain much the same.

Yet the point about that need for external support still remains. Who or what will direct the service managers? Who or what will coordinate this service with other services? Who or what will ensure that quality is established and maintained? There's not much for that that's in the core nine-cell service structure as such: and yet there's a real need for some forms of support or guidance to make sure that all of those things *do* happen. Hence, although in principle every service is a "delivery service," every service also needs the support of those three other key categories of service: direction services, coordination services, and the validation services that help to create, maintain, and pervade quality throughout every part of the enterprise. Collectively, these other services provide the overall guidance support needed by every service.

We might instead describe "direction services" as "management services," though that can be misleading as their role is actually quite a bit broader than simple management of a business unit or service. An alternative term for "validation services" would be "pervasive services," because while they do ensure that everything holds to the values of the chosen shared enterprise, they also need to pervade *everywhere* throughout the whole enterprise.

The relationships between each of these three types of guidance services are that they are almost orthogonal to each other, as shown in Figure 10-2.

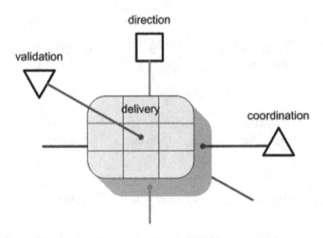

***Figure 10-2.*** *Delivery service and its guidance services*

As described in the note about Viable System Model earlier, we represent delivery services with a circle or a rounded-corner rectangle; direction services with a square symbol; coordination services with an upward-pointing triangle; and validation services with a downward-pointing triangle.

For Enterprise Canvas, we show the guidance services in relation to the service to be guided by linking them to the frame of the overall "delivery service," with the frame shown in Figure 10-3 as a dotted line around the standard nine-cell Canvas.

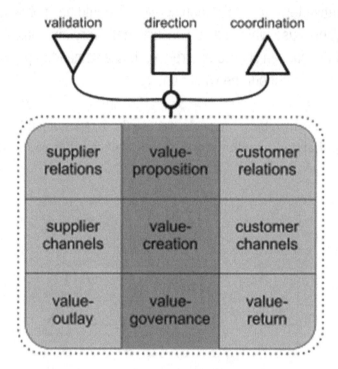

***Figure 10-3.*** *Guidance services and nine-cell Canvas*

Note that each of these will attach *at the respective layer or "row,"* as described in Chapter 5, "Service Layers." The same layering and recursion will apply to these services too, from most abstract (Row–0 Enterprise) to most concrete (Row-6 Action Records).

Each of these services also has their own flows that pass between them and the service in focus in the Enterprise Canvas. Each type of guidance service also has its own emphases within the cells of the Enterprise Canvas, as shown in Figure 10-4.

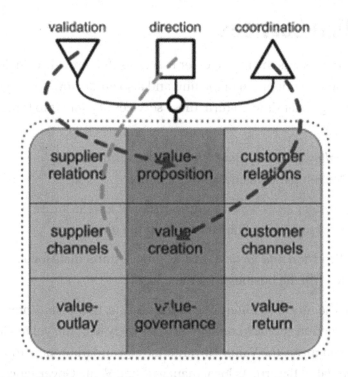

***Figure 10-4.*** *Emphases of the guidance services*

With the exception of some of the coordination services, few of these services have much direct or immediate impact on the day-to-day running of most of the delivery services – they're more in-the-background rather than in-your-face. Their real role is to assist in the *dynamics* of services – the ways in which the services can, may, and must change over time to adapt to changing context and to align more strongly with the enterprise vision.

# Direction Services

**Direction** represents the management services that provide oversight of the direction and operation of the unit and also guide how the service may need to change over time. In turn, these services are split into three distinct categories:

- *Policy, purpose, and identity*: Long-term view to "develop the business" for the unit

- *Strategy and context* ("outside/future"): Near-future view to "change the business" for the unit

- *Direction and tactics* ("inside/now"): Immediate focus to "run the business" for the unit

Within the nine-cell Enterprise Canvas frame, the "inside/now" group of direction services connect most strongly with the Value-Creation cell and, even more, the Value-Governance cell and from there to Value Outlay and Value Return. As local management, Value Governance does have a natural tendency to look to the past – the "bean-counters" – or at best to include the near future for local planning purposes with a view that's tightly constrained to local needs. The role of the direction services is to connect the governance of this service to the big picture and to the present and future direction of the enterprise as a whole. The "strategy and context" and "purpose, policy, and identity" groups of support services probably connect most strongly to the Value-Proposition cell, with its emphasis on future rather than present or past.

From the perspective of a single delivery service, there will usually be only one overall set of these direction services attached to it. Much as in a classic organizational hierarchy, though, a "run the business" direction service will typically provide guidance for several delivery services, often be shared across different levels; a "change the business" direction service will typically cover an entire business silo, such as marketing, finance, or IT; and a single "develop the business" direction service will provide guidance for the entire organization, and sometimes beyond.

In our ZapaMex example, the "purpose, policy, and identity" direction services are mostly the responsibility of the executive board, with support from their immediate teams in making these decisions and distributing them throughout the organization as a whole. The "strategy and context" direction services are provided on one side by the strategy team, working with the change team, and on the other by the marketing team. The "direction and tactics" direction services are provided by middle management and line management, following the management hierarchy all the way down to the front line.

# Coordination Services

**Coordination** represents the coordination services that link units together to create webs of cross-functional processes as required. As with the "direction" services, these can be split into three distinct categories:

- *Develop the business*: Coordinate portfolios of longer-term change across units – also provides cross-functional bridge between direction's "policy purpose and identity" and "strategy and context"

- *Change the business*: Cross-functional coordination of change projects – also provides cross-functional bridge between direction's "strategy and context" and "direction and tactics"

- *Run the business*: Cross-functional coordination of run-time processes – also provides cross-functional bridge between direction's "direction and tactics" and the unit's own processes and interfaces, connecting everything end-to-end along the organization's part of the respective supply chain and value web

Within the nine-cell Canvas frame, these connect most strongly with Value Creation and the "supply-chain" interfaces – Supplier Channels and Customer Channels. Value Creation has a natural tendency to focus only on the here-and-now, on doing the same things the same way to maximize local efficiency and reliability without concern for whole-system effectiveness. The coordination services ensure that this service is connected to others as required at run time and is also connected to organizational and enterprise change.

There's often only one organization-wide "develop the business" strategy-coordination service, though a variable number of "change the business" services, dependent on the organization's portfolio/project-management mix. There will be a large number of "run the business" links, often forming a complete "shadow network" that is almost invisible to the standard hierarchy.

In ZapaMex, the portfolio development, product development, and strategy teams work together on the "develop the business" tasks, reporting directly to the executive board. The overall change group, consisting of the project managers, project leads, and architecture teams, do the bulk of the "change the business" work, though they also do some coordination with the marketing and procurement teams. The "run the business" coordination work is done by line managers and team leads, with support from IT systems as appropriate, some occasional help from architects and like, and also a few people with often-blurry job titles who wander around in the background *between* the departments and silos and keep everything working together across the whole.

# Validation Services

**Validation** represents the broad range of support services that underpin overall governance and that guide the organization toward ever-stronger alignment with the enterprise vision and values such as safety, security, efficiency, and so on. These services need to touch *every* part of the organization, without exception, ultimately as part of the background ethos, culture, and collective habits – hence, that alternate label of "pervasive services." As with the other guidance services, these types of support services can be split into three distinct categories:

- *Develop awareness*: Advertise and evangelize to create awareness of the importance of the respective values and their practical implications.

- *Develop capability*: Educate in practices and metrics to implement and monitor compliance to the enterprise values via their derived principles, etc.

- (Use that developed awareness and capability to take action at run time, to support the value as an embedded part of every activity.)

- *Verify and audit*: Review records and lessons learned to assure compliance to the values

Within the nine-cell Canvas frame, these connect most strongly with the Value-Proposition cell. From there, they link with the "relations" cells – Supplier Relations and Customer Relations – to "spread the word" outward to the supply chain, the market, and the broader enterprise. Internally, though, they *must* link with and become embedded in every cell of the service.

In principle, there should be one matched set of these services, organization-wide, for *each* key value of the enterprise, such as safety, security, quality, innovation, knowledge-sharing, and the like, depending on the vision and values of the enterprise and of the organization itself. There will usually be a distinct quality team for each of those respective values and provide the respective services as appropriate. Note, though, the real purpose of those validation services is to reaffirm that upholding the respective value is ultimately *everyone*'s responsibility – *not* solely that of the respective quality team.

The full set of services needed will be different for every enterprise, aligning with the different needs and different values of the respective enterprise. Note that for some values such as financial probity or occupational health and safety, various laws or other constraints may mandate that the "verify and audit" services should or must be kept separate from the respective "develop awareness" and "develop capability" services.

For ZapaMex, the highest-priority value concern is health and safety – the company has a proud record of one of lowest injury rates in the industry, and is keen to maintain that reputation. The next priorities are its product quality, its relationships with customers, suppliers, and others, and in creating a culture of continual improvement in everything that they do. There's also a focus in the society as a whole about business ethics and financial probity, so those need to be addressed as well.

Within ZapaMex, the "develop awareness" aspects for each of these concerns are tackled in on-boarding of new staff and the like, in conversations with suppliers and with government, in marketing materials and customer-service channels, and in business reports both outside and inside the company. For "develop capability," training on health and safety and on business ethics is provided by external specialists, whereas training on the other values is mostly done in-house; in the manufacturing areas, the team leads maintain a continuous watch for potential hazards and are quick to help staff learn how to resolve production problems in ways that can avoid unsafe practices. For "verify and audit," much of "verify and audit" is done by external services, particularly for equipment safety and financial review; in each case, though, the reviews are also assessed by the quality teams and change teams, working together to look for any options to support further improvements on the respective quality concerns.

# Into Action

In the next sessions with the team leads of your business-transformation project, you want them to show how they'll ensure that every service will have the right management and governance, coordination with other services, and strategic oversight and coordination of change. You'll recommend that they should use the "guidance-services" section of Enterprise Canvas as a template and completeness checklist. Use the ideas in this chapter and the following questions to help you guide those conversations.

# Direction Services

- Who or what is responsible for policy, purpose, and identity for this service? Who or what within this service is responsible for ensuring that this service connects to organizational and enterprise policy, purpose, and identity? What flows are needed between this service and other services to ensure that this happens? What is the content of such flows? What events and decisions will trigger and guide such flows? What functions, capabilities, and assets are needed in this service to enact those requirements?

- Who or what is responsible for strategy and context for this service? Who or what within this service is responsible for ensuring that this service connects to organizational and enterprise strategy and context? What flows are needed between this service and other services to ensure that this happens? What is the content of such flows? What are the events and decisions that trigger and guide such flows? What functions, capabilities, and assets are needed in this service to enact those requirements?

- Who or what is responsible for near-future direction and tactics for this service? Who or what within this service is responsible for ensuring that this service connects to organizational and enterprise direction and tactics, and for connections to whole-of-system support such as finance, HR, and infrastructure? What flows are needed between this service and other services to ensure that this happens? What is the content of such flows? What events and decisions will trigger and guide such flows? What functions, capabilities, and assets are needed in this service to enact those requirements?

## Coordination Services

- Who or what is responsible for engaging everyone in "develop the business" whole-context review and change? Who or what within this service is responsible for ensuring that this service connects to "develop the business" review and change? What flows are needed between this service and other services to ensure that this happens? What is the content of such flows? What are the events and decisions that trigger and guide such flows? What functions, capabilities, and assets are needed in this service to enact those requirements?

- Who or what is responsible for engaging this service in broad-scope change programs and change projects? Who or what within this service is responsible for ensuring that this service connects to such "change the business" activities? What flows are needed between this service and other services to ensure that this happens? What is the content of such flows? What are the events and decisions that trigger and guide such flows? What functions, capabilities, and assets are needed in this service to enact those requirements?

- Who or what is responsible for engaging this service in process choreography and other run-time coordination? Who or what within this service is responsible for ensuring that this service connects to broader-scope run-time coordination? What flows are needed between this service and other services to ensure that this happens? What is the content of such flows? What are the events and decisions that trigger and guide such flows? What functions, capabilities, and assets are needed in this service to enact those requirements?

# Validation Services

For each value, principle, or quality required by the enterprise vision and for the organization's chosen role within the enterprise:

- Who or what is responsible for developing general awareness of the importance of this value to the organization? Who or what within this service is responsible for ensuring that this service engages in developing the awareness of that value? What flows are needed between this service and other services to ensure that this happens? What is the content of such flows? What are the events and decisions that trigger and guide such flows? What functions, capabilities, and assets are needed in this service to enact those requirements?

- Who or what is responsible for developing the capability to enact this value within the organization? Who or what within this service is responsible for ensuring that this service develops its capability to enact this value in its operations? What flows are needed between this service and other services to ensure that this happens? What is the content of such flows? What are the events and decisions that trigger and guide such flows? What functions, capabilities, and assets are needed in this service to enact those requirements?

- Who or what within this service is responsible for ensuring that this value is expressed in the real-time operations of this service? What flows are needed within this service, and between this service and other services, to ensure that this happens? What is the content of such flows? What are the events and decisions that trigger and guide such flows? What functions, capabilities, and assets are needed in this service to enact those requirements?

- Who or what is responsible for auditing and verifying the practical expression of this value within the organization and across the enterprise? Who or what within this service is responsible for ensuring that this service connects appropriately to the processes for auditing and verifying this quality within the service? What flows are needed between this service and other services to ensure that this happens? What is the content of such flows? What are the events and decisions that trigger and guide such flows? What functions, capabilities, and assets are needed in this service to enact those requirements?

# Summary

In this chapter we noted that no service stands alone: it always exists within a broader context and needs to be connected with other support services that can provide guidance and governance to link the service into its place in that context. These support services also help to coordinate it with other services, provide direction on future change, and keep it on track with enterprise values. We saw how to identify the various types of these support services that each service will need, the roles they play relative to the service in focus, and how to model the respective relationships in Enterprise Canvas.

In the next chapter, we explore how a service connects to and interacts with its investors and beneficiaries.

# CHAPTER 11

# Service Investors and Beneficiaries

Another set of flows that we will often need to include in our service-design assessment are those that link the service with its investors and beneficiaries:

- *Investors* provide an investment of some value in order to help get the service started or to maintain its operations, in ways or forms that are distinct from and/or cannot be provided by either the main "horizontal" value flow nor the guidance services.

- *Beneficiaries* receive some value as a *benefit* or dividend from the operation of the service, in ways or forms that are distinct from and/or cannot be provided by either the main "horizontal" value flow nor the guidance services.

- Appropriate *balance* needs to be maintained in the relationship between investor flows and beneficiary flows – between what comes in and what goes out.

The simplest example of this is monetary investment in a company:

- As an *investor*, someone invests money in the company.

© Tom Graves 2023
T. Graves, *Mapping the Enterprise*, https://doi.org/10.1007/978-1-4842-9836-7_11

- As a *beneficiary*, that person receives a monetary dividend or repayment from the company – the "return on investment."

- In terms of *balance*, there's usually an expectation that, in compensation for taking on some of the financial risk, the monetary return to the investor will be greater than the initial investment – that the person will receive more money out than they paid in.

---

ZapaMex is a privately owned company: as investors, the founders provided most of the start-up funding and took on most of the financial risks to get everything started; and they and their families, as beneficiaries, retain much of the financial return.

From time to time, the company's owners have also taken out bank loans, such as to pay for new facilities and equipment to support the company's growth. For the duration of each loan, the bank has thus been a financial investor, receiving payment both in interest charges and other fees, and in the eventual repayment of the loan.

---

Note, though, that this is often about far more than merely money alone. These are value flows, so just as we've seen with the main "horizontal" value chain from supplier to self to customer, *any* form of value can bridge across that flow: money, goods, information, connections, reputation, access to services, whatever. The forms of value received from investors and returned to beneficiaries are also not necessarily the same and in some cases can be very different indeed.

At ZapaMex, the owners acknowledge that their staff are each investing a significant part of their lives in working with them toward the aims of the enterprise. In return, they offer benefits to their staff, not just in monetary form, such as wages and the like, but also in support for healthcare and product discounts for themselves and other members of their families – each of these non-monetary benefits being aligned to the enterprise values.

In line with the country's culture, ZapaMex has a strong focus on family. They acknowledge that the families of their staff are making another kind of investment, in family life disrupted by the absence of that staff member while they are away at work. Some of the benefits offered in return for this absence come in the form of wages and the like that are being shared with the family. The company do also organize "bring your child to work" days and whole-of-company family events, and offer training and priority for employment to family members.

The outcome from this is that not only may the investors and beneficiaries for a service be different, but the content of the respective flows may be different too; and all of these may be different again for each of the different services with different roles at different levels of the organization's services. This can make it challenging to find the right balance between investment and return across the enterprise – yet we do need to face that challenge in our work on service design, because there can be very real consequences to the organization and enterprise if we don't get the balance right.

To make sense of this, it's best to explore the flows first and then tackle the question of balance once that's done.

# Investor Flows and Beneficiary Flows

In Enterprise Canvas, we model the main parts of these investor flows as an up arrow from Investor to Value Outlay and beneficiary flows as a down arrow from Value Return to Beneficiary. As we'll see later when we explore that question of balance, both Investor and Beneficiary also connect to Value Governance, but we can skip over that for now.

---

Conventionally, investors and beneficiaries are often described as the stakeholders or "owners" – which *is* valid, though it can sometimes become very complicated to explain this point once we start to look at the value flows in anything more than the most simplistic of monetary terms!

---

Figure 11-1 provides a visual summary of how these flows relate with the core of the service itself.

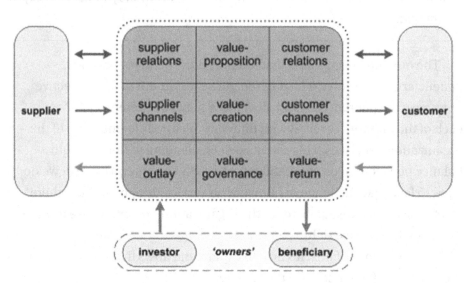

***Figure 11-1.*** *Flows: investment and dividend*

In practice, an **investor** is a kind of supplier – but the flow usually goes the opposite way to what we would expect, feeding into the right-to-left return channel rather than the left-to-right main channel. Invested value is an *input* to the service, but often no further value will be added by the Value Creation of the service before it is sent onward to a supplier.

As we've seen, the simplest example of this kind of investment is in monetary terms: for example, a new business will typically need to buy in some supplies in order to be able to sell them onward with some form of added value. But since there are many kinds of value, there are also many other kinds of investment, which can include

- Entrepreneurs provide a start-up with ideas, commitment, drive.

- Friends and family provide entrepreneurs and employees with material, emotional, and aspirational support.

- Business references or a government export certificate provides a new business with vital credibility in the marketplace.

- A community invests sufficient trust to grant a social "license to operate."

- An analyst firm invests their personal reputation, status, and credibility when recommending the company as a suitable financial investment.

- A customer does likewise in recommending the company's products and services.

For example, a ZapaMex customer makes a video about "unboxing" her newly delivered shoes, commenting on the quality of the packaging and presentation as much about the shoes themselves. Putting the shoes on, she comments on the look, the fit, the comfort, on how they make her feel – linking her to the enterprise vision of "helping your feet feel happy and healthy." She then posts the video on the net for anyone to see.

In doing all of this, she invests her effort, her trust, her own reputation, her pleasure in both the company and the ZapaMex brand. She's not been paid to do this – the opposite, in fact, in that she has *paid* for the privilege to do all of these things. It's therefore in the company's interest to make sure that to her it continues to *feel* like a privilege, and that her investment has for her been worthwhile.

Perhaps, the simplest way to explore investment is to identify the respective assets as a mix of the *tetradian* asset dimensions, as described in Chapter 3, "Service Context and Market":

- *Physical*: Alienable "things" and tangible products from services

- *Virtual*: Non-alienable items such as ideas and information

- *Relational*: Person-to-person connection

- *Aspirational*: Personal commitment to an idea, belief, brand, or enterprise vision

Note that others may have multiple roles relative to the service in this respect and may also invest multiple forms of value. A supplier who extends a financial line of credit to the company is investing both money and trust. That satisfied ZapaMex customer who tells her friends about how much she likes her new shoes is both a customer *and* an investor because she's investing her own reputation in the company.

The inverse may apply if a ZapaMex customer, for example, is *not* satisfied with their purchase: they become an *anti-client* who "anti-invests" their reputation and their effort *against* the company, and will usually try to induce others to withdraw their investments too. In former times this usually didn't matter all that much – a single complainant wouldn't be able to do much on their own. But it now matters much more than it did, because in these days of social media, a single disgruntled customer can cause a *lot* of damage.

---

Probably *the* textbook example of this is Dave Carroll's song *United Breaks Guitars*. A professional musician, he became annoyed with United Airlines, having been given the run-around for almost a year by the customer-service department after his beloved Taylor guitar was damaged in baggage handling. He wrote a song about his troubles, which he and his band performed in a low-cost music video that they then posted up on YouTube.

The song's catchy tune and chorus and the bright, ironic humor of the video were enough to make it an instant Internet hit: it passed the million-views mark in well under a week. Quickly becoming a lightning rod for anger at *all* airlines' often customer-hostile "customer-service" systems, it appeared on national TV only a day or two after release; on international TV a day or two after that. United, caught completely off-guard, probably spent upward of $20million in urgent damage control; the damage to brand was incalculable, but the incident certainly played a part in triggering a short-term hit of almost a billion dollars off their share value.

The irony, of course, was that United could reasonably claim that none of it was their fault: the initial incident fell into one of those awkward gray areas where many different organizations were involved and no one of them could be assigned exclusive responsibility to repair the damage. But no matter: it was United that wore the blame – and the costs, in every sense.

So don't ignore the risks that your anti-clients can represent: anyone could become one, for any reason, at any time, and any one of them could kill the company – yet you have no way at all to know in advance which one of them it might be.

---

Many companies will acquire some of their anti-clients as a direct consequence of the nature of the work that they do: oil drillers and miners opposed by environmental activists, for example, or a family-planning clinic challenged by those who hold opposing religious beliefs. In a sense, every competitor, of whatever kind, is an anti-client too, although that kind of anti-investment is to be expected and should be planned for from the start: it shouldn't much matter unless the competitor is able to incite a more general anti-client attack – as may happen often in politics, for example.

---

Note that the only certain way to tackle the risk (and opportunity) represented by anti-clients is to go to the visible effort of building a reservoir of trust and reputation with the broader community. At some point you *are* going to have to draw on that reserve, and – courtesy of the naturally chaotic nature of real-world interactions and events – you have no way to know when or why that will be. One of the few proven tactics to do this is to build dialogue connections with the broader enterprise by being clear on your enterprise vision and demonstrating *by explicit action* that you hold yourselves accountable to that vision. The alternative is simply to sit and hope that nothing will happen: not a wise move, as United Airlines discovered the hard way.

---

Going the other direction, a **beneficiary** is a kind of customer, as the recipient of a benefit from the service. Again, though, the flow will usually go the *opposite* way to the usual customer flow, coming from the return channel rather than the main channel. Value here is an *output* from the service, but usually no value will have been added by the Value Creation of the service itself.

As before, the simplest example is in monetary terms, such as a dividend payment to a stockholder. Once again, though, there are many other kinds of value that may be returned: for example, the government gets payback for its export license in terms of enhanced credibility for the country as a whole, while the local community may see returns in terms of "good citizen" behavior by the business and also the wages and employment of its citizens supporting the local economy.

# A Question of Balance

Most investors will expect some form of return on their investment, either direct or indirect. The complication here, as we've seen, is that the dividend may not necessarily take the same form of value as in the initial investment. Someone who invests time may expect to be paid in money; someone who invests money in a social project may simply want the satisfaction of seeing the job done well, with a good social outcome. You will see that there could be an almost infinite array of possible permutations in this.

It's therefore important to avoid any reliance on the usual overly simplistic notion of "double-entry life-keeping" and instead take care to identify what each potential investor's expectations may be. Otherwise, again, there's a risk of creating another dangerously disgruntled anti-client, where, with a little extra effort, we could instead have ensured strong satisfaction all round for everyone.

From a simple monetary perspective, especially in a commercial context, the investors and beneficiaries will often seem to be the same – the stockholders or shareholders, for example, or the members of a cooperative. But in reality, and especially in a not-for-profit or government context, they will often be different, at least in terms of a money-only calculation. In addition, as we've seen above, invested value and returned value may take on very different forms: a financial investment may be returned in a form such as reputation or social standing. In many cases, simple book-keeping may be more of a hindrance than a help.

Whichever way we may choose to do it, it is always essential that the various "books" balance up in some appropriate way. Often the key test criterion is simply that the investor feels satisfied with the effective return on their investment – in whatever form each of those investments and returns may take. The result, though, is that achieving that proper balance across all forms of investment can sometimes be anything but simple.

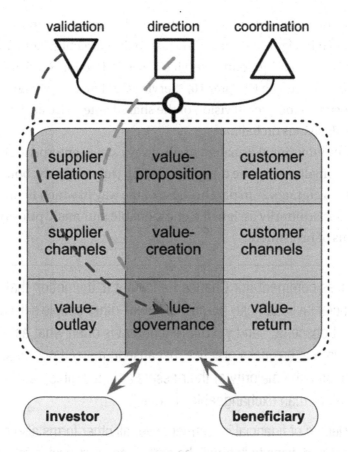

***Figure 11-2.*** *Investors and beneficiaries: maintaining the balance*

In the Enterprise Canvas, as shown in Figure 11-2, most of this work will fall to the Value-Governance cell. There will often need to be distinct activities and flows associated with that cell – such as an investor-relations unit, for example. (Note again, though, that the actual task there will need to address *all* investors and forms of investment – *not* solely monetary forms.) These flows will need to link both to investors and to beneficiaries – who, once again, may in many cases be different people. And a major focus is not just to maintain appropriate relations with all of these stakeholders, but to ensure also that an appropriate balance is

145

maintained on either side of the investment/dividend equation. As also shown in Figure 11-2, a strong link to the "direction" and, in some cases, the "validation" guidance services – see "Direction Services" and "Validation Services" in Chapter 10, "Service Guidance" – will help in keeping focus on the overall vision of the shared enterprise as the ultimate arbiter for decisions on balance.

While unintentional imbalance will always create enterprise risk, deliberate imbalance can be downright lethal. Unfortunately, both of these can be all too common – in part because of the way in which financial investment is arbitrarily assigned a questionable automatic priority over all other forms of investment.

---

As business commentator Charles Handy put it, the notion that the financial investors can purport to "own" other people's lives is downright obscene – and yet at present that is often what actually happens in real business practice, because in many if not most organizations, the majority of their assets are intangible, residing in people rather than exchangeable "things."

The privileging of financial investment over all other forms also enables all manner of options to "game" the enterprise, from hostile takeovers to asset-stripping to overt dumping and worse. That such activities may technically be legal does not change the fact that in almost other any context, they would be classed as serious crimes: and the point here is that every other investor in the enterprise will know it. In short, such game plays can create a time bomb for the overall enterprise, and at some point – as is already starting to happen in some cases – that bomb will eventually explode, with messy results all round. It's likely that the only people who can take appropriate action on this are senior executives and lawmakers – and whether they will have the courage to bite the bullet on this is another question entirely. But in the meantime, this section of the Enterprise Canvas can help to surface serious concerns such as these: and that at least will give us something to work with when the appropriate time comes.

---

# Into Action

You want your team leads to understand that, for your business-transformation project, investment and benefit can take many forms and can apply to almost any type of service, even right down to the detail level. You'll recommend that they should use the "investors and beneficiaries" section of Enterprise Canvas as a way to explore this in the service designs. Use the ideas in this chapter and the following questions to help you guide those conversations.

## Investment and Dividend

- What investments are made in this service? In what forms of value do these investments occur? Via what flows are these investments made in the service? Who or what is responsible for making these investments? Within the service, who or what is responsible for receiving these investments, and for ensuring satisfaction of the investor in the investment?

- What dividends are disbursed by this service? In what forms of value do these dividends occur? Via what flows are these dividends disbursed by the service? Who or what is responsible for receiving these dividends? Within the service, who or what is responsible for disbursements, and for ensuring satisfaction of the beneficiary in the dividend?

# Balancing Investors, Beneficiaries, and the Enterprise

- What facilities exist within the service to ensure appropriate balance between investors and beneficiaries, between investments and dividends?

- What facilities exist to ensure satisfaction both of investors and beneficiaries? Via what flows do these facilities communicate with investors and beneficiaries? Within the service, who or what is responsible for each of these facilities, for their appropriate operation, and verification of appropriate results?

- What facilities, mechanisms, or flows are used to ensure appropriate linkage to the enterprise vision?

- What action is taken in the event of unintentional imbalance between investment and dividend, or between different investors and beneficiaries? Who or what is responsible for taking such action?

- What action is taken – or can be taken – in the event of deliberate imbalance between investment and dividend, or between different investors and beneficiaries? Who or what is responsible for taking such action?

- Where such action to correct imbalances is prevented by current corporate law or other "external" forces, what else may be done to minimize damage to the overall enterprise?

# Summary

In this chapter we saw that many services will require some form of investment to start them going; and some services also provide some form of value return to beneficiaries. Although stockholders and other "owners" are an obvious example of this at the larger scale, similar relationships can occur right down to the code level, with automated services. We also noted that investors and beneficiaries are not always the same, that the respective value flows may not be the same, and that we may need to take active measures to ensure a proper balance of value across the whole context.

In the next chapter, we explore service decomposition, the way that services are often assembled from collections of other smaller and more focused services.

# CHAPTER 12

# Service Decomposition

The Enterprise Canvas provides a kind of idealized view of the services of which the enterprise is composed, what each service does, and how they interconnect. In the real world, of course, few things match up exactly to that nominal ideal. In the upper layers of abstraction – above Row-3, Service Model – this should not matter at all; in fact most of the time there we should take some care to *avoid* paying too much attention to how things will work out in practice, or, especially, to what already exists.

As we move downward, though, we do need to pay more and more attention to the various constraints and practicalities of the real world. In Row-3 we need to bounce back and forth between the "ideal" of the Canvas and the real-world services that either do or will implement each cell and flow of the Canvas, including the guidance services and the links with investors and beneficiaries.

---

In Rows 3, 4, and 5, we also need to become much more explicit about the content and structure of each service and flow, and the Row-6 metrics for each, but we'll look at those in more detail in Chapter 13, "Service Content" and Chapter 14, "Services as Systems."

---

© Tom Graves 2023
T. Graves, *Mapping the Enterprise*, https://doi.org/10.1007/978-1-4842-9836-7_12

For example, for ZapaMex, the company may want to explore the options for its real-world Customer Channels, as shown in Figure 12-1. At present the company sells only through its retail stores, but would it be practical to do sales via direct mail as well? If so, what about phone sales, to complement the direct-mail order forms? In which case, what would be the cross-over with the existing customer-service call center – in what ways would those Customer-Relations services need to change? And what about e-commerce, via a web store? The company might plan to do that only in a year or so in the future, but it would be wise to think about those services now – especially as they would impact on the way we would handle Value-Return payments from the customer, and the Customer-Relations services too.

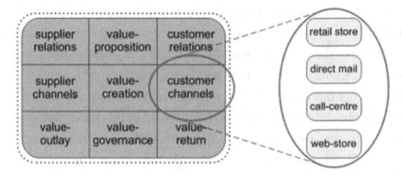

**Figure 12-1.**  *ZapaMex: decomposition of Customer-Channels services*

Each step in this process of *service decomposition* brings us closer to the real world. (This detailed decomposition is often also known as describing the *granularity* of a service.) Yet, as shown in Figure 12-2, each of these items is still also a service in its own right – and hence a candidate to model on its own Enterprise Canvas, complete with its own flows, guidance-service links and possibly its own service-specific links to investors and beneficiaries as well.

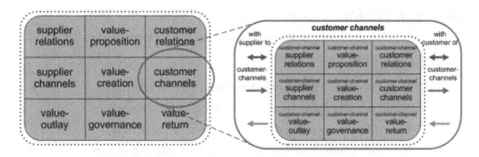

*Figure 12-2.* *Each cell is also a service in its own right*

In the same way, we can, and often should, apply the same decomposition to each of the cells within an Enterprise Canvas. Each cell is a service; hence, it also has its own subsidiary services and flows. This also means that there'll almost certainly be flows *between* cells within an Enterprise Canvas, which we will likewise need to map in the same way as for any other service.

---

In theory this decomposition could go on ad infinitum – but that's a quick way to get stuck in "analysis paralysis," so in practice we do need to know when to stop that analysis! The simplest guideline here is that we should aim always to do the *minimum* decomposition needed to make sense of the service, and stop as soon as we've reached that point.

---

# Into Action

Your team leads in the business-transformation project will all be familiar with decomposition and granularity of services, but are likely to want a simple means to introduce their less-experienced team members to these concepts and practices. You could suggest that they might use the fractal "services-within-services" structure of Enterprise Canvas to illustrate this

153

point, and to provide the templates and completeness checklists that they would need. Use the ideas in this chapter and the following questions to help you guide those conversations:

- What are the services within each cell of a service? What are the flows between each cell of a service? Going down into the detail of a lower-level Row if necessary, what are the cells and flows of each of these subsidiary cells of the service?

- What real-world services implement each service in a high-level Enterprise Canvas? How does the view change as you delve deeper into finer-grained partitioning of services?

- Which real-world services bridge between two or more of the cells in the idealized structure of the Enterprise Canvas? Why is it necessary that they should do so? What implications and trade-offs does this suggest for the service's orientation (to its suppliers, to its own value creation, or to its customer) or its time focus (future, present, or past)?

# Summary

In this chapter we saw how and why, as we move more toward realization of the service, we'll often need to split the generic descriptions in each Canvas cell into the more explicit "child" services and sub-services of which it is composed in real-world practice. We can use the Canvas with our stakeholders as a guide to elicit details about these "child" services – and, if appropriate, model each of them on their own Enterprise Canvas.

In the next chapter, we explore more detail about service content – the various elements that enable the service to work *as* a service.

# CHAPTER 13

# Service Content

The previous chapters outlined the core principles for Enterprise Canvas as a service-design pattern, describing it in terms of overall structure and relationships, as if seen from the outside. To put it into practical use, we now need to look at the *inside* of each service and flow and the elements that make it work *as* a service.

As with all previous chapters, we only address a single concept here: the *internal* content of services and products. However, there is a lot that we need to cover in this one chapter. We need to address the differences between services and products, and how to describe service content in terms of three distinct dimensions: *content detail, content categories,* and *content types.* The level and type of content detail that we need for our service models will change as we move from big-picture intent to strategy to plans to real-world operations, and we will use the Service-Layers model to provide guidance there. Later in this chapter, we will use the Service-Content model to provide guidance on content categories such as Asset, Function, Location, and so on, and on content types such as physical, virtual, and the like. And finally, we will need to explore how to bring all of these elements together to describe this single thing called "the service."

The shared enterprise is like a holograph: every service ultimately connects with everything else. Hence, any assessment we do in any part of the enterprise implicitly contributes to the detail of everywhere else. And because everything ultimately connects with and depends on everything else in the enterprise, we can choose somewhere to start: any service,

© Tom Graves 2023
T. Graves, *Mapping the Enterprise*, https://doi.org/10.1007/978-1-4842-9836-7_13

anywhere, at any layer, any level, any item of content, any area of interest, any aspect of the organization or enterprise where something happens. We model only what we need for that specific task; then link the models together as required, and allow the overall detail to emerge over time through the layering and interconnections of the Canvas structure.

The process for modeling is essentially the same in every case, whether we want to do an as-is, an as-was, or a to-be model for the respective service that is the focus of this Canvas. The key is to get started at all, and then let the Enterprise Canvas pattern guide us in how to connect everything together from there.

# Service and Product

Before we go into the detail of service content, we need to do a brief exploration of the differences between services and products, their respective roles in the flow of value around the enterprise, and the differences in how we need to describe their respective content.

A service represents where something happens in the enterprise, where value is *created or changed*; a product represents the *current state* of some aspect of value within the enterprise. A service is *active*, while a product is *static*; or to describe the difference in a shorthand form, a service *does*, whereas a product *is*.

As described in Chapter 9, "Service Flows," any flows between services are realized as products: products are the outputs of services, which then become inputs for other services. Note, though, there may be no actual "flow" as such: in practice, that term really applies to only physical assets. For the other asset types, a flow is more implied than real: for example, a change in a relational asset may be an outcome of one service, that is then referenced in another service, but the relational asset does not actually move in a physical sense between the two services.

Services have boundaries: these may be boundaries of place or time, or where responsibility is passed from one agent to another, or just some point where we choose to place a boundary. Yet as shown in Figure 13-1, wherever there is a boundary or gap between services, then at least one product *must* exist there, to provide a means to bridge across that gap.

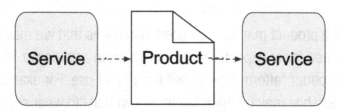

***Figure 13-1.*** *Products bridge the gap between services*

As described later in this chapter, a service must be a complete composite of any appropriate mix of Assets, Functions, Locations, Capabilities, Events, and Decisions. In turn, as described in Chapter 12, "Service Decomposition," a service may itself be assembled from any other appropriate "child" services, each of which is made up of its own mix of Assets, Functions, and so on.

In the same way, a product may be assembled from any number of "child" products, each of which may be any appropriate mix of asset types. Unlike a service, though, a product can *only* be composed of Assets: it cannot incorporate any of the other content categories. However, a product can represent or imply a service: for example, an insurance product represents a promise of future service to be provided whenever certain conditions are met. A product may also embed Asset content that can be unpacked into a form that may then be used as a service: for example, a smartphone app is a product that includes executable code that enables the app's services when it is run.

The purpose of a product is to be used as an input to another service, often run by someone else: for example, a ZapaMex shoe is intended for use in the new owner's self-service of "to wear shoes." We can use the existence of a product to identify the probable services in which it might be used.

---

Note that a product may also be used in services that we may not have planned for or expect. This is known as an *affordance*, in that the product "affords" the possibility of that use. For example, a ZapaMex shoe may be intended for use in that "to wear shoes" service, but it could also be used in other purposes – and services – such as a door-stop or a decorative item on a shelf, or as a projectile to throw at a night-time caterwauling cat. This point about affordances can be important in some service-design issues such as identifying potential product liability and service risk.

---

To summarize all of this: In the flow of value around the enterprise, a service is where some aspect of that overall value is created or changed, whereas a product represents some aspect of value; a service *does*, a product *is*. In terms of service content, a service must always incorporate a *complete* set of the service categories, whereas a product can *only* incorporate elements of the Asset service-content category.

# Service Layers and Service Content

The Service-Layers model, as described in Chapter 5, "Service Layers," plays a crucial role in identifying content for a service when modeling with Enterprise Canvas. This is because, for most purposes, each Enterprise Canvas will describe only a single service at a single layer of abstraction, in context of the flows and interchanges it shares with each of its stakeholders. In that sense, the layer we choose for an Enterprise Canvas instance indicates the type of information and level of detail that needs to be acquired and modeled for that Canvas instance. Figure 13-2 shows the Service-Layers model, summarizing the content role and level of detail needed for each respective Row in that model.

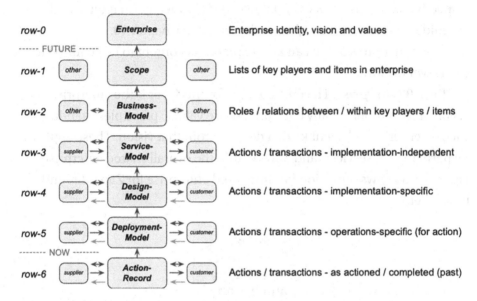

***Figure 13-2.***  *Service-Layers model – layers of abstraction*

Again, note that important point here: in general, use only *one* layer for each Enterprise Canvas, and *don't mix layers.* Each layer has a different role for architecture, design, deployment, and operations, and we would create architectural and other risks if we blur them together. By keeping the models separate and distinct at each service layer or Row, we can then link "downward" through the layers to build trails of derivation from most-abstract to real-world most-concrete, or link "upward" to build trails of provenance to show how action records and real-world services support and maintain the vision for the organization and the overall shared enterprise.

If we need to see how something changes across layers – such as going from Row-3 Service-Model to Row-4 Design-Model implementation design, for example, or from an actual Row-5 Deployment-Model implementation back up to Row-3 to rethink alternate options – then we should use a separate Canvas for each layer, and link them together via the respective service interfaces and flows, as described in Chapter 9, and/or via guidance-service oversights, as described in Chapter 10.

Given that proviso, we can now explore the content to be acquired for each layer or Row.

**Row-0** *Enterprise*: The only content for this layer is the enterprise vision, and, optionally, any enterprise-wide values, principles, standards, success criteria, and suchlike that devolve from that vision. These apply to *all* participants, services, and flows within the overall shared enterprise. Figure 13-3 shows the vision for the shared enterprise for ZapaMex and its market.

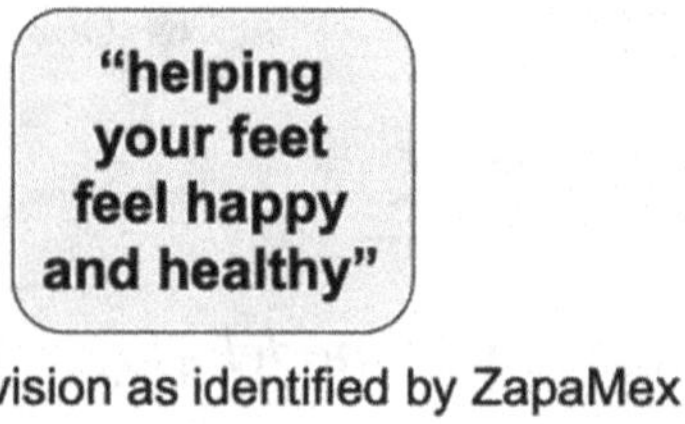

"helping
your feet
feel happy
and healthy"

enterprise-vision as identified by ZapaMex

***Figure 13-3.*** *Row-0 content*

Use the methods described in Chapter 4, "Service Vision and Values," to derive that content for the service's Row-0 "Enterprise."

**Row-1** *Scope*: For this layer, we need a summary of the content elements that would be needed to support the enterprise *as a whole*, and make it work for all of its participants and stakeholders. These elements would then be addressed and used as required in a value web of interlinked services that would each, in their own way, support the vision, values, standards, and success criteria of that shared enterprise.

As shown in Figure 13-4, the content elements would typically be sorted into a predefined set of categories such as the interrogatives *What, How, Where, Who, When,* and *Why*.

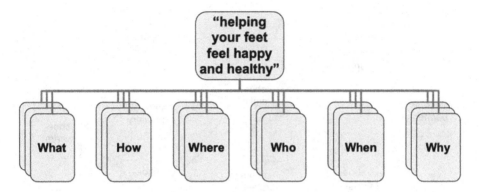

*Figure 13-4. Row-1 content realizes Row-0 vision*

Use the methods described in Chapter 6, "Service Actors and Other Entities," to derive that content for the service's Row-1 Scope.

**Row-2 *Business Model***: For this layer, the content that we need would be drawn from the Row-1 Scope layer, but packaged in two different forms. The first is a model of roles and relationships between those roles – in essence, services, and products that move between them – that, across the whole, cover *all* of the content from Row-1. In effect, this Row-2 model outlines all elements of business that should or must occur within the overall shared enterprise. This "enterprise business model" for the ZapaMex example is shown in Figure 13-5.

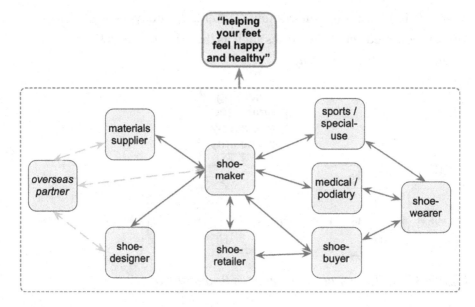

**Figure 13-5.** *Row-2 content for shared enterprise*

The second form of Row-2 Business Model represents the subset of that Row-1 Scope content as seen from the perspective of *one* participant or role within that overall shared enterprise. Figure 13-6 shows the high-level business-model relationships for ZapaMex itself.

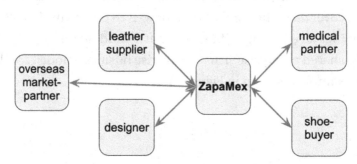

**Figure 13-6.** *Row-2 content for ZapaMex as one player within its shared enterprise*

In both forms, services realize any appropriate subset of Row-1 elements, whereas flows realize an appropriate subset of the "What" column in the Row-1 elements. Use the methods described in Chapter 7, "Service Roles and Relationships," to derive the content for any required views for the services' Row-2 Business Model.

**Row-3 *Service Model*** (also known as "logical model"): For this layer, the content we need is an abstract overview of the *internal* workings of the service and of the flows that pass between services.

A typical first step would be to apply decomposition, to derive a set of "services-within-services," with implicit flows between them. In Enterprise Canvas, we start this decomposition with a "horizontal" split between service for inbound, core and outbound, and a "vertical" split for before, during, and after the main transactions along the value chain, as described in Chapter 8, "Service Structure." This gives us a standardized nine-cell initial decomposition, as shown in Figure 13-7.

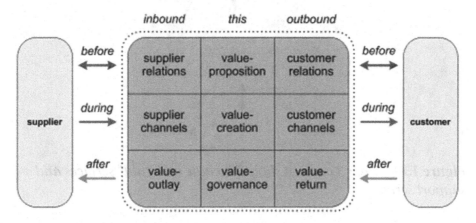

***Figure 13-7.*** *Row-3 content from initial decomposition*

We also need an overview for the content of the flows, as described in Chapter 9, "Service Flows." This should include both external flows shared with suppliers, customers, and others, and flows between those internal services.

As shown in Figure 13-8, we also need to extend the same decomposition review "outward" to any "child" services of this service; to the flows shared with its support services, as described in Chapter 10, "Service Guidance"; and to the flows shared with any investors and beneficiaries, as described in Chapter 11, "Service Investors and Beneficiaries."

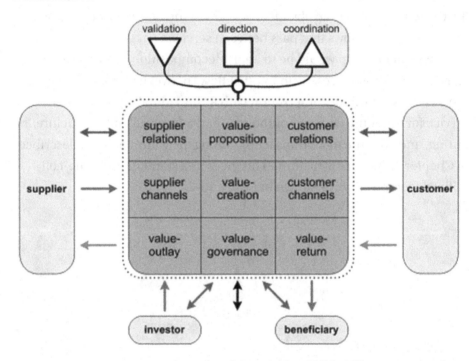

***Figure 13-8.*** *Row-3 content should include all "child" services and support services*

We can then repeat the same process to the various child services and flows, applying any further internal decomposition that may be needed there, to any required depth, as described in Chapter 12, "Service Decomposition."

Note, though, that in Row-3 all of this is still at an abstract level: we identify the *type* of service and flows required for each item in the decomposition, to detail how it is to be implemented.

To find the content for this layer, we first expand out the overall set of service elements from Row-1 and Row-2, adapting them from the simple interrogatives of What, How, Where, and so on, into more real-world categories such as Asset, Function, Location, and the like, using the Service-Content model described in the next section of this chapter. We then apply those to the services and products we identified in our business models and service decomposition, to the level and type of detail required for this Row-3 Service-Model layer.

For Zapamex, its Row-3 first-level decomposition would be as shown in Figure 13-9.

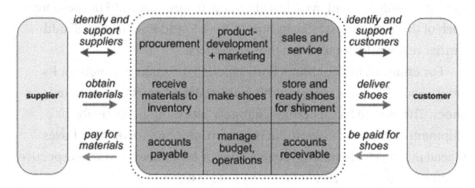

**Figure 13-9.** *Initial Row-3 content for ZapaMex internal services and external flows*

By asking broad questions about the nature of the service and its flows, we can derive useful ideas about content for specific cells and flows. For example, if we ask about what the service *does*, about the services, products, and/or other "deliverables" that this service creates through its work, that then gives us the role and content for the Canvas' Value-Creation cell. If we ask about *why* the service does what it does, about the value that it creates and adds for each of its stakeholders and for the enterprise as a whole, that gives us the role and content of the Value-Proposition cell and key aspects of the Customer-Relations, Supplier-Relations, Value-Outlay, and Value-Return cells, the "before" flows, the Validation, Investor, and Beneficiary flows, and interactions with the non-transactional stakeholders. And if we ask about who or what it works for, that it would *relate* with, actions it shares, whom or for what the service does what it does, and with whom or what it would *relate*, the transactions that share with others, that would give us the roles, content, flows, and interfaces needed for the Supplier-Channels and Customer-Channels cells, and the respective transaction stakeholders for those flows. We can gain a lot of useful information from those kinds of questions.

Flows are realized as products – we will see more on that in the "Service and Product" section later in this chapter. Here in Row-3 we need to capture only a broad overview about the nature, role, and purpose for each of those products; later, in Row-4, Row-5, and Row-6, we will add further real-world detail about those products.

For example, in ZapaMex's Row-3 model, the main products for its "make shoes" Value-Creation service are matched pairs of completed shoes. These go to its Customer-Channels "store and make ready for shipment" service, whose products are cartons or crates of shoe-boxes placed into a vehicle for delivery to shops or customers, and the respective invoice and delivery docket for each of those items.

**Row-4 *Design Model*** (also known as "physical model"): For this layer, the content we need is a more specific overview of the internal workings of the service and of the flows that pass between services. To derive this content, we do the same kind of process as for Row-3 Service Model, but at a more implementation-specific level of detail.

For example, if ZapaMex decided in their Row-3 Service Model that they would need some kind of vehicle to move finished goods from the factory to their retail stores, here in Row-4 they would specify that the vehicle would be a mid-sized truck, and probably also identify the specific model of truck to be used.

Note too that, as shown in Figure 13-10, services may be implemented by *any appropriate mix of people, machines, and IT*. The same service may also need multiple ways to implement it, such as to cope with business continuity and disaster recovery; and those various implementations may often each need their own specific mix of people, machines, and IT.

***Figure 13-10.*** *Row-4 content describes services provided by people, machines, and/or IT*

For ZapaMex, invoices to be sent out by its "store and make ready for shipment" Customer-Channels service may be sent out in either physical or electronic form. The Row-4 model needs to specify how these products are to be created, and also how delivery crews will know that a physical invoice will not need to be attached to a package if it has already been sent in electronic form.

**Row-5 *Deployment Model*:** For this layer, the content would be the exact detail needed for real-world operations, for services, products, and coordination between services. To identify and derive this content, we do the same kind of process as for Row-3 Service Model and Row-4 Design Model, but at an operations level of detail.

For example, ZapaMex's Row-3 model specified the need for a delivery vehicle, and Row-4 specified the make and model of mid-sized truck that they would use for this. Here in the Row-5 model, the delivery roster would have to include the full details for each delivery, including the driver's name or ID, the truck's registration number, and the intended delivery route. There would then need to be a service that could prepare and present that delivery roster, with the roster itself as the product from that service.

**Row-6** *Action Records*: For this layer, the content we need is about the outcomes of service operation. Where Row-5 will describe what is *intended* to happen, Row-6 represents what *actually* happened.

Everything in this layer will be some kind of product – usually as information, but also other forms as well. In most cases these will be for *internal* use or reuse, though some will also go outward, such as for review by auditors and the like.

In each case we will need to identify which service will create these products and also the intended recipient for each product – such as for procurement planning, "run the business" performance reviews, and "change the business" or "develop the business" strategy development.

For ZapaMex, its Row-6 model for its Customer-Channels services would include a record of the actual driver, vehicle and route used for a delivery, and the packages loaded onto the vehicle at that time. These records would be used for pay calculation, delivery tracking, vehicle maintenance, insurance, and more. A physical product of the operations would be the internal pallet to be returned to the factory floor, or sent onward for repair.

# The Service-Content Model

For each Row in the Service-Layers model, we need to describe the required detail in terms of the respective content categories and content types.

The Row determines the content categories that we need for the respective stage of modeling. In Row-0, we only need the vision and values; for Row-1, we can use simple interrogatives such as What, How, and Where; for Row-2, we begin to translate those interrogatives into real-world categories such as Asset, Function, and Location; in Row-3, Row-4, and Row-5, we will need to expand out our descriptions to include both content category and content type; and in Row-6, products are the only content, which must be comprised solely of Assets. Figure 13-11 provides a visual summary of these changes from layer to layer.

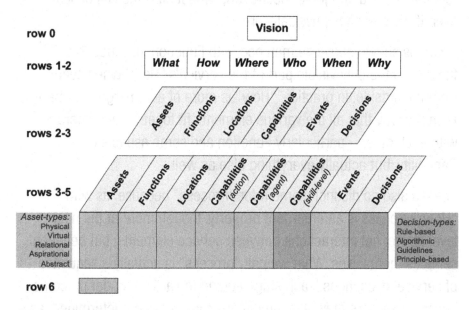

***Figure 13-11.*** *Row-0 to Row-6 – content summary*

In Row-2, the interrogatives translate roughly as follows: *What* becomes Asset; *How* becomes Function; *Where* becomes Location; *Who* becomes the agent for a Capability; *When* becomes Event; and *Why* becomes Decision.

For most of that translation, there's a close match between interrogative and content category, but there are some challenges around "*Who*" and "*How.*"

"*Who*" is shown above as the agent for a Capability, but note that an agent also be a machine or an IT system. In practice, "Who" is also represented by the *relational* asset type, though people themselves should *never* be described as "assets" in an architecture or anywhere else: *the relationship is the asset*, not the person. The relationship with the person creates the access to that person's capabilities: if the relationship is damaged or destroyed, almost all value will be lost, even if the person is physically present.

"*How*" is shown above as matched with Function, because the function is the only visible part of the service's "How" when seen from the outside. In practice, "How" is more of an emergent property from the way that all the various elements fit together and interact with each other – particularly Function and some aspects of Capability, but actually everything else as well.

There's also no distinct element for "Process" because, as with "How," process is an emergent property, though more at the next level above: not interactions between service elements, but between services themselves. What we call "process" is actually a sequence of service invocations, each stage adding toward a broader outcome. Those sequences may take almost any form, from predetermined, as often seen "hard-wired" into software, to free-form, as in many types of case management. In that sense, "Process" is itself just another kind of service, as a wrapper around other services.

The Service-Content model then links *content categories* with *content types*, as shown in Figure 13-12.

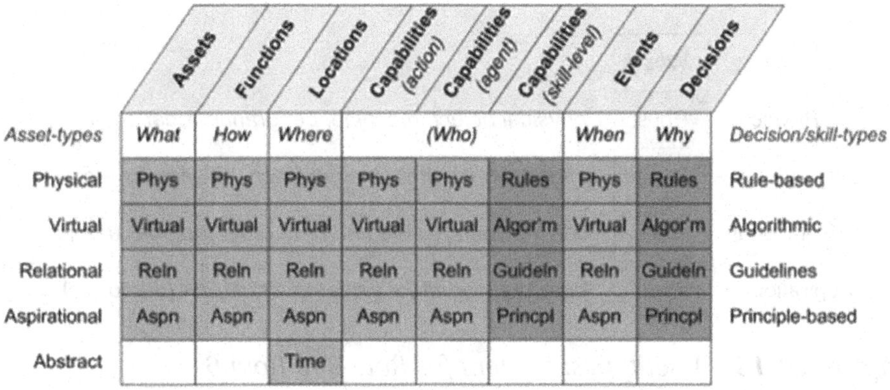

| Asset-types | Assets | Functions | Locations | Capabilities (action) | Capabilities (agent) | Capabilities (skill-level) | Events | Decisions | Decision/skill-types |
|---|---|---|---|---|---|---|---|---|---|
| | What | How | Where | (Who) | | | When | Why | |
| Physical | Phys | Phys | Phys | Phys | Phys | Rules | Phys | Rules | Rule-based |
| Virtual | Virtual | Virtual | Virtual | Virtual | Virtual | Algor'm | Virtual | Algor'm | Algorithmic |
| Relational | Reln | Reln | Reln | Reln | Reln | Guideln | Reln | Guideln | Guidelines |
| Aspirational | Aspn | Aspn | Aspn | Aspn | Aspn | Princpl | Aspn | Princpl | Principle-based |
| Abstract | | | Time | | | | | | |

*Figure 13-12. Service-Content model*

There are two distinct sets of content types: the *asset-types* set, used for Asset, Function, Location, Capability action (including what the capability acts on), Capability agent, and Event; and the *decision-types* set, used for Decision and for Capability skill levels.

The *asset-types* set is as described in the market metaphor in Chapter 3, "Service Context and Market":

- *Physical* "things"

- *Virtual* items such as data and information

- *Relational* links between real people

- *Aspirational* links between people and abstract ideas, represented by brands, and also by morale, by values, and by the idea of the enterprise itself

Figure 13-13 provides a visual checklist for asset types.

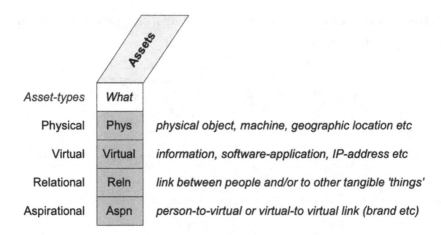

**Figure 13-13.** *Asset types: content for Row-3 to Row-6*

---

In the Service-Content model, *time* is an abstract asset type that is best understood as a *location*. While events do occur *in* time, time *itself* is not an event; and although time could be described as a kind of resource, it's not an asset as such: it can't be possessed, it can't be changed, and nor can it be directly exchanged for anything else.

People often regard *money* as a special type of asset, but in architectural terms it's best understood as an enumeration for a belief about value. In the Service-Content model, we would describe it as a composite of *virtual* and *aspirational*, representing information about a belief in future rights of access to assets.

---

The *decision types* set describes levels of complexity. There is a close relationship between complexity levels for decisions and complexity levels for skills, so this set is used for both:

- *Rule-based* trainee-level decisions and skills

- *Algorithmic* apprentice-level decisions and skills

- *Guidelines and patterns* for journeyman-level decisions and skills

- *Principle- and value-based* master-level decisions and skills

Figure 13-14 shows a visual summary for the decision types.

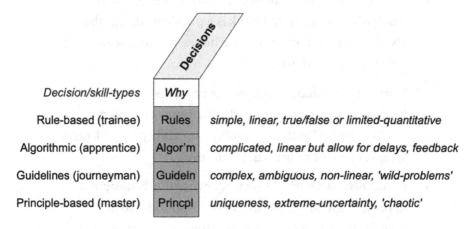

| Decision/skill-types | Why | |
| --- | --- | --- |
| Rule-based (trainee) | Rules | simple, linear, true/false or limited-quantitative |
| Algorithmic (apprentice) | Algor'm | complicated, linear but allow for delays, feedback |
| Guidelines (journeyman) | Guideln | complex, ambiguous, non-linear, 'wild-problems' |
| Principle-based (master) | Princpl | uniqueness, extreme-uncertainty, 'chaotic' |

***Figure 13-14.*** *Decision types and skill types: content for Row-3 to Row-5*

Note that the *decision-types* set is only used for Row-3 to Row-5; it is not relevant for Row-6, whose content consists solely of products, which can only be described in terms of *asset types*.

Although not an exact match, the asset-type and decision-type sets do roughly align with each other and are shown as such on the Service-Content model. For example, a physical machine can only follow simple mechanistic rules; algorithms work well with virtual information.

The cells in the Service-Content model define a set of *primitives*, which we can then combine as required into *composites*. A primitive is something that can be defined or described in terms of a single cell in the model, whereas a composite straddles across cells. The links for a composite can go either vertically, horizontally, or both ways across the model, for example:

- *Vertical composite*: Raw data is a primitive, a *virtual asset*, whereas a printed book is a physical "thing" that also contains information, and hence is a composite *physical + virtual asset*.

- *Horizontal composite*: A *function* provides an interface to change *assets*, yet cannot do anything on its own until combined with a *capability* – an ability to work on an asset type at a particular skill-level.

- *Combined composite*: A security *capability* is designed to protect specific types of *assets*, responding to any type of *event* with an appropriate type of *decision*.

In terms of the Service-Content model, a *service* is a combined composite that, at run-time, *must* link together a complete set of *assets, functions, locations, capabilities, events*, and *decisions*, with any appropriate mix of the asset types and decision types for each.

---

A composite should not be able to straddle framework layers – the Rows of the Service-Layers model – but that doesn't concern us here, because we should only be working with a single Row at a time on any given Enterprise Canvas model. Note, though, that a design pattern *can* straddle more than one Row: for example, in data architecture, a "many-to-many" data-relationship pattern in a Row-3 service model would typically be shown in a Row-4 design model as implemented by a cross-reference table.

---

One of the main roles of service architecture is to apply abstraction – moving "upward" through the service-detail layers toward Row-0 Enterprise – to split the real-world composites back into smaller composites and primitives, so as to enable reconfiguration and redesign into other, more effective "solutions" for the given context. Design and implementation go the other way, moving "downward" through the service-detail layers toward the "Now" between Row-5 as immediate future and Row-6 as the past. At that point, by definition, everything must be an "architecturally complete" composite across all the content-model columns, which we could summarize as

- With *Asset* do *Function* using *Capability* at *Location* on *Event* because *Decision*

"Architecturally complete" composites may use *any* appropriate mix of segments. For example, in ZapaMex's Row-4 service-design model for its Value-Creation cell, the same nominal business function of "make shoes" might be implemented using a machine (physical capability), a manual process (relational-linked physical capability), or an IT-driven CNC system (virtual-linked physical capability). One of the keys to design for business continuity and disaster recovery is to structure the service functions such that one type of capability may be swapped for another at any time – such as a manual process that can take over when the regular IT system fails.

Another key value of these distinctions between entity types is that it helps us identify additional services that we may need to include in our architectures. For example, consider a printed book in a library:

- It is a *physical "thing"*: We will need services to manage it as a physical asset, with storage, location tracking, physical maintenance, and so on.

- It contains *virtual information*: We will also need services that manage it as a virtual asset, with possible concerns about copying and suchlike.

- There are *ownership relationships* with various people, sometimes temporary (as a library loan), but maybe also nominally permanent (as owned by the library): We will probably need services to track those relationships.

- There are value relationships or *meaning relationships* with or for various people: We might need services to track what people feel about the book in general, or even this specific copy.

Or, to give another example, the location of a room within an office building:

- It has a *physical location*: We will need our services to note the physical schemas that apply, such as geographic location, building floor, corridor position, and so on.

- It may have a *virtual location*: We will need our services to note any virtual schemas that might apply, such as room ID, role ID, and suchlike.

- It will imply various *relational locations*: We may need services that note who uses this office at this time, or in the past, or is listed to do so in the future; and/or where each of those people sit within the organizational architecture, or reporting relationships, or other relational schemas.

- It may imply *meaning locations*: We might need to connect with "organizational-history" services if, for example, this was where a famous scientist worked, or where the first transistor was created, or where the treaty was signed.

The trap here is that all of this could easily go on to infinity, so we do need to remember always that core principle of Just Enough Detail. Start with the business need in mind, and then do just enough assessment to satisfy that need – no less, but also no more than that.

# *Asset* Content Elements

**Assets** are resources for use in a service, and for which the respective service accepts and acknowledges responsibility. A product is likewise an asset for which the respective "owner" assumes responsibility.

---

This point about responsibility is perhaps the key distinction between assets and generic "resources." We will see more about that later in this chapter, in the section on "Cross-checks for Service Content."

---

Assets may be composed of any appropriate mix from the *asset-types* set: *physical, virtual, relational,* and *aspirational*. An asset may also be represented by any *composites* between these types. Many real-world assets are composites in this sense: for example, a key point in marketing is creating emotional attachment to objects – in other words, a composite asset of *physical* and *aspirational*.

For ZapaMex, its physical assets include its buildings, furniture, shoe-making machines, shoe-making materials and completed shoes, and its delivery vehicles. Its virtual assets include the information that it uses to run its business, the content of its website, and the stories told by its customers. Its relational assets include its connections with employees and their families, suppliers, customers, recruiters, regulators, and many more. Its aspirational assets include its vision, values, reputation, and brand. Its composite assets include its CRM (customer-relations management system), which incorporates virtual information about relational assets, and the point-of-sale displays in its stores, which combine physical shoes and virtual product information in support of the aspirational asset of the brand.

See the "Asset Content Elements" checklist in the "Into Action" section at the end of the chapter for more on how to apply this to your own organization's services.

## *Function* Content Elements

**Functions** implement the external interfaces to and from a service. The simplest example is a code function, which specifies the types and formats for virtual-asset parameters that it will accept and return, and will also indicate what actions will be taken by the service as a whole, and the expected outcomes from that action. Overall, functions may use, reference, work with, and/or return any appropriate mix of assets, described in terms of the *physical, virtual, relational,* and *aspirational* asset types.

Although a function forms part of the overall "How" for a service, it does nothing in itself other than to act as an interface. The actual work of a service will be done by the capabilities hidden behind that interface. Figure 13-15 summarizes the relationships between *function* as an external interface, *capability* as an internal "ability- to-do-work," and the *service* as a whole.

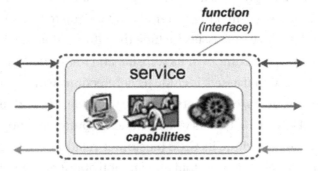

***Figure 13-15.*** *Service as function plus capability*

A well-designed service should be able to switch between different capabilities, to cope with different needs such as load balancing and emergency business continuity and disaster recovery, without requiring significant changes in the service's function interface. To support this, the function should specify the *parameters* for the respective service-level agreement (SLA), but allow different *parameter values* to permit variance in the conditions for the SLA to support those different operational needs.

---

These distinctions between service, capability, and function can sometimes seem confusing at first, in part because function and service may seem to be the same thing when seen from the outside, and also because function and capability can often become merged together in machine design and in some common forms of IT-systems design. Yet we need to note that merging will *not* apply when services and processes are enacted by real people, or when we move back to the abstract for process or service redesign. Architecturally, it's important to keep the functions and capabilities separate at a conceptual level and be aware of how and why we merge them in each service implementation.

---

For ZapaMex, its physical functions include the work surfaces and controls for the shoe-making machines in the factory; its virtual functions include the user interfaces of the applications upstairs in the office. Its composite functions include the entryway for the warehouse, which receives physical goods and the virtual information associated with those goods; the bar-code scanners in the stores that likewise link physical shoes and shoe-boxes with their virtual tracking information for stock management and sales management; and the physical front door of each store, which enables person-to-person relational-asset sales connections and aspirational-asset links to brand, guided by virtual assets such as sales protocols.

See the "Function Content Elements" checklist in the "Into Action" section at the end of the chapter for more on how to apply this to your own organization's services.

# *Location* Content Elements

**Locations** are "places" in terms of some context or schema. We describe locations via the *asset-types* set: *physical* locations; *virtual* locations such as a URL or an IP address; *relational* locations, such as displayed in an org chart; and *aspirational* locations, such as relationships between brands. There may also be composites of these types, such as the *physical plus virtual* location of a data server.

We can also describe *time* as an abstract location: for example, events are located *in* time, though are not actually part *of* time itself.

For ZapaMex, its website has several linked virtual locations, in terms of its IP address, domain name, and associated URLs and also the merchant ID used for credit-card transactions on the website and in its stores. Its factory building has a complex composite location: it has a geographic physical location; its mail address is a virtual location; as a place where people work, it is an anchor for person-to-person relational locations, and also where work roles and positionings in work hierarchies represent relational locations relative to each other; and it is also the aspirational location of the brand and of the company's history.

See the "Location Content Elements" checklist in the "Into Action" section at the end of the chapter for more on how to apply this to your own organization's services.

# *Capability* Content Elements

**Capabilities** provide the core "How" for a service. However, the content for a capability is always a composite and should be described in terms of three distinct subsidiary strands: *action, agent,* and *skill level.*

The *action* for a capability identifies what the capability will do to deliver its value, outcomes, and products. This in turn is determined in part by the assets on which it will work, which may be any appropriate mix of asset-type content: *physical, virtual, relational, aspirational,* and/or *composite.*

The *agent* for the capability is someone or something that will do the *action* for the capability and will work on the assets for the action. The agent itself is an asset-types element, such as a *physical* machine, a *virtual* IT application, a real person accessed via a *relational-asset* link, an *aspirational asset* such as a purpose or brand, or any appropriate composite such as a person providing guidance and override for a computer-automated machine.

---

For this aspect of capability, the "Who" interrogative does sort-of make sense when the agent is a real person, but does *not* make sense wherever the capability is enacted by a machine or IT system. Describing the agent of a capability in terms of "Who" versus some kind of not-"Who" can lead us into a modeling trap where human agents, computer-based agents, and machines are each placed in different content-based layers, and it then becomes impossible to describe how one type of agent may be substituted for another within the same capability. For service models at Row-3 and above, it is best to use the more abstract concept of "agent" and only worry about the specific type of agent at Row-4 or below.

---

The ***skill level*** for the capability is the set of competencies or decision abilities required from the *agent* in that *action*. Skill levels for capabilities are closely related to decision levels and are based on the *decision-types* set of *rule-based, algorithmic, guidelines,* and *principle-based.*

For skill levels, it is useful to cross-map the decision types with repeatability types such as simple, calculated, ambiguous, and not-known. Figure 13-16 summarizes the relationship between those two themes.

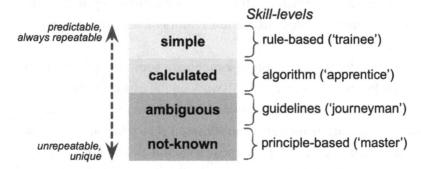

***Figure 13-16.*** *Capabilities: repeatability and skill levels*

This gives us a skill-levels set of simple *rule-based* decisions such as following a predefined step-by-step process or checklist; calculated *algorithmic* or "hard-systems" decisions that follow predictable rules but can accommodate branching, delayed feedback, damping, and the like; *heuristic* or "soft-systems" decisions using guidelines, patterns, and heuristics to interpret "wicked problems" and complex and emergent uncertainties; and *principle-based* or values-based decisions for contexts that are inherently unpredictable and unique.

These distinctions about skill levels are important for capabilities in service design, because physical machines, IT, and people have very different capability curves. In general:

- Physical machines can usually work only on physical assets and are best suited to following rule-based decisions.

- IT systems can work on virtual assets and, via control of physical machinery, physical assets, using rule-based or algorithmic decisions, but are still limited in capability for pattern recognition, and in general should *not* be used for decision-making in inherently unique contexts.

- People can work on any types of assets, with varying skill levels, though in many cases are notoriously *not* well-suited to the rigid rule following and mechanical repetitive tasks of classic "scientific management."

Attempts to use inappropriate types of systems and capabilities in a given context will usually lead to ineffectiveness and, in many cases, "unexpected" failure.

For ZapaMex, its capability for shoe-making acts on physical materials such as leather, plastics, and thread, using virtual information to keep track of those actions. The agents for those actions include physical injection-molding machines to make the soles for shoes, information-driven CNC machines to cut shoe leather, and people to do hand-stitching of shoe parts. In terms of skill levels, the machines must follow simple rules, always doing the exact same thing; the CNC cutter can adapt algorithmically for different materials and material thickness; and craftspeople make the complex decisions and adjustments needed for custom-fitted shoes for disabled people.

See the "Capability Content Elements" checklist in the "Into Action" section at the end of the chapter for more on how to apply this to your own organization's services.

# *Event* Content Elements

**Events** are triggers for action, or the ending of an action. We can describe these in terms of the asset-types set: *physical* events such as the operation of a mechanical safety switch or the arrival of a vehicle; *virtual* events such as an error condition or a counter reaching a predefined level within a computer application; *relational* events such as a phone call or a business meeting; and *aspirational* events such as a change of brand or an event causing damage to morale. There can also be *composite* events: for example, in Japan a ground sensor will send a signal to a mobile phone app for people to warn others about an incoming earthquake.

---

Note that perhaps most real-world events will be composites of these types: for many purposes, a broader notion of event as a naturally composite "package" may be more useful than trying to force all events to fit to a single type.

Note also the previous point about *time*: events may occur *in* time, but are not actually part of time itself.

---

For ZapaMex, typical events in its warehouse include the physical arrival of a truck, and an electronic or in-person request for materials to be moved to the factory floor. For its retail store, its sales process begins with the physical event of a potential customer entering the door, sending the virtual information event to the sales staff that a customer has arrived, leading to the relational and aspirational event of a conversation about shoes.

See the "Event Content Elements" checklist in the "Into Action" section at the end of the chapter for more on how to apply this to your own organization's services.

# *Decision* Content Elements

**Decisions** represent the "why" or "because" for a service and for the enterprise as a whole. These are usually built up in layers or hierarchies of dependencies, with the question "why?" typically moving upward through the layers, and "because" decisions moving down.

To describe individual decisions, use the *decision-types* set: simple *rule-based* decisions such as following a predefined step-by-step process or checklist; *algorithmic* or "hard-systems" decisions based on calculations that can accommodate variables such as branching, damping, and delayed feedback; more adaptable *guideline-based* or "soft-systems" decisions, using heuristics or patterns to interpret emergent events and contexts; and *principle*-based or values-based decision-making for contexts that are not-known, inherently unpredictable, or unique. Most real-world contexts require composites of those decision types, such as in a chain of exception capture and escalation.

---

We may need to be careful about over-reliance on predefined "because" decisions, but they do help in keeping decision-making simple and fast. The enterprise vision is also the ultimate "*Because.*" for that enterprise: note the period/full stop in that "Because." which indicates that the layering of "Why" stops here!

---

In service design, we not only need to identify the decisions that must take place within that service, but also ensure that the *ability* to make appropriate decisions does indeed exist at each escalation level in the respective context – otherwise the overall process is almost guaranteed to fail on some unexpected and unplanned-for event. To do this, we need to link each decision within a service to the skill-level type required for each agent in the respective capability.

For ZapaMex, everyone is responsible for safety on the factory floor. The decisions in the safety processes there rely mainly on simple checklists, cross-checks between machines and the different parts of each machine, and heuristics and historical patterns of wear for particular types of machine, but also on a more subtle experience-based sense or "feel" that something may not be right.

See the "Decision Content Elements" checklist in the "Into Action" section at the end of the chapter for more on how to apply this to your own organization's services.

# Cross-checks for Service Content

The Service-Content model shows us what to identify within each element of a service and also helps us to distinguish between the roles in each part of the service. Conversely, the Enterprise Canvas cells each specialize in different areas of the content-model frame:

- The core changes to enterprise value take place within the Value-Creation cell.

- Tracking of value, and value flow between services, takes place within the Value-Outlay, Value-Governance, and Value-Return cells.

- The supplier-side and customer-side Channels deal with the main transaction events.

- The Relations cells focus on dealing with relational and/or aspirational assets.

We can also use the Service-Content model with the Service-Layers model to identify which Canvas layer we're working in at any given point:

- If we're looking at *lists* of things, we could be anywhere up to Row-1.

- If we're looking at *relationships* between entities, we cannot be above Row-2.

- If we're looking at *attributes* of things, we cannot be above Row-3.

- If we're looking at a *specific technology or technique*, we are working on Row-4 or below.

- If we're looking at *records* that represent the past, the "as-was," then by definition we are in Row-6.

With regard to products, we should also note

- A product can be comprised only of *asset-type* content: if we're looking at a supposed product that incorporates any other content categories, it is either a mis-defined product or an incompletely defined service.

These checks can also help to prevent us from treating any prepackaged "solution" as an architectural requirement unless we explicitly choose to do so. Note that *the only absolute architectural requirement for the organization is the enterprise vision, with its associated core values*: everything else is an implementation of that requirement, at varying levels of abstraction.

The relationships between primitives and composites are also important here. In essence one of our most important architectural cross-checks comes down to this:

- Services are usable to the extent that they are architecturally "complete."

- Services are *re*usable to the extent that they are architecturally *in*complete.

To enable new architectural options, we need to be able to split our composites apart; to then enable new service implementations, and new business options, we need to be able to re-combine the resultant primitives into new combinations.

---

For example, as an author, I might think of myself as "a writer of books." But a printed book is actually a composite, a "bundling" of information in a specific physical form – and as an author, my actual product is the *information*, not the physical book. (It would be the other way round for someone who worked in a printing business, of course.)

Once I understand that point, it opens up a whole raft of new possibilities, new options to deliver the service represented by that information. For example, I could dispense with the physical book and present the same content in electronic form, as an e-book. I could split up the content in different ways, perhaps serialized in smaller chunks in an online magazine. I could present it in another virtual medium, via video or voice. Or I could deliver it via a relational-asset channel, in a form such as in-person consulting. All of these options become possible once I split "the book" into its real root primitives – or, perhaps more to the point, the options remain entirely invisible unless I do that split.

---

To make something reusable, we need to move up the layers of abstraction, to split apart the implementation composites, and to expose any "bundling" that could perhaps be recombined in new ways. To make something usable, we need to go down the layers, linking each item into more "complete" implementation bundles. At the point where it touches the real world, between Row-5 and Row-6, *everything* must be architecturally "complete," with all Assets, Functions, Locations, Capabilities, Events, and Decisions fully defined and addressed.

The other key point about the Content Model is that it acts as a checklist to make sure that we line things up correctly: for example, that we *don't* try to use IT for something for which it is not well-suited, or which it can't handle at all.

---

Another common trap here is that it can be easy to forget that a record of a "something" is *not* the same as the thing itself. The record is information, a virtual asset, whereas the item referred to in the record could be any type of asset at all – a physical object, a data event, a business relationship, whatever. As soon as we find a record of something, we need to look for the matching audit processes and the like, such as data-cleansing and de-duplication, that would ensure that the records *do* line up correctly with the respective items – because if that audit process doesn't exist, we have an architecture that almost guarantees service failure.

---

We can also use the same checklists to ensure proper coverage not just for everyday operations, but also for exceptions such as disaster recovery and business continuity. Machines, computer systems, power supplies, or network connections may all fail, and whole buildings can be swept away in a natural or man-made disaster: we may well need "manual" processes to take over at a moment's notice. For those cases, we would need the respective special-conditions processes to exist, and people with the appropriate skills to do them – and also know how to switch over to those "manual" processes, too. All of those are items that we can check by using the Content-Model checklists in a layered way.

Another item to check is the content for the flows shared with support services and others, and the service functions, capabilities, events, decisions, and the like that support those connections. Cross-check these with the descriptions of the support services in Chapter 10, "Service Guidance," and the roles of investors and beneficiaries in Chapter 11, "Service Investors and Beneficiaries."

We also need to ensure that all of the necessary links are in place to connect each part of the service all the way back up to the enterprise vision and values, as described in Chapter 3, "Service Context and Market," and Chapter 4, "Service Vision and Values." For example, Figure 13-17 shows how the service's core functionality relates to its role, mission, and goal within the vision of the organization and the broader shared enterprise.

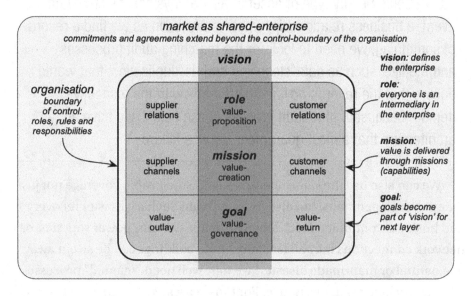

***Figure 13-17.*** *Connecting the service to vision, role, mission, and goal*

Finally, we may also need cross-checks on *responsibility* and *governance*: for example, a key part of the "Who" for a service will relate to questions about responsibilities. This in turn draws on another crucial distinction between responsibility and possession: for example, a process owner is the person who is responsible for that process, not the person who "possesses" it. In essence, service architectures only work when we use a responsibility-based model throughout, such as where "resources" become assets only when we take on responsibility for them.

At any given time, there should always be exactly *one* person who is uniquely responsible for any service element or product element. Conversely, every element needs one person who is uniquely responsible for it at all times. Look for any overlaps in responsibilities, such as those occurring in transitions between layers: for example, one person may have operational responsibility for an item, another has tactical responsibility, another the strategic responsibility. Look also for gaps in responsibilities, where *no one* has apparent responsibility, or where the responsibility has nominally been assigned but not actually taken up or enacted.

---

Note that merely assigning a responsibility to someone does not necessarily mean that that responsibility is taken up! Functional responsibility is an active *choice*, not an arbitrary label.

Also note that responsibility can only be held by a real person: a machine or an IT box is *not* capable of taking responsibility for anything in any legal sense of the term. Hence, especially where IT or machines are involved, it may at times be necessary to follow lengthy trails of non-responsibility, or evasions of responsibility, in order to identify the actual responsible person. For a service architect, this can often be a challenging task, especially in dysfunctional organizations.

---

As a final note, remember that responsibility is literally "response ability," the ability to choose and act on appropriate responses within a given context. That means that a person can *only* be responsible for something if they also have the *authority* and *competence* to make the

191

required decisions. If they do not have that authority or competence, they *cannot and must not* be considered responsible or accountable for the item, and hence a further search will need to be made for someone who *can and does* have the required competence and authority.

See the "Dependencies Between Content Elements" checklist in the "Into Action" section here for more on how to apply this to your own organization's services.

# Into Action

You want the change teams in your business-transformation project to use a consistent way to describe the internal content and structure of services and products, and also ensure that every product and flow that may be needed is properly accounted for and properly described. You'll suggest that they should use the Service-Layers and Service-Content models in Enterprise Canvas to provide guidance, cross-checks, and completeness checklists. Use the ideas in this chapter and the following questions to help you guide those conversations.

## Service and Product

- What products are used as inputs to this service? Which capabilities use them, in what ways, for what purpose? Which function interfaces and service-level agreements apply to their use as inputs?

- Which products are output from this service? Which capabilities produce them? Which function interfaces and service-level agreements apply to them as outputs? Which services, for which stakeholder, are the intended users for these products? What other affordances might arise for use of these products?

- Who is *responsible* for this service or its products? How is that responsibility identified, assigned, accepted, maintained, and/or transferred to some other person? What happens if that responsibility is not identified, accepted, acted on, or appropriately transferred?

## *Asset* Content Elements

- What *physical assets*, as physical "things," are important to this service? What roles do these assets play in the service – for example, as input supplies, as output products, or used as consumables in business processes?

- What *virtual assets*, as data, information, or knowledge, are important to this service? What roles do these assets play in the service – for example, as records, as metrics, as content for delivered services, as controls in business processes?

- What *relational assets*, as relationships with other organizations and actual people, are important to this service? What roles do these assets play in the service – for example, as links with employees, suppliers, customers, shareholders, regulatory bodies, other stakeholders? How are these links used in business services and processes – such as through contracts and other agreements?

- What *aspirational assets*, as the personal sense of belonging, commitment, and shared purpose, are important to this service? In what ways do others connect to the service – for example, morale and

commitment of employees, customers' sense of
"belonging" via a brand, or community perception
of reputation? To what does the service and its
organization itself belong – for example, to a nation, to
an industry, or to the shared enterprise as represented
by its vision and role? What impacts do these assets
have in business processes such as in HR, productivity,
marketing?

- What apparent types of perceived *abstract assets*, such
  as finance, credit, or energy, are important to this
  service? What roles do these assets play in the
  service – for example, as access to resources for
  business processes, as measures of success, as
  relational factors in transactions? What are the
  underlying composites, in terms of the asset-types set,
  on which each of these types of "abstract asset" are
  actually based?

- What *composite assets*, or combinations of asset-type
  "primitives," are important to this service? What are
  their base asset types? In what ways is it possible, or not
  possible in practice, to split the composite into its base
  asset types? What are the consequences of *not* being
  able to split the composite into its base types?

- What value does each type of asset have for the service?
  For relational and aspirational assets, by what means
  does the service identify when these assets need to be
  created, or have been changed, damaged, or deleted,
  by the entity at the *other* end of the link? How are these
  assets obtained, maintained, monitored, managed
  through their life cycle, and disposed of at the end of it?

- Who is *responsible* for each asset, or type of asset? How is that responsibility identified, assigned, accepted, maintained, and/or transferred to some other person? What happens if that responsibility is not identified, accepted, acted on, or appropriately transferred?

## *Function* Content Elements

- What functions and their interfaces are used in this service? What service-level agreements and the like apply to each of these functions? How do these functions relate with each other, in terms of service categories and service layering?

- What *assets* does each function use, create change, update, delete, destroy? What asset type, or combination of asset types, is involved in each case – physical, virtual, relational, aspirational, abstract? What type of function, or combination of function type, is involved in each case – physical, virtual, relational, aspirational, or abstract?

- What *locations* are related to each function? What category of location, or combination of location categories, is involved in each case – physical, virtual, relational, aspirational, abstract?

- What are the underlying *capabilities* for each function? In what ways do the respective actions, agents, and skill levels affect the service-level agreement for each function?

- What *events* trigger or are triggered by the function? What type of event, or combination of event types, is involved in each case – physical, virtual, relational, aspirational, abstract?

- What *decisions* or reasons apply to or impact on the function? What type of decision, or combination of decision types, is involved in each case – rule-based, algorithmic, guideline, or principle-based?

- What *composite functions*, or combinations of function-type "primitives," are important to this service? What are their base function types? In what ways is it possible, or not possible in practice, to split the composite into its base function types? What are the consequences of *not* being able to split the composite into its base types?

- Who is *responsible* for each function, or type of function? How is that responsibility identified, assigned, accepted, maintained, and/or transferred to some other person? What happens if that responsibility is not identified, accepted, acted on, or appropriately transferred?

## *Location* Content Elements

- What types of *physical locations* and their associated location schemas – geographic, building floor, etc. – are important to this service? What roles do these locations play in the business – for example, as retail contact points, manufacturing locations, physical storage, or resource sites?

- What types of *virtual locations* and their associated location schemas – networks, naming, web addresses, contact numbers, etc. – are important to this service? What roles do these locations play in the business – for example, as virtual contact points, or as nodes for information routes?

- What types of *relational locations* and their associated location schemas – such as market segments, or nodes in reporting relationship trees and social networks – are important to this service? What roles do these locations play in the service, or in broader business processes?

- What types of *aspirational locations* and their associated location-schemas – in particular, the end-nodes of aspirational-assets – are important to this service?

- What types of other *abstract locations* and their associated location schemas, such as time and time zones, are important to this service? What roles do these locations play in the service – for example, as reference points for measurement of performance?

- What types of *composite locations* – combinations of any location-type "primitives" – are important to this service? What are their base location types? In what ways is it possible, or not possible in practice, to split the composite into its base types? What are the consequences of *not* being able to split the composite into its base types?

- What value does each type of location have for the service? For relational or aspirational locations, by what means does the service identify when relational

197

locations need to be created, or have been damaged or deleted, by the entity at the *other* end of the link? How are all of these locations identified, obtained, maintained, monitored, and, where feasible, managed throughout their life cycle?

- Who is *responsible* for each location, or type of location? How is that responsibility identified, assigned, accepted, maintained, and/or transferred to some other person? What happens if that responsibility is not identified, accepted, acted on, or appropriately transferred?

## *Capability* Content Elements

- What *capabilities* are implied as required by the overall enterprise? What capabilities are implied as required by the functions of this service? How would you categorize each capability, in terms of *asset-type acted upon, asset-type* of *agent*, and required *skill level*?

- What *capabilities* are implied by each key asset type, location, and event identified in assessments here? What is the required skill level in each case?

- What *capabilities* are implied by each key *decision*, reason, constraint, standard, or suchlike identified in the assessments here? What is the required skill level for appropriate decision-making in each case? What asset types would be involved in each case? What events or functions would call for this capability?

- Does the capability need to vary in different locations? If so, what location category is implied in each case?

- Who is *responsible* for each capability, and for each of the actions, assets, agents, and skills used in that capability or type of capability? How is that responsibility identified, assigned, accepted, maintained, and/or transferred to some other person? What happens if that responsibility is not identified, accepted, acted on, or appropriately transferred?

## *Event* Content Elements

- What types of *physical events* are important to this service?

- What types of *virtual events* – messages, signals, data values – are important to this service?

- What types of *relational events* – arrivals, departures, contacts, other events in relationships with other organizations and actual people – are important to this service?

- What types of *aspirational events* – such as reputation- or public-relations events, or changes to brand – are important to this service?

- What types of other *abstract events*, such as cycles of time, are important to this service?

- What types of *composite events* – combinations of any of the event-type "primitives" – are important to the organization's business? What are their base event types? In what ways is it possible, or not possible in practice, to split the composite into its base types? What are the consequences of *not* being able to split the composite into its base categories?

- What roles do each of these events play in the service, as input or output triggers for routine or exceptional business processes? What value does each type of event have for the service? How are these events identified, monitored, and managed within an overall life cycle?

- Who is *responsible* for each event, or type of event? How is that responsibility identified, assigned, accepted, maintained, and/or transferred to some other person? What happens if that responsibility is not identified, accepted, acted on, or appropriately transferred?

## *Decision* Content Elements

- What decisions, business rules, principles, and guidelines apply within this service? What decision levels and skill levels are required in order to appropriately enact each decision? Who or what would enact each decision? Who would be ultimately responsible for each of these decisions?

- What laws and other regulations apply to this service? To what extent and in what ways are they binding on the service and the organization? In what ways do these vary in differing jurisdictions and the like?

- What standards, such as quality standards, technical standards, interface standards, language standards, and suchlike, will apply to this service? To what extent and in what ways are they binding on the respective areas of the organization? In what ways do these vary in differing regions and the like?

- What social expectations and social standards, on ethics, environment, general "good neighborliness," and so on, will apply in each aspect of this service and its business context? To what extent and in what ways are they binding on the respective areas of the organization? In what ways do these vary in differing regions and the like?

- What constraints and/or opportunities do these decisions imply for the organization and its business in the enterprise? What trade-offs do these imply against the business requirements?

- By what means would the service confirm its compliance with these constraints? What actions and information would be required? How would you monitor and measure compliance? What would be the consequences of failure to comply? What opportunities arise from the required compliance with these constraints?

- Who is *responsible* for each decision, or type of decision? If a decision is embedded within the operations of a machine or IT – such as in an autonomous vehicle or machine-learning application – who is responsible for embedding those decisions, and for the operational validity of those embedded decisions? How is that responsibility identified, assigned, accepted, maintained, and/or transferred to some other person? What happens if that responsibility is not identified, accepted, acted on, or appropriately transferred?

# Dependencies Between Content Elements

- Given the asset-types list, what capabilities are needed to work on them?

- Given the decision-types list, what exceptions will cause a decision to be escalated, maybe all the way up to truly unique yet business-critical events?

- Does the skill and capability exist to resolve that escalation? If so, via what means will that capability be delivered?

- To what extent can we design the service interfaces to be "implementation-agnostic" – for example, such that people can take over when an IT system fails, or a machine can take over when people are overloaded?

- What interchanges, flows, and interfaces are needed to support, guide, coordinate, and validate all aspects of the service?

- What are the trade-offs across the service, and between services?

- What are the costs of the service, in any given sense of "cost"?

- Who is *responsible* for the service as a whole, and for its own operations and within broader processes? How do they ensure that all other responsibilities for elements within the service, and for its connections and coordination with other services, are all appropriately enacted, and link together appropriately at all times? How is that responsibility identified, assigned, accepted, maintained, and/or transferred to some other person? What happens if that responsibility is not identified, accepted, acted on, or appropriately transferred?

# Summary

In this chapter, we reviewed how to acquire the detail about the internal content that is needed for each service and its products. We did this by applying checklists to each cell in the service structure and its flows, to enquire about the assets, functions, locations, capabilities, events, and decisions at play in each case, and how they link together to deliver the service itself.

In the next chapter, we explore how Enterprise Canvas can support us in making sense of services as systems and within systems-of-systems.

# CHAPTER 14

# Services As Systems

Some aspects of systems theory can provide a useful support for modeling services with Enterprise Canvas, with an emphasis on recursion, flow, strategy, and overall integration. However, we do need to keep this as simple as practicable, and also make it clear that this is about the term "system" in its more generic sense rather than solely about IT systems. The diagrams here should help to explain the concepts and their applications for a general business audience where required.

There's one important warning here: we need to know when to stop doing a systems analysis! Systems contain other systems, intersect with other systems, and form parts of other systems or systems-of-systems, and so on ad-infinitum. If we're not careful, we'd end up trying to model the entire world and everything in it: not a good idea.

To keep things simple, we apply the "Just Enough Principle": we only do "just enough analysis" to satisfy the immediate business question. Then leave it alone until the next business question comes up, for which we'll do a bit more systems analysis in that specific area of concern; and then another business question comes up, for another concern; and so on.

© Tom Graves 2023

T. Graves, *Mapping the Enterprise*, https://doi.org/10.1007/978-1-4842-9836-7_14

The trick is to leave "hooks" on the outer edges of each piece of systems analysis, to which other pieces can connect as appropriate. After a while we'll quietly discover that we've actually created a systems view across quite a large, broad, fully interconnected scope, with maybe a few identifiable gaps that you could fill in later whenever the need might arise. But the important point is that we've let that model evolve in its own way, in its own time, and we haven't tried to do it all in one go.

---

These assessments apply especially in Row-3 Service Model, Row-4 Design Model, and Row-5 Deployment Model, though much of it – particularly the section on strategic completion – could also apply all the way up to Row-1 Scope.

# Enterprises As Systems

Everything in the enterprise is, implies, or represents a service. In the same way, *everything* is a system, is part of a larger system, contains other systems: systems ad infinitum. In dealing with anything on the scale of an enterprise, we need to be able to think in terms of systems and systems-of-systems if we're to have any chance of making sense of what's going on.

In a systems sense, much of what we need here can be summarized as shown in Figure 14-1, in five straightforward principles: *rotation, reciprocation, resonance, recursion*, and *reflexion*.

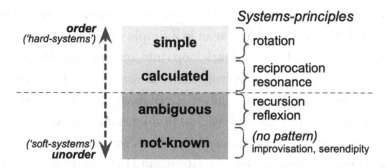

**Figure 14-1.** *Repeatability and systems principles*

**Rotation** is the simplest of the systems principles. Any real-world system is too large and too complex to be seen in its entirety from one view alone: to make sense of it all, we need to be able to *rotate* through a variety of different views and viewpoints and merge those different views together to build a more complete picture of the whole.

This is straightforward enough: every checklist does it. One of the aims of the Enterprise Canvas is that it provides us with a set of visual checklists to give us a range of different interlinked views on the service in scope. We can then use it *as* a checklist, *as* a systematic rotation through multiple views.

**Reciprocation** and **resonance** present a matched pair of principles that apply mainly to flows. In a simple world, flows will all need to balance somehow: "for every action there is an equal and opposite reaction" and suchlike. In that sense, flows need to be *reciprocal*; at the market level, there needs to be "fair exchange," "quid pro quo" – or at least a verifiable perception of that. Reciprocation is a key part of what we explore when we do an assessment of service-flow content.

The complication is that although things do have to balance up somehow, the flows may not be a simple "tit for tat." Often there will be delays in a feedback loop, or translations from one form of energy to another – for example, financial donors to a charity typically receive a return in the form of a different kind of satisfaction. In terms of point-to-point physics, each transaction can be seen as a simple win/lose; but when we take the *resonance* of those feedback loops into account, win/lose turns out to be a special case in a full spectrum between win/win and lose/lose.

That last point applies especially in social flows and transactions – and frequently leads to "unexpected" wicked problems if we're not aware of what's actually going on. To help us make sense, we can use the Enterprise Canvas to describe resonance and reciprocation in the interactions and flows across the whole system, especially over time.

**Recursion** and **reflexion** provide another matched pair of principles that become particularly important when dealing with true complexity.

*Recursion* will occur when the same pattern repeats, or, in fractal-recursion, is "self-similar," at different levels of the same system. A conventional reporting hierarchy is recursive: the pattern repeats at different levels of management. A service-oriented architecture is recursive: the same concept of services – the same *pattern* of services – applies in much the same ways at every level of the enterprise.

*Reflexion* is the inverse of this: if recursion means that every part in some ways reflects the whole, then we can also infer the whole – or some aspects of the whole – from within every part. Note, though, that it's like the holograph, in that every discrete part of the image also contains *all* of the image, but in less detail – and that loss of detail can sometimes be misleading if we extrapolate anything out too literally.

Within the Enterprise Canvas, one of the most immediate examples of recursion is that every cell within the overall service shown on the Canvas is also itself a service. The Supplier-Relations cell, for example, not only provides "supplier-relations" services on behalf of the service that we depict on the Canvas, but to do so it must also have its own Value Proposition in presenting those services. It has its own Supplier Channels and Customer Channels (the latter rather than the former being how, in this case of Supplier Relations, it actually delivers its services); it has its own Value Creation in which it creates the value of those supplier relations, and so on. And each of those sub-cells too has its own flows, some of them linking externally on behalf of the main service, others linking to other cells and sub-cells *within* the service.

The inverse is also true. Whenever we come across a business entity or function that delivers what we might interpret as "supplier-relations services," we need to ask who or what service it delivers these services *for*. We also need to look for and identify its matching Supplier Channels, Value Creation, Customer Channels, Value Outlay, and the like that provide its "sibling" services in terms of the Enterprise Canvas.

Typically, whenever we go "down" a level into the recursion, we move closer toward real-world implementation, and whenever we go "up" a level in the recursion, we're usually also moving up a layer of abstraction, as described in Chapter 5, "Service Layers." In that sense, abstraction and recursion are closely linked within the Canvas – which is also another reason why abstraction (rather than, say, management hierarchy) is the most effective framework for layering here.

# Impact of Time Compression

The spectrum of repeatability, from predictable to unique, can tell us a great deal about what skills are needed in any given context. However, there is an important rider to this, which relates to the amount of time available for decision and action. Introducing this additional dimension in effect forces that simple linear spectrum into a more complex two-axis frame, as shown in Figure 14-2.

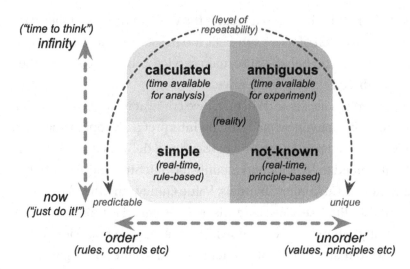

**Figure 14-2.**  *Repeatability, time, and order*

---

Note that there are several other axis pairs and interpretive frames that can be used with this model of repeatability – see my book *Everyday Enterprise Architecture* for a range of other practical examples.

---

The key point about this variant of the repeatability model is that it describes what may happen at different timescales. The split between "order" and "unorder" is fairly straightforward:

- *Order*: Repetition of a rule or formula will always deliver the same results; there is an identifiable "right way" or "best practice" for any context; analysis is the most reliable approach; key driver is logic or "truth."

- *Unorder*: Repetition of a rule or formula will either not ensure the same results (Ambiguous) or will never repeat the same results (Not-known); there is

no identifiable "right way" or "best practice" that will
always deliver the same results in a given context;
iterative experimentation is the most reliable approach;
key driver is value or feelings.

At different timescales, different options become emphasized. As "time for thinking" becomes available, the emphasis can shift toward experimentation (ambiguous) or analysis (calculated). At the extreme, with infinite time seemingly available, there tends to be a drift toward "analysis paralysis," or endless experimentation that seems to lead nowhere.

But in the other direction, as time becomes more compressed into an increasingly urgent "do it *now!*" the available choices become squeezed into a narrow spectrum between simple rule following, at one extreme, to a kind of impenetrable real-time improvisation, dancing with the chaos in a way that would be incomprehensible to anyone else – or, in some cases, even to those doing the work. In effect, it presents a savage split between the limited competence of the raw trainee – unable to adapt to anything outside of the rules – and the hyper-competence of the multi-year master – who has no time to explain – and no apparent means or time to learn how to move from one capability to the other.

In practice, the Value-Creation and the main-channel interfaces – Supplier Channels and Customer Channels – tend to fall naturally into this time compression: the nature of the work is that there will be no time available to stop and think. Other cells will often fall into much the same pattern, simply as a result of day-to-day pressures of work. Yet *skills development can only take place if there is sufficient "time-to-think" to reflect on action.* Hence, it is *essential* that every service, and every cell in every service, is backed up by learning processes – usually delivered via the Validation and/or Coordination guidance services. The aim would be that time-to-think is available *before* action – as planning – and time-to-think is available *after* action, as reflection on performance, so that there is no need to think *during* the real-time action of the service itself.

# Systems and Cycles

Another useful frame here is **Five Elements**. This provides a set of distinct perspectives into a service that also link together into a continuous change cycle, as an internal counterpart to the external Service Cycle. It is based in part on what is perhaps the oldest-known systems framework, the ancient Chinese *wu-xing*, which has been used to guide systems-based sensemaking and decision-making across many types of contexts for more than two thousand years. Classic *wu-xing* describes a context in terms of five distinct element-like perspectives that cross-check and interact with each other: *wood*, new developments, new beginnings; *fire*, the energy for change, Adam Smith's "the animal spirits of the entrepreneur"; *earth*, providing the material for change; *metal* (or, in the earliest versions, *stone*), the action of change; and *water*, the outcomes of change, feeding back into the new.

In the Five Elements model, these "elements" translate into a set of business-oriented terms: respectively, as *Purpose, People, Preparation, Process*, and *Performance*. This frame is shown in Figure 14-3.

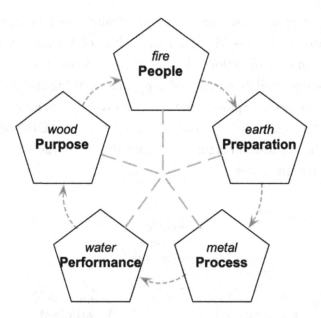

**Figure 14-3.** *Five Elements frame*

We can use the Five Elements perspectives as a set of themes or "lenses" through which to explore issues relating to overall effectiveness:

- *Appropriate*: Supports and optimizes support for business purpose

- *Elegant*: Clarity, simplicity, consistency, self-adjusting for human factors

- *Efficient*: Optimizes the use of resources and minimizes wastage of resources

- *Reliable*: Predictable, consistent, self-correcting, supports "single source of truth"

- *Integrated*: Creates, supports, and optimizes synergy across all systems

We need to apply these themes systematically across the entire enterprise, to each of its services, to each of that service's cells and "child" services, and to each of its flows. The aim here is to ensure that every aspect of a service will fit in with and support everything else throughout the overall enterprise: exploring these themes will help to identify where they support overall effectiveness, where they don't, and if they don't, what to do about it. As shown in Figure 14-4, each theme also acts as a cross-check to each of the others.

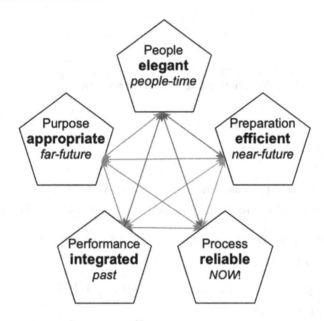

***Figure 14-4.***  *Five Elements: effectiveness*

As also seen in Figure 14-4, each of these perspectives also has its own view of time: far future, "people-time," near future, "*now!*" and past, respectively. It's important to note these differences in time perspectives when assessing effectiveness. They can often lead otherwise to "inexplicable" clashes between work groups and across the organization and enterprise.

We can also connect the Five Elements perspectives together, as phases of *action* or focus in a mutually supportive sequence. This usage for Five Elements is derived in part from Bruce Tuckman's well-known Group Dynamics model of distinct phases in the life sequence of a project: *forming, storming, norming, performing,* and *adjourning.* Here, though, we link the end of one sequence to the beginning of the next of a new sequence, to form a continuous *cycle* with each new sequence starting at "forming" and Purpose, as shown in Figure 14-5.

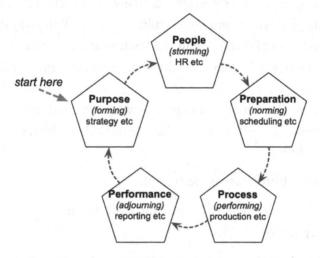

***Figure 14-5.*** *Five Elements: five phases in the continuing lifecycle*

The same pattern will also repeat across an organization, with different business units enacting different parts of the cycle:

- *Purpose*: Strategy, futures, business intelligence, corporate identity, brand

- *People*: HR, training, organizational development, narrative knowledge, health and safety, security

- *Preparation*: Planning, scheduling, project management, procurement, infrastructure, logistics

- *Process*: Production, manufacturing, sales [in a sales context], any "service-delivery" function

- *Performance*: Book-keeping, performance records, accounting, audit, archive; also "lessons-learned" review

In effect, each of these business units is a service in its own right, with its own mix of service content: assets, functions, locations, capabilities, events, and decisions. The same applies likewise to each of those business units' subsidiary services, and *their* "child" services, all the way down to the smallest level of detail – again each with their own mix of service content and each activity following the same Five Elements sequences and cycles.

Yet there are also small elements of service content that act as connectors *between* each of the Five Elements nodes, which we could summarize as follows:

- *Values* bring Purpose for People.

- *Policies* provide the overarching guidance for Preparation.

- Start-*Events* signal the transition from Preparation into the main action of Process.

- *Completions* mark the end of Process and the start of Performance review.

- *Satisfaction* for all parties at the end of Performance review connects back to Purpose.

---

This aspect of the Five Elements model is based in part on ideas from the VPEC-T framework developed by Nigel Green and Carl Bate – see Chapter 16, "Integration with Architectures."

---

As summarized in Figure 14-6, the Five Elements nodes identify the sets of activities that need to occur in the respective phases of this internal service cycle, and the connectors signal the boundaries between the phases in the cycle – all of it centered around Trust, exactly as in the external Service Cycle for all flows between services.

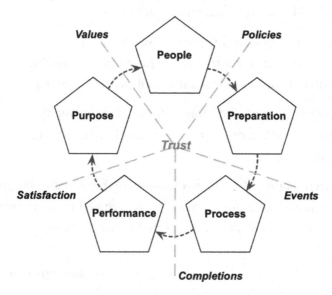

***Figure 14-6.*** *Five Elements: service-activity cycles*

These types of Five Elements reviews of service effectiveness and service-activity sequences will provide key cross-checks for successful service design and service operation. They can also highlight important risks and opportunities, and surface options for potential service improvements that might otherwise be hidden from view.

# Strategy and Lifecycle Completion

The Five Elements model also provides an important view into the relationships between strategy, tactics, and operations:

- *Strategy* is about the relationships between the organization and the enterprise, between the organization and the people who work within it, and between the organization and its various "external" stakeholders – relationships which mostly center around identity, belonging, and *feeling*.

- *Tactics* is about translating those relationships into explicit plans for action in the near future – activities which mostly center around analysis and *thinking*.

- *Operations* or "execution" is focused on *action* in the immediate present – everything here will center around *doing*.

As shown in Figure 14-7, the overall flow of the activities lifecycle passes through each of these modes in turn – which in practice means that an explicit balance needs to be maintained between them.

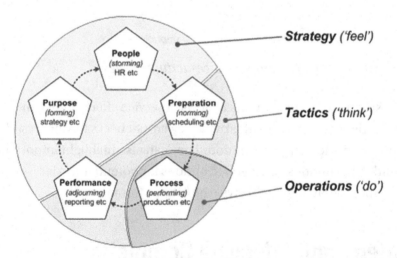

*Figure 14-7.* *Strategy, tactics, operations: links to Five Elements*

However, the modes also often represent fundamental differences in mindset and worldview – which can lead to serious problems if any one of the modes comes to dominate over the others. We can perhaps see this most easily via a cross-map to the market cycle.

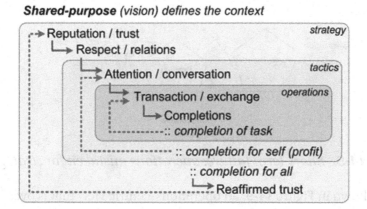

***Figure 14-8.*** *Operations, tactics, strategy, and the market cycle*

In this view of the market cycle, as shown in Figure 14-8, there are three distinct stages of completion – each of which offers a choice as to whether to continue in the cycle, or loop back to an earlier stage.

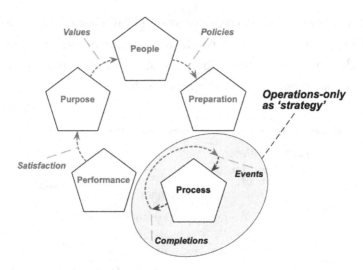

***Figure 14-9.*** *Short-term failure: operations mistaken for strategy*

As shown in Figure 14-9, an operations-centric view that is over-focused on the short term will loop back to the next task as soon as the current main-channel task is complete, without checking for completion of anything coming back along the return channel. This is typical for any production-oriented service, though can often work quite well if there is linkage to another service that can take over the main cycle at that point. The catch is that it *must* assume that there are no changes at all in the context, because it has no means within itself to adapt to change: if there *is* any change in the context, the service will usually fail. If an obsessive focus on "doing" comes to dominate so much that operations itself is taken as "strategy" – as in the fixed Five Year Plans of the old communist era, for example – then system failure is *guaranteed* in the relatively short term.

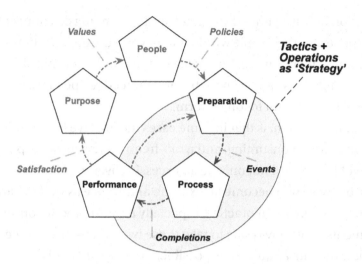

***Figure 14-10.*** *Medium-term failure: tactics mistaken for strategy*

A more common source of failure risk, as shown in Figure 14-10, occurs at the second Completions choice, which occurs early in the Performance phase. In a commercial context, this is the "monetization point," the point at which payment has been received and in which the financial part of the transaction is complete: from the service's perspective, a basic "satisfaction for self" has been achieved. In services that are dominated by notions of "results" – as is all too common in business – there is then a tendency to want to loop back straight away to a point somewhere within the Preparation phase, to set up the next transaction and get back to "monetization" as quickly as possible. This also leads to a situation where relatively short-term tactics are mistaken for strategy – as in the classic pseudo-strategy of "our strategy is last year's target plus 10%."

The problem is that the *overall* transaction – "satisfaction for all" rather than solely "satisfaction for self" – was never completed, there is no reaffirmation of mutual Trust, and the all-important reconnections with Purpose and People were never made, often dismissed as "unnecessary overhead." The resultant "quick-profit failure cycle" does deliver higher profits in the short term, but leads to an initially slow yet accelerating deterioration of trust within the market, and a widening disconnect from the enterprise and the people within and beyond the organization – setting the stage for an increasingly desperate yet apparently "inexplicable" slide into irrelevance. This can be an all-but-guaranteed recipe for service failure over the medium to longer term.

The reality, though, is that in some cases the full Five Elements cycle can be overly time-consuming, and a too-frequent review of Purpose and even of People will not only be an excessive overhead in most contexts, but will soon become an extreme annoyance as well: "change is mistaken for progress." In practice, especially in most production-oriented environments, it usually *is* safe to take those two "short-cuts," to keep the overall flow moving as quickly as possible, for *everyone*'s satisfaction. The keyword, though, is "usually": the trick is to know when it's safe to do so, or when we *do* need to work our way through all of the Completions, carefully, and in sequence. There are key questions there that need to be asked in any service design with the Enterprise Canvas.

# Into Action

You have some concerns that your change teams might miss potential issues that could arise through how services interact with each other across the whole context and scope of your business transformation, perhaps particularly when timescales become a factor in the story. You want them to use systems perspectives as a cross-check – and also understand that the term "system" applies to much more than just the IT. Use the ideas in this chapter and the questions below to help you guide those conversations.

## Enterprises As Systems

- What checklists could be used in this context to build a more complete view of this service?

- How do we move between the different views and tests indicated by the checklist? What do we need to do to avoid becoming stuck on a single view as "the truth"?

- What checklists and checklist items are missing from this view? What other views or checks do we need?

- How do we link all the different views together? Since all of them present some form of "truth," how do we resolve any conflicts that may occur between all of these different forms of "truth"?

- How do we ensure that there is balance – reciprocation – across all flows for this service?

- Given that forms of value may change across the service, or between the relations channel, main transaction channel, and return channel, how do we keep track of these changes? How do we ensure that there is "fair exchange" even when the form of value has changed?

- At what point do simple notions of balance – "double-entry life-keeping" – become more of a hindrance than a help in understanding the flows of this service? At what point do we need to accept natural resonance – increasing or decreasing – within the flow?

- How would we create a resonance in a flow, to increase a desirable effect, or dampen (reduce) an undesirable one? And who decides which resonances are "desirable" or "undesirable"?

- How do we ensure that changes in balance – such as created by resonance – are shared appropriately between all parties in the enterprise? Who decides how that changing balance is to be shared? How can we ensure that those decisions are in line with the enterprise vision?

- What patterns of recursion can you identify within the structure of the service and its flows? In what ways could you use such patterns to reduce complexity across the overall system? What advantages and potential problems are implied by those patterns?

- In what ways can aspects of the whole be seen reflected in any or many of the system's individual parts? In what ways could you use such patterns to reduce complexity across the overall system? What advantages and potential problems are implied by those apparent patterns?

## Impact of Time Compression

- What are the skills and capabilities required in the service?

- If the service requires delivery in very short timescales, what checklists and other Simple-domain tools and techniques are available to reduce the risk of falling into an unmanaged Chaotic state? What "master"-level skills are required in order to bring the service out of such a Chaotic state? From where are these skills available?

- What time is available for analysis and experimentation within the service itself? If none, where does planning and reflection take place? Who or what guides this planning and reflection?

- If there is no time within the service for planning, reflection, or capability development, and there are no links to outside services that can provide these, what impact does this have on the effectiveness of the service in the long term, medium term, or even short term?

# Systems and Cycles

For the service overall, for each of its cells, and for each of its flows:

- Who or what is responsible for the *Purpose* of this item? (This should link strongly with the Value-Proposition cell, for example, and also the "Direction" guidance services.)

- Who or what is responsible for the *People* issues for this item? (This is where the "Validation" guidance services are likely to play a key part in the service and, for external links, the Supplier/Customer-Relations cells.)

- Who or what is responsible for the *Preparation* and scheduling for this item? (This should link strongly with the Value-Governance cell, and also the "Coordination" guidance services.)

- Who or what is responsible for the *Process* and action of this item? (This should link strongly with the Value-Creation cell, probably the Supplier-Channels and Customer-Channels cells, and probably also the "Coordination" guidance services.)

- Who or what is responsible for the overall *Performance* of this item, including completions and lessons learned? (This should link strongly with the Value-Governance cell, the Value-Outlay and Value-Return cells, and also the "Validation" guidance services.)

- Who or what is responsible for *integration* between all of these domains – such as in resolving clashes in time perspective between the groups?

- Who or what is responsible for assessing effectiveness for each item, and its relationships and interactions across the whole? What actions, if any, need to be taken to improve that effectiveness?

- Who or what is responsible for ensuring continuity of connections for the sequences and cycles of activities for this item? What actions, if any, need to be taken to improve those activities and connections?

# Strategy and Lifecycle Completion

- Is there a choice in the service's handling of Completions where it can short-cut back to start straight away on the next task? If so, to what other service is the responsibility passed to handle the remainder of the service's Completions? What processes and decisions ensure that the service *does* continue on through the whole of the Five Elements cycle at appropriate intervals?

- Is there a choice in the service's handling of Completions and Performance where it can short-cut back to set up the next transaction? If so, to what other service is the responsibility passed to handle the remainder of the service's Performance activities? What processes and decisions ensure that the service *does* continue on through the whole of the Five Elements cycle at appropriate intervals?

- What decisions and processes are needed to ensure an appropriate balance at all times between strategy, tactics, and operations – between *feel*, *think*, and *do*?

## Summary

In this chapter, we learned that it can be useful to take a "systems" view of a service and its context. We reviewed a range of systems-type techniques and perspectives that can help us to assess integration issues, strategic concerns, and other related themes for service modeling with Enterprise Canvas.

In the next chapter, we explore a variety of service patterns in which Enterprise Canvas can help us make sense of the respective service and its context.

# CHAPTER 15

# Example Patterns

One of the more valuable uses for Enterprise Canvas is that it provides a consistent pattern to guide a basic completeness check for service designs. As with the core principles for Enterprise Canvas, we can apply this kind of completeness check at any level, from whole-organization to detail-level service. This chapter shows five brief examples of this completeness-check review as applied to various types of service:

- For-profit business, at whole-of-organization level

- Not-for-profit charity, at whole-of-organization level

- IT service management, as a business unit within the organization

- Simple IT-based business process, described as a BPMN model (Business Process Modeling Notation)

- Military squad, as a people-based capability

See "Appendix D: Enterprise Canvas As Service Viability Checklist," for a more detailed description of the review process.

## Example 1: Publicly Owned For-Profit Business

This example shows the type of pattern for a larger for-profit business that will tend to arise as an outcome of mainstream notions of "scientific

© Tom Graves 2023
T. Graves, *Mapping the Enterprise*, https://doi.org/10.1007/978-1-4842-9836-7_15

management" and the legal mandates of current corporate law for publicly owned corporations, particularly in the USA.

In this structure, "the enterprise" and "the organization" share the same boundary. The two terms are considered to be exact synonyms for each other: there is no real link with, or even awareness of, a shared enterprise beyond the organization, and relations with suppliers and customers alike are often characterized by a combative "us against them."

By custom and sometimes by law, monetary return is defined as the only meaningful form of value: it is assumed that the only reason that the organization exists is to make money for the stockholders, as the purported owners of the enterprise. Given this requirement, the enterprise vision is straightforward and exclusive: "make money" from the market, as much of it as possible, to optimize or maximize the returns to the stockholders over the short to medium term.

All of the guidance functions – Direction, Coordination, and Validation – are subsumed into an expanded notion of "management" which takes over the Value-Governance cell, in part to gain a more direct connection to the "owners." This also has the effect of replacing Direction's future focus with an over-emphasis on past performance, in effect flipping the Enterprise Canvas structure upside down and usually forcing any business model to run on the "quick-profit failure cycle" described in the "Strategy and Lifecycles" section in Chapter 14, "Services As Systems." Structurally, Validation and Coordination are replaced by "command" and "control," respectively, and, other than as required by law, often explicitly disconnected from anything beyond the organization. That self-isolation can also result in an insistence on proprietary standards, a tendency toward a "not invented here" syndrome, and increased risks of regulatory challenge.

Figure 15-1 shows an Enterprise Canvas overview of the probable structure of the organization-as-a-service that would arise from that description above.

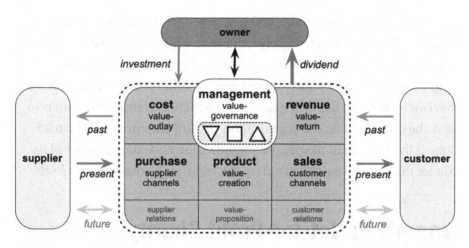

***Figure 15-1.*** *Overview Canvas for publicly owned for-profit business*

Within the service functions represented in the main Canvas, the natural boundaries between the cells tend to be exaggerated and reinforced as distinct silos. There is often a rigid separation between development and production, and even more so between line management against all other parts of the service: the classic Taylorist separation between "management" and "workers." Management also often claims the entire return channel as its own private domain, asserting rigid control over budget and all monetary matters and using the resultant scarcity of resources as a substitute for values-based governance.

With the loss of any real focus on the future, and the absence of any means to connect the organization to the vision of a broader shared enterprise, there is no available option for a "pull"-based marketing model via a shared Value Proposition. Its only alternative is some form of product development derived from internal assumptions about "something we can sell." Without any direct engagement in the value proposition, the organization's potential customers are unlikely to feel much inherent engagement in the product; hence, it becomes the unhappy role of marketing to attempt, via "push," to manufacture a sort-of-"relationship" with customers where no real reason for any such relationship actually exists.

Overall, although common in the business world, this inherently dysfunctional structure is unlikely to be successful or effective in the longer term, for anyone involved – not even for the stockholders. Yet a comparison of this structure with the generic Enterprise Canvas indicates what *can* be done to improve matters – of which the most important is to break the delusion that the organization "is" the enterprise and instead connect the organization with the shared vision and shared values of its broader market and extended enterprise beyond the organization itself.

# Example 2: Not-for-Profit Charity

Not-for-profit organizations and charities operate under different laws and social expectations than those that apply to for-profit organizations, which in turn gives rise to a different typical structure for the organization-as-a-service.

---

Much the same principles as here *should* apply to the government context, since that too is nominally "not-for-profit." In practice, though, the "guidance" functions there often tend to be subsumed into the executive, much as in the dysfunctional for-profit model, and with much the same dysfunctional results.

---

In this example, the charity aims to deliver a service to its recipients, yet to do so must engage donors to provide the resources needed in order to deliver those services, and hence must also act as a direct and explicit intermediary between donors and recipients.

The same principles apply to almost any charity, but charities in practice often have very complex relations between many different types and roles of providers; for this example we'll keep it simple, and imagine a charity that provides clothing to victims of natural disasters.

Here the boundaries of the organization may include the "direction" guidance functions – as in a conventional for-profit business – but the "coordination" and "validation" functions *must* extend beyond the organization itself. On the "coordination" side, this charity *must* coordinate its service delivery with other charities and services that operate in the same disaster zone – medical, shelter, food, rescue, security, and suchlike; and on the "validation" side, the charity's services and activities will only make sense to donors and recipients alike if they connect to a shared vision such as "keeping people safe, warm, and comforted after an emergency."

Many charities start off with something like a "product-development" model, designing support services of some kind as a metaphoric equivalent of "something we can sell," and then delivering those services. As a "push"-type activity, though, it may be difficult for it to make sense even to the nominal recipients, and unless the connection is made to a "higher cause" that will engage others, the charity will soon run out of resources, and fail. All the problems and potential mistakes faced by commercial "startups" apply just as much to charities and other not-for-profits: the only difference is that resources and "profit" may be measured in a different way.

The Value Proposition here is straightforward: given the shared vision, there is a clear need for clothing to replace items lost in natural disasters – a need which will be all too evident to the intended recipients, and will also make immediate sense to potential donors. This in turn implies the need for a service to deliver such clothing in a disaster-recovery context (the Value-Creation cell, here described as "service operation"); and for some form of management, in donor locations, on the spot in the disaster-affected region, and in logistics in between (the Value-Governance cell, here labeled "service management"). The linkage to value and enterprise values is therefore reasonably clear, though we will have to drill down from this very simple Row-2 model all the way to a Row-5 detailed-implementation model to get a proper picture of what all of this would entail in practice.

On the donor side, we need to explain what the need is, and why it should be seen as important (Supplier Relations, here labeled "cause marketing"), and encourage *two-way* conversations that will engage people directly in the enterprise values and thence in the charity's value proposition. Assuming that this engagement does happen, we'll also have created the space for transactions to occur, much like a supplier relationship in a commercial context – in this case, the donors supplying either clothing or money to assist in delivery of that clothing, or both (Supplier Channels, here labeled "fundraising/collection").

On the recipient side, we need to identify appropriate "customers" for our clothing service. Given that this will take place in a disaster-recovery context, gaining their *trust* will also be crucial here – hence, again, the importance of *two-way* communication to create engagement in the shared vision (Customer Relations, here shown as "recipient relations"). We then need to match their needs with the available resources, both on-the-spot and via requests further back along the charity's logistics chain (Customer Channels, here labeled "service delivery").

In both cases, the return channel (Value Return and Value Outlay, here labeled "recipient results" and "cause results," respectively) is *significantly* different from that in a commercial context. For a business, "success" is a profitable sale; income and costs alike can, it seems, all be reduced to monetary metrics, which makes the measurement of "success" a mere matter of quick calculation – all very simple and straightforward. But as soon as we realize that there are other forms of value in play than money alone – as is immediately evident here, if perhaps less so in a commercial context, then we need to look for a much broader definition of "success," in fact drawn directly from the shared values of the extended enterprise.

In this case the charity would probably not expect any payment from the recipients for the clothing. What will matter much more instead will be some form of proof that the service delivery was in accordance with the shared values of the enterprise – hence, for example, all those photos of happy, smiling, *well-clothed* children that we would expect to see passing through the return channel, to appear as "cause results" on the charity's website and in reports to donors. The return channel closes the loop of value; and its balance overall, across all relevant forms of value, provides the proof that the organization has indeed delivered *added value* in terms of the extended enterprise's vision and values.

Figure 15-2 shows an Enterprise Canvas overview of the probable structure of the organization-as-a-service that would arise from that summary mentioned previously.

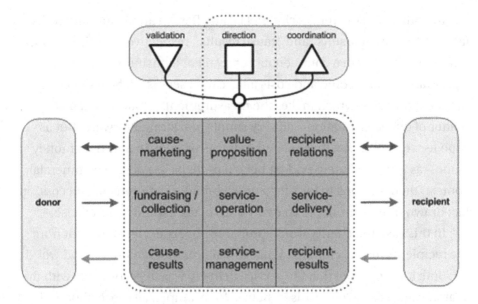

**Figure 15-2.**  *Overview Canvas for a charity*

Note that it's not true that money doesn't matter here: it does. In fact, it matters a *lot*, not least because potential donors are very quick to withdraw support from any charity that is perceived to carry too much overhead in any form, monetary or otherwise. The key point here is that money is not the *only* form of value in play in the overall transactions of the charity – a point which, in an architectural sense at least, also applies in every "for-profit" organization as well.

# Example 3: ITIL IT Service Management

For this next example, we will explore something more in the mid-range: IT service management within a large organization. The typical reference for this is Version 3 of ITIL, the IT Infrastructure Library.

For our purposes here, ITIL Version 3 is a better fit than the later Version 4, because it is more generic and implementation-neutral in its description of service management, whereas Version 4 reverts to being focused almost exclusively on IT services – as one would expect for an IT standard, of course.

This standard describes service management overall in terms of five distinct strands: Service Strategy, Service Design, Service Transition, Service Operation, and Continual Process Improvement. We can map those core ideas onto the Enterprise Canvas, and see what we get in terms of an overall pattern for service management. The result, as shown in Figure 15-3, shows that it does all fit quite well.

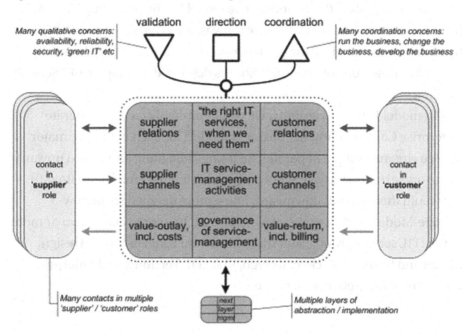

*Figure 15-3.* *Overview Enterprise Canvas for IT service management*

237

One immediate point is that the definitions of "customer" and "supplier" are fairly fluid here: many actual stakeholders will take both types of roles at various times, so it definitely does help if – as the Canvas allows us to do – we take a symmetric view of the respective relations, main-channel and return-channel interfaces.

Another key point is that it does depend strongly on a clear value proposition, here summarized as "the right IT services, when we need them." All of the ITIL processes revolve around that core idea and the values that lie behind it. The ITIL specification helps in this, too: for example, in describing Service Strategy, the Overview document states that "customers do not buy products, they buy the satisfaction of particular needs."

All of this requires very strong linkages beyond the service itself – almost the exact antithesis of the Taylorist-style model for the preceding "for-profit business" example. In the Enterprise Canvas, these linkages are provided by (or rather, modeled as) the guidance services: the structured layers of validation, direction, and coordination, as described in Chapter 10, "Service Guidance."

To model ITIL in its entirety, we would probably create a separate Enterprise Canvas at Row–2 "Business Model" for each of the five major service streams, shown in parallel on a single diagram, and linked upward to the organization (Row-1 Scope) and the extended enterprise (Row-0). We would then expand downward, into a more detailed set of Row-3 Service-Model models, some of which would be shared across two or more of the ITIL service groups; and then downward again to Row-4 Design Model and beyond. It's clear, though, that ITIL Version 3 and Enterprise Canvas do work well together here.

# Example 4: BPMN Process Model

This pattern may help to demonstrate why there should be serious concerns about the limitations and incompleteness of so many of our current service-design methods and so much of current enterprise architecture. To illustrate this, let's return to the simplified BPMN diagram from Chapter 9, "Service Flows," as shown in Figure 15-4.

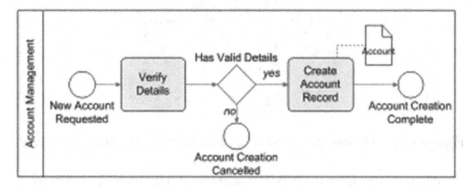

***Figure 15-4.*** *Simple BPMN model of account-creation process*

The process model purports to describe the *service* of creating an account – in other words, something that we would expect to model on the Enterprise Canvas. But in terms of service design and service completeness, Figure 15-5 shows what we would *actually* get from that form of service model when we map it onto the Canvas.

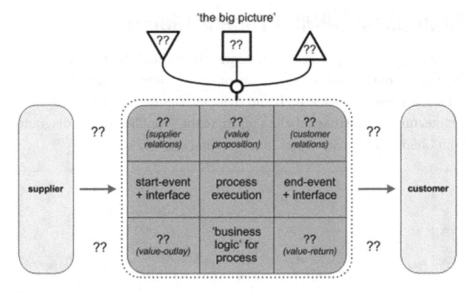

**Figure 15-5.** *Derived Enterprise Canvas for account-creation service*

What we have from the BPMN model is only a tiny subset of what we actually need in order to make sense of it *as* a service:

- There's no concept of any precursors to transactions – the content and interfaces for the usual Supplier/ Customer-Relations cells.

- There's no concept of any return channel – the content and interfaces for the Value-Outlay/Return cells.

- There's only the most minimal of content for Value Governance, namely, the small part that deals with the decision-making and business logic with the execution of the process.

- There's no "why" *anywhere* in the process model – no Value Proposition, no known reason why this particular process and service should even exist.

- There's no linkage anywhere to "the big picture," the guidance services that link this process to the various qualitative concerns, or even to the inter-service choreography needed to coordinate the execution of the complete end-to-end business process.

---

To be fair, the equivalents of "Supplier" and "Customer" and their interfaces could be represented by headers in parallel swimlanes – but that still wouldn't tell us anything about the coordination of the full *end-to-end* business process.

---

The Canvas itself doesn't show the assets such as the account record, for example, or the triggering events, or the location, which is also absent from the BPMN model; yet all of those are items that we would expect to pick up straight away by applying a service-content assessment (see Chapter 13, "Service Content") to the respective cells – particularly the Value-Creation cell, here shown as "process execution." In the same way, a service-flows assessment of the interfaces (see Chapter 9, "Service Flows") would tell us much more about the respective flows than we have here in the BPMN model.

What this pattern *does* show us, though, is how to use a BPMN diagram to populate this part of the base content for an Enterprise Canvas. We would then go on from there to fill in all of the blanks, to build a complete model of the service that we need for the required purpose.

# Example 5: Military Squad

For our final example, imagine the classic military squad, working their way out on active patrol in the hinterland somewhere. If they're troops from Britain, it might have been in Afghanistan in the recent past, or the exact same place a century and more ago; or if we go back in time a couple more millennia, it might have been a Roman squad somewhere out the back end of Britannia. It doesn't really matter which military it might be, because at the squad level, most armies have worked much the same way since forever, as a closely coupled network of mutual services that we might summarize visually as in Figure 15-6.

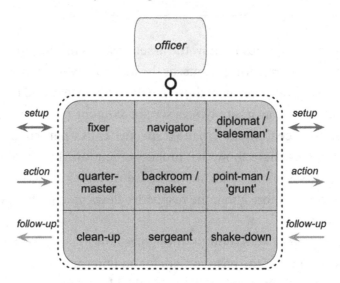

***Figure 15-6.*** *Overview Canvas for a military squad*

These are *roles* rather than individual people, and we'll often see the soldiers moving about between these roles from time to time: when it turns into a fire-fight, everyone is instantly a "point-man," for example. But over time, natural tendencies will start to emerge, individual soldiers falling more often into one role than another, either because of specific training, or just as a matter of habit.

We can summarize these roles from Figure 15-6 in the respective Enterprise Canvas groups, with the Canvas tasks shown in [..] for each role.

The **guidance services** are kind of outside that dotted-line boundary of the squad itself, yet connect it to the broader world. Although in the full Enterprise Canvas there are a fair number of these "external" service relationships, they're represented here overall by one archetypal role:

- The *Officer* [Direction, Coordination, Validation] connects the squad to the big picture, the overall vision and values, the "proper channels," and suchlike.

The **inbound** roles, on the left hand or "supplier" side, work on interactions coming "inward" to the squad, typically bringing stuff in that the squad needs or that come from the overall environment:

- The *Fixer* [Supplier-Relations] searches around to find appropriate sources for what the squad needs or smooths the way for things to be found.

- The *Quartermaster* [Supplier Channels] receives inbound resources and maintains and distributes them around the squad as needed.

- The *Clean-up* [Value-Outlay] settles up, pays the bills, and generally quietens things down again after the resources have been acquired or received.

The **value-construction** roles, "within" the core of the squad, identify what value is, create that added value, and keep everything within the squad itself moving toward delivery of that added value:

- The *Navigator* [Value Proposition] identifies the pathway (literal or metaphoric) that would best achieve the purpose as outlined by the "commander's intent" of the Officer.

- The *Maker* [Value-Creation] takes internal action to follow the pathway identified by the Navigator, using the resources obtained by the Quartermaster, locally guided by the Sergeant.

- The *Sergeant* [Value-Governance] provides local guidance and internal coordination, in context of the pathway identified by the Navigator, and in accordance with the overall intent identified by the Officer.

(The Sergeant is more connected to decisions for the here-and-now, whereas the Navigator is more connected to the big picture, as map reader and the squad's external radio operator.)

The **outbound** roles, on the right hand or "customer" side, work on interactions going "outward" from the squad, typically putting into action whatever it is that the squad needs to do to deliver its added value to the overall story:

- The *Diplomat* [Customer Relations] "spies out the land" and sets up outward connections with the world in the direction (literal or metaphoric) identified by the Navigator.

- The *Grunt* [Customer Channels] takes outward-facing action along the connections set up by the Diplomat.

- The *Shake-down* [Value Return] receives and verifies return from the outside world and distributes it through the squad as guided by the Sergeant.

Note here that "customer" may not be a good metaphor here – especially not if we try to describe a nominal adversary as a "customer" of military services! The actual relations with an adversary are closer to a clash between mutual anti-clients – "someone in the same nominal shared enterprise who fundamentally disagrees with how the Other is acting within that enterprise."

---

For a great example of this team structure, see the 1963 film *The Great Escape*, about the real mass escape from the Stalag Luft III prisoner-of-war camp in Germany in March 1944. True, some parts of that film are very much fictionalized – particularly the role played by US actor Steve McQueen, none of which actually occurred in the real world. But all of the others – "Big-X" Bartlett, "Forger" Blythe, "Surveyor" Cavendish, and the others – were based on real people, with real roles in the escape attempt that map exactly to those in the Enterprise Canvas shown in Figure 15-6.

---

There's also another variation of this for a smaller group, such as in a skirmishing team or reconnaissance unit. For that case, we might reframe the squad's roles into two trios rather than three, as shown in Figure 15-7. One trio takes on the "inward-facing" roles (shown on the left of the diagram), and the other trio taking on both sets of "outward-facing" roles (shown on the right), but still with the same split of roles for what needs to happen before, during, and after the main action.

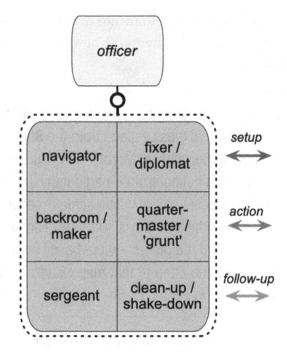

**Figure 15-7.** *Overview Canvas for a military skirmish squad*

In effect, it's still the same overall set of roles, but the outward-facing roles deal with all interactions with the "outside world," rather than splitting between "inbound" and "outbound." We'll particularly see that type of setup when the context is more of a bidirectional partnership with others, rather than a "through-flow" of stuff coming in on one side and going out the other.

# Into Action

You want your change teams in the business-transformation project to ensure, before they move toward implementation, that their service designs are structurally complete and do actually make sense in terms of what they are intended to do. You'll suggest that they should use the

Enterprise Canvas pattern as a sanity check and completeness checklist for their service designs. Use the ideas in this chapter and the following questions to help you guide those conversations:

- In your work context, what patterns do you use to guide service design?

- Who is responsible for acquiring and applying those patterns?

- If different patterns are used at different levels and/ or in different business departments or service implementations, how do you ensure continuity and consistency across those various usages of patterns?

- In what way does each pattern support service completeness, in the sense that Enterprise Canvas defines and describes completeness?

- Who is responsible for ensuring service completeness, both for each service, and across the enterprise as a whole?

## Summary

In this chapter we reviewed five example patterns that summarize a range of ways to use the Enterprise Canvas in typical enterprise-architecture assignments.

In the next chapter, we will explore how to use Enterprise Canvas in conjunction with other enterprise architecture and service-design tools and methods.

# CHAPTER 16

# Integration with Architectures

(Note: See the "Other Resources" section in "Appendix E: Sources and Resources" for links and references to models and techniques mentioned below.)

## Architectural Frameworks and Model Types

**VPEC-T** is probably one of the most useful frames with which to assess the various themes and drivers in an information system.

As indicated in Figure 16-1, the VPEC-T acronym stands for **V**alues, **P**olicies, **E**vents, **C**ontent, **T**rust, that represent five different views or "lenses" through which to view and make sense of the respective business context. The framework is described in detail in the book *Lost In Translation*, by Nigel Green and Carl Bate.

© Tom Graves 2023
T. Graves, *Mapping the Enterprise*, https://doi.org/10.1007/978-1-4842-9836-7_16

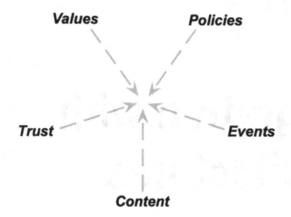

**Figure 16-1.** *VPEC-T as five views into a context*

---

Some of the underlying ideas from VPEC-T were adapted and re-imagined into the VPECS connector nodes between phases in the Five Elements change cycle, as described in Chapter 14, "Services As Systems." Note that, as a set of steps in a sequence rather a set of dimensions, VPECS adaptation is fundamentally different from the original VPEC-T framework, and should *not* be described as "VPEC-T."

---

**Archimate** is a standard notation for enterprise architectures, originally developed in the Netherlands, and later adopted as an international standard by The Open Group. Although its coverage of enterprise content has expanded over successive versions, it still essentially focused on IT. It defines an architecture in terms of three content-based layers (Business, Applications, and Technology) and three interlinked structural emphases (Static Structure such as data and other assets, Behavior such as services and functions, and Active Structure such as roles and interfaces).

From an Enterprise Canvas perspective:

- *Archimate layers to Enterprise Canvas layers*: "Business" primarily sits in the Row-2 to Row-3 Canvas layers; "Application" and "Technology" sit *in parallel domains* in the Canvas Row-3, Row-4, and sometimes Row-5 layers.

- *Static Structure*: "Data Object" and other types of artifact would translate either to asset-type content within Canvas cells or to asset-type products within Canvas flows between services.

- *Behavior*: The various types of "Service" in each Archimate layer would typically each be modeled on its own Canvas; the various types of "Process" would typically sit in the Value-Creation cell of the respective Canvas; the various types of "Function" would typically sit as interfaces for the outward-facing cells of the respective Canvas.

- *Active Structure*: Roles would typically translate as Supplier, Customer, or other external parties for a Canvas; interfaces as Canvas flows; and components ("Device," "Application Component," "Network," and suchlike) as asset-type content for the respective Canvas cell.

**TOGAF** (The Open Group Architecture Framework) is another well-known framework in IT-oriented enterprise architectures that includes a well-defined process – the Architecture Development Method, or ADM. Its underlying metamodel aligns somewhat with that used in Archimate and is based on the same general principles. The ADM can be used with Enterprise Canvas for IT-oriented service design, but it can be problematic for use in service-design contexts that are not centered primarily or solely around IT.

---

Note that there are ways to adapt the ADM for use beyond IT and/ or for a whole-of-enterprise scope, as documented in my books *Bridging the Silos* and *Doing Enterprise Architecture*; however, as with the VPECS adaptation of VPEC-T, these adaptations must *not* be described as "TOGAF."

---

The **Zachman Framework** is probably the best known of all enterprise-architecture frameworks. It is a simple two-axis matrix with either five or six rows representing stages of change from initial intent to real-world action, and six columns representing the interrogatives What, How, Where, Who, When, and Why, with each cell in the resultant matrix representing a specific architectural "primitive." The standard version is somewhat IT-centric: for example, the only asset type listed in the "What" column is Data. The Service-Layers model and Service-Content model for Enterprise Canvas are based in part, though with some significant adaptations and extensions, on the rows and columns, respectively, of the Zachman framework, as described in Chapter 5, "Service Layers," and Chapter 13, "Service Content."

Stafford Beer's Viable System Model or **VSM** is one of the best-known and most proven of systems-theory design tools, and was one of the core inspirations for Enterprise Canvas. Although the original VSM focused mainly on information flows, the same concepts can be applied to flows of any asset types, both simple and composite. As shown in Chapter 8, "Service Structure," and Chapter 10, "Service Governance," the VSM "systems" are represented in the Enterprise Canvas model as follows:

- VSM *system-1* (operations or service delivery) is shown as a rounded-corner box and is represented by the nine-cell core of the Canvas.

- VSM *system-2* (coordination) is shown as an upward-pointing triangle and is represented by the "coordination" guidance services for the Canvas.

- VSM *system-3\** (audit) is shown as a downward-pointing triangle and is represented by the "validation" guidance services for the Canvas.

- VSM *system-3* (planning and control), *system-4* (near future), and *system-5* (far future) are shown as square boxes and are represented by the "direction" guidance services for the Canvas.

Beer's concept of an algedonic high-priority feedback path that can bypass the normal channels is extremely important, and should be considered when assessing any or all of the Canvas flows.

---

For more information on the standard VSM model and its usage in business, see Patrick Hoverstadt's *The Fractal Organization*; for more on its adaptation for service-oriented whole-enterprise architectures, see my book *The Service-Oriented Enterprise*.

---

**Context-space mapping** is the underlying framework and process on which the Enterprise Canvas is based, and is described in more detail in my book *Everyday Enterprise Architecture*. The core of context-space mapping comes down to just four keywords:

- *Sensemaking*: Making sense of the context.

- *Strategy*: Deciding what to do with what we've discovered.

- *Structures*: We look for patterns, for structures, for something that's stable enough for us to build something on it or with it or around it.

- *Solutions*: We identify and/or define the detail of what we're going to do within the chosen context.

The underlying process for context-space mapping draws strongly on John Boyd's **OODA** (observe, orient, decide, act) model for agile problem-solving, crosslinked to a concept of sensemaking domains as discussed in my book *Inventing Reality*. In context-space mapping, we choose a base-frame as a core model and then cross-map to other compatible model types while we "go for a walk" – metaphorically speaking – through all of the different perspectives offered by the base model and the cross-maps. As described throughout this book, the Enterprise Canvas was designed for use as a base-map in context-space mapping for service design.

# Strategic Frameworks and Model Types

The **Business Model Canvas** was another key inspiration for this work, and Enterprise Canvas was intentionally designed to be compatible with it. The book *Business Model Generation* by Alex Osterwalder and others is an essential companion for any Row-2 or Row-3 service-design work for business architectures with Enterprise Canvas. In addition, as shown in "Appendix B, Working with Business Model Canvas," business models developed with Business Model Canvas can be mapped directly onto Enterprise Canvas for expansion "downward" toward implementation and "upward" for verification of alignment with the vision and values of the shared enterprise.

The OMG/BRG **Business Motivation Model** provides a standard framework to assess business drivers and business goals, and, for Enterprise Canvas, would particularly apply to the connections between the core Canvas and its "direction" guidance services. Do note, though, that its definition and role for "vision" is significantly different from that in the ISO9000-based approach used for Enterprise Canvas, and the two definitions are essentially incompatible with each other. (Business Motivation Model defines "vision" as a description of a desired future state, subordinate to "mission"; Enterprise Canvas, as described in Chapter 4, "Service Vision and Values," defines "vision" as the ultimate anchor for the quality system, to which "mission" and everything else are subordinate.) Both definitions are valid in their own context, but we do need to take some care to avoid mixing them up when working on service design with Enterprise Canvas.

Other common strategy frameworks that would work well with the Enterprise Canvas include **Porter's Five Forces** model, **Blue Ocean Strategy**, and the ubiquitous **SWOT**. In each case we would typically use the respective framework to assess the service or organizational unit in the Canvas, comparing it against others (such as for competitiveness analysis) or assessing the flows between the service and other players in the shared enterprise (supply-chain partners, competitors, etc.). SWOT would be used to assess strengths, challenges, opportunities, and the like in the usual way, on the service as a whole, on individual cells, on flows, and on stakeholder relationships, as summarized in Chapter 13, "Service Content."

# Structural and Operational Frameworks and Model Types

Industry-specific structural frameworks such as **SCOR** (supply chain), **eTOM** (telecoms), and **ITIL** (IT service management) fit well with Enterprise Canvas. Each of these frameworks describes its context in terms of services, which in turn provides a template and checklist for modeling on a Canvas. The main value of linking these frameworks to modeling with Enterprise Canvas is that the latter adds distinctions between types of flows that occur before, during, and after the main service transactions and also documents the necessary "guidance-service" linkages to overall direction, cross-functional coordination, and whole-of-enterprise values.

**SCOR** is a layered, hierarchical model whose structures map to Enterprise Canvas as follows:

- Levels 1, 2, and 3 for SCOR roughly correspond to Enterprise Canvas Row-2, Row-3, and Row-4, respectively.

- The SCOR level-1 structure of Source/Make/Deliver corresponds almost exactly to the Enterprise Canvas transaction linkage to the supply chain: SCOR "Source" corresponds to the Supplier-Channels flow and cell; SCOR "Make" corresponds to the Value-Creation cell; and SCOR "Deliver" corresponds to the Customer-Channels cell and flow.

**eTOM** is another layered model: eTOM's levels 0 to 3 roughly correspond to Enterprise Canvas Row-1 to Row-4, respectively. As a matrix structure, the eTOM services are defined within intersecting cells of the matrix, as well as within the row/column overlays themselves; but in each case the respective service and its relationships can be mapped onto its own Canvas. At the highest level, the eTOM "Strategy Infrastructure and Product" grouping has strong links to the "direction" and "coordination" guidance services as modeled in Enterprise Canvas; the eTOM "Enterprise Management" grouping is in part shared across the "direction" and "validation" guidance services; the eTOM "Operations" grouping summarizes what happens within the nine-cell core of the Canvas. Also note the strong emphasis in eTOM on "Customer": this would typically be linked to the Customer-Relations cell and flows on the Canvas.

We reviewed a mapping between **ITIL** and Enterprise Canvas in Chapter 15, "Example Patterns." At the topmost Row-1 level, there might be a single Canvas for ITIL "service management"; but at Row-2, where relationships come into the picture, we would need to model each of ITIL's five main service groups as a separate entity – in other words, a separate Canvas for each. We would then devolve downward as required, detailing each of the services first in generic form for Row-3, and then in more context-specific form for Row-4.

The **ISO-9000** quality-system international standard aligns almost exactly with the Enterprise Canvas layers:

- ISO-9000 "vision" layer: Enterprise Canvas Row-0 to Row-1

- ISO-9000 "policy" layer: Enterprise Canvas Row-2 and generic part of Row-3

- ISO-9000 "procedure" layer: Enterprise Canvas detail of Row-3 and generic part of Row-4

- ISO-9000 "work-instruction" layer: Enterprise Canvas detail of Row-4 and Row-5

**Balanced Scorecard** is another useful frame to apply across the Canvas, particularly in context for the Value-Governance cell, which is where performance data and post-transaction records should naturally accumulate. It may be useful to augment or review Balanced Scorecard's four standard perspectives – Financial, Internal Business Processes, Learning and Growth, and Customer – with other themes derived as appropriate from enterprise vision and values. The single most important point, especially in a commercial for-profit business, is to loosen the stranglehold of finance-centric metrics, and to instead cover the full range of meanings of "value" that apply in the shared enterprise.

Standard review processes and process-improvement models, such as Deming/Shewhart **PDCA** (Plan/Do/Check/Act), **Root-cause analysis**, **Value-stream mapping**, and, where appropriate, **Six Sigma**, can all be usefully applied to the models developed on a Canvas, and in some cases modeled in relation to the activities shown on the Canvas. Conceptually and operationally, they belong as part of what the Canvas would model as its guidance services – in practice usually a collaboration between the "validation" and "coordination" services. Note that in general Six Sigma should not be used unless the service on the Canvas handles literally millions of nominally identical events.

# Into Action

As your change teams move down into the detail of their service designs for your business-transformation project, they will need to use a wide variety of more specialist models, standards, and tools to guide and cross-check their work. You want to recommend that they should use Enterprise Canvas as a shared anchor to link together all of those disparate approaches and methods. Use the information in this chapter to help you guide those conversations.

# Summary

In this chapter, we reviewed how Enterprise Canvas can provide a unifying frame through which many different frameworks and model types can be linked together and support each other to create an overall integration across the architecture.

In the next, final chapter, we will explore how to invert the "top-down" approach that we have used so far, and instead derive the enterprise vision by working "bottom-up" from real-world innovations.

# CHAPTER 17

# Rethinking Vision Bottom-Up

For Enterprise Canvas, everything links back to the vision for the shared enterprise that defines a service's context. As described in Chapter 4, "Service Vision and Values," the enterprise vision is the ultimate anchor for the quality system, the meaning of value in and throughout the enterprise, and the rules and standards that apply in that context. It also provides the core reason for the relationships between each of the players and stakeholders in that shared space. From there, the vision then defines the context for the market within which the organization can position itself, and the supply chains through which the organization connects with its suppliers, customers, and other partners. Given those rules, roles, responsibilities, and relationships, the organization can identify and design all of the services that it needs in order to fulfill its chosen role within that supply chain, market, and shared enterprise.

We can summarize all of that, from the organization's perspective, as shown in Figure 17-1.

© Tom Graves 2023
T. Graves, *Mapping the Enterprise*, https://doi.org/10.1007/978-1-4842-9836-7_17

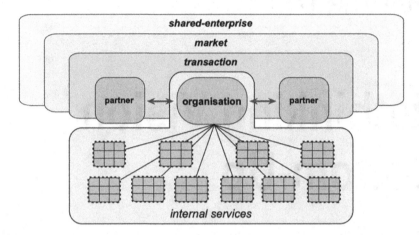

**Figure 17-1.**  *Enterprise, market, supply chain, organization, and services*

Throughout this book so far, we have kept things simple by describing these relationships in the way that we would for a startup business: start from the organization and what it wants to do, with the capabilities that it has or knows that it can build; identify a shared-enterprise vision that it would see as a desirable context; and then work top-down from there, identifying the respective market and preferred positioning within that market and shared enterprise, that would then place it in the right relationships with other players in its preferred supply chain or value web.

For an existing organization, though, this can often be a lot more complicated – particularly when the organization or industry is undergoing change, either to respond to a new opportunity or when the market itself is facing turmoil from the outside. In those cases, we will often need a more freeform approach, one that allows us to rebuild the vision and strategy either bottom-up or sideways-out, rather than the startup's simpler top-down style.

Undergoing major change of that kind can be challenging enough for an organization that, in essence, runs a single business model within a single market and which has a single, identifiable shared enterprise – the "unitary enterprise," as shown in Figure 17-2.

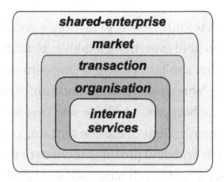

***Figure 17-2.** Unitary enterprise: organization within a single shared enterprise*

Even in that type of enterprise structure, any significant change to the business model may well require the organization to position itself in a different market, which has a different shared enterprise as its context, with its own distinct and different vision, values, and so on. If that happens, then all of those respective context-related changes will need to ripple all the way down through the organization, requiring detail-level changes to operations, direction, coordination, validation, and more, potentially in every single one of its internal services.

---

The Enterprise Canvas approach of "everything is, represents, or implies a service," in which the same consistent methods apply the same way everywhere, provides perhaps one of the few ways to stay even somewhat sane when facing the complexities of that level of whole-of-system change.

---

This becomes even more complicated, though, if the change will require the organization to operate multiple business models that each connect with a different market, each of which in turn will sit within a different shared enterprise, with different vision, values, standards, rules, and more.

The only way to make this work is to identify some kind of unifying theme that can help to hold everything together, typically in the form of a consortium or other similar structures. One common structure for this purpose is the "shared-services consortium," which places one organization in the background whose sole "market" is the more visible front-facing organizations of the consortium. This "background organization" transacts with and provides services or products to the front-facing organizations, each of which have their own distinct market and enterprise. All of the organizations within the consortium then sit under the umbrella of an overarching "enterprise-of-enterprises" that provides the unifying theme, as shown in Figure 17-3.

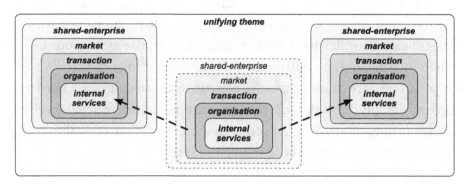

***Figure 17-3.*** *Enterprise-within-enterprise: consortium with shared services*

Another structure, perhaps less common, is the classic "industrial conglomerate" type of consortium. This consists of a collection of subsidiary organizations, again each with their own market and enterprise, yet have nothing to link them together other than that they all sit under some kind of unifying theme, as shown in Figure 17-4.

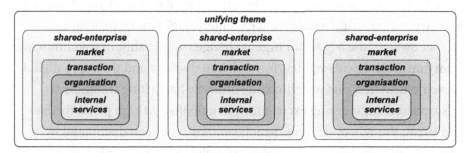

***Figure 17-4.** Enterprise-within-enterprise: conglomerate*

This can work if the unifying theme is a broader overarching enterprise such as an entire industry, or a broad domain such as healthcare, government, social service, or defense. However, if the conglomerate is simply an outcome of arbitrary merger-and-acquisition activities or similar poorly defined organizational aggregations, without any unifying shared enterprise to provide the reason and purpose to stay together, there is a high risk of failure from infighting between the organizations, or as a result of no common direction.

To summarize, responding to change at a whole-of-organization level can bring real benefits, yet also real risks, which can only be managed by careful attention to the framing of the shared enterprise.

In the remainder of this chapter, we will explore five real-world examples where an organization either reinvented their business or created a new one, and reframed the overarching definition and structure of the enterprise to make the change work. In each case we will assess the context and the *trigger* for change; the relationship between the new *market* and the old; the role of *technology* in the change; and the impact on the overall *enterprise vision*, echoing back down through the organization itself.

# Example 1: Swatch

Swatch created a new market and enterprise for a country's watchmaking industry, built around a new "unitary-enterprise" type of structure.

For Swatch, the *trigger* for urgent change was the shift in watchmaking from fine mechanical engineering to digital displays and thence to digital movements. The Swiss watchmaking industry had a long tradition of unsurpassed engineering excellence, though often at high price. By the late 1970s, though, even its mid-range *market* had been decimated by competition from Japan, using new technologies at a much lower cost. The only apparent market that remained was for luxury craftsman watches, and even that seemed under threat. In the early 1980s Nicolas Hayek combined business restructure, technological innovation, and radically different marketing to reframe the Swiss watch industry – most of it under the then-new "Swatch" brand – and reclaim its previous preeminent position.

The *market* for the new type of watch was a new "Blue Ocean" niche, presenting a new concept of the watch as a low-cost, almost transitory fashion statement, where the notion of "the watch" is linked less to the raw function of timekeeping than as a statement about identity and self. Watches and watch-straps can also be customized for the individual, creating a sub-market similar to that in the MyM&Ms example here. In recent years, Swatch has extended the same concept to watches designed specifically for children, under their Flik-Flak brand. In effect, all of this is actually closer in concept to the "luxury" end of the market: both types of market are more about an emotive or aspirational relationship to time or with time, rather than solely about timekeeping itself.

New *technology* included the use of plastics, ceramics, and ultrasonic welding, underpinned by a Deming-type continuous-improvement approach to manufacturing and reduction of number of components. This experience was also carefully echoed back into the legacy Swiss-watch industry, retaining its "craft" focus but combined with lessons learned from bulk manufacture.

The marketing for each of the Swatch sub-markets is different, though they do seem to use the same overall *enterprise vision* – in other words, using a "shared-services consortium" enterprise structure. There does not seem to be any explicit vision statement shown on their website, but from the language used for marketing, we could guess it to be something like "expressing the joy of time."

# Example 2: Mars MyM&Ms

MyM&Ms is a service by global food-manufacturer Mars Incorporated, providing a variant of the popular M&Ms chocolate candy that is personalized for events such as weddings, birthdays, conferences, and more. At the present time, the service is available only in the USA and some parts of Europe. The new business is built around a "shared-service consortium" type of enterprise structure.

For Mars, the *trigger* for what became MyM&Ms was an idea from within their Advanced R&D unit, rather than their marketing department.

The new *market* – gifts, promotions, and special events for individuals and event organizers – is significantly different from the regular market for M&Ms – retail candies/sweets for foods wholesalers. However, it leverages strongly from the main market on the basis that the underlying product is well-known: in fact, the unique selling proposition for MyM&Ms largely depends on the idea that this is a special personalized version of something that is otherwise *not* new and different.

The *technology* is much the same as in the main market: real-time labeling of mass-produced product. The main difference is that the new version of the labeling technology permits mass personalization. This is then linked to a website that enables creation of the customized label, and that manages ordering, payment, fulfillment, and delivery of the personalized product. The market could not exist without this mass-personalization technology.

The core *enterprise* for MyM&Ms is significantly different from that of the main Mars company. Although the enterprises are related, the focus here is on personalization rather than on the underlying product – a point emphasized by the fact that Mars are also beginning to provide mass personalization for some of their other products. A "shared-services consortium" enterprise structure is implied by the fact the M&Ms website is separate from the main Mars Incorporated website: the background enterprise focuses on manufacture of the base product, which is passed to the MyM&Ms front-facing enterprise for personalized labeling and delivery to individuals, and to the main Mars front-facing enterprise for standard labeling and delivery to food wholesalers.

In recent years, the "MyM&Ms" term has been phased out in favor of the original "M&Ms" term, supported by the provision of a product-specific personalized M&Ms website. The M&Ms website shows a three-part tagline of "celebrate the moment: we believe in celebrations of all kinds – big and small. Memories happen in moments where we care and share with each other." It presents its vision, described as its mission, as "We believe in championing the power of fun to create a world where everyone feels they belong."

# Example 3: Play-Doh

Play-Doh is a non-toxic, non-staining, reusable modeling compound, used by children in 75 countries around the world. The business is now based on a "unitary-enterprise" structure.

For Cincinatti-based soap-manufacturer Kutol Products, the *trigger* for the creation of Play-Doh was a request in 1955 from a school teacher, a relative of the company founders, for a substitute for modeling clay that would be safe and fun to use. They sent her a sample of an existing compound used to clean wallpaper, which the children then used to make Christmas decorations. The response was such that the company recognized that the compound could be repurposed as a product they could sell to parents and children.

The new *market* was fundamentally different from the existing one: from trade cleaning products to children's toys.

The *technology* in use is essentially the same for both markets. In later developments, the Play-Doh formula included colorants and changes to improve plasticity, but the basic bulk-mixing technology remained almost identical.

The new *enterprise* is radically different in the two markets: on one side, an enterprise vision of something like "effective and reliable cleaning for the building trade"; on the other, more like "safe and fun modeling" – an enterprise vision which also does not restrict the market solely to parents and their children. Although the base technology was largely unchanged, the two enterprises were so different that it mandated a "shared-services consortium" overarching enterprise structure for the organization. Eventually the divergences and differences in markets became so extreme that the Play-Doh division was sold off as a separate company, with the latter's own enterprise centered around the toy industry. Meanwhile, the original parent-company Kutol continues as a manufacturer of cleaning products, reverting to a "unitary-enterprise" structure focused on hand hygiene.

# Example 4: Oceaneering Animatronics

Oceaneering is a large engineering company specializing in hydraulics, control systems, and remote-operated vehicles for harsh or extreme environments including deepwater, defense, and aerospace. The provision of animatronics for theme parks at first seemed to be a surprise addition to their portfolio, initially causing a disconnect across the enterprise structure, but has now settled back into a straightforward "shared-services consortium" type of structure.

Oceaneering describes the *trigger* for the new market for entertainment-industry systems as "a call for help" from a theme-park engineering team who were having difficulty maintaining large animatronic "creatures" that needed to operate partly underwater.

Functionally, the new *market* is similar to the old, namely, specialist engineering applications for hydraulic technologies and control systems. The main challenge was that the organization had been positioned as a provider primarily for the deepwater-oilfield industry, and at the time had not fully set itself up to work across multiple markets.

The *technology* involved was broadly the same as for their main deepwater-engineering market: hydraulic and other actuators, control systems, and so on, to be repurposed into animatronics and hydrodynamics.

Because the organization had positioned itself with the oil-industry enterprise, the engagement into an animatronics and entertainment-industry *enterprise* at first exacerbated an already-existing enterprise disruption that had arisen from the previous inclusion of engineering services for aerospace. This risked falling into a "conglomerate-consortium" enterprise structure in which both aerospace and animatronics would be "second-class citizens" in the organization's portfolio, and in which the unifying theme for the conglomerate would be little more than the organization's name. This situation was reflected in the organization's website during the early 2010s, in which its services for the aerospace industry were barely mentioned, and those for the entertainment industry were not mentioned at all, despite providing a sizeable proportion of the organization's business. More recently there seems to have been a major shift, such that all industries that the organization now serves are listed on the current website, with specialist engineering as the unifying theme. This would enable a "shared-services consortium" enterprise structure, where the focus on special-purpose engineering provides both the unifying theme and the background services shared by all of the organization's market-specific subsidiary enterprises.

# Example 5: Nokia

At the present, Nokia presents itself as provider of hardware, software, and research on communications technology and information systems. Given the organization's history, that might well change to something completely different at any point in the future – because Nokia is perhaps the most extreme example of an organization that has mutated and reinvented itself and its enterprise many times over the decades.

Nokia started out in the mid-1860s as a lumber company, named after the town in which it was located.

In the 1900s it moved into the new *market* for electricity generation. This would have required significant changes in *technology*. The *trigger* for that change was recognition of market opportunity.

In the 1910s, Nokia was essentially taken over by another company, a rubber-products manufacturer, which later, in the 1920s, acquired a cable manufacturer. The *trigger* for the first change seems to have been commercial opportunity, retaining the organization's name because of the location; the *trigger* for the later acquisition would probably have been driven by parallel interests, in that rubber products would have been used for electrical insulation. In both cases, the new *technology* was related to and supported the technology of the previous enterprise.

In the 1930s, and onward into and beyond Finland's engagement in the Second World War, Nokia changed into more of "conglomerate-consortium" type of enterprise structure, spread across multiple *markets* that included products such as paper, bicycle and car tires, footwear, cables, televisions and other consumer electronics, electricity-generation equipment, communications equipment, plastics, aluminum, and chemicals. The *trigger* for each of these expansions is not clear, and in some cases the new *technology* would have been radically different from that already in use. There was some enterprise continuity, though, in that all of these products and related business lines can be traced back to the four historical roots of the corporation, in lumber, electricity generation, rubber, and cables.

However, the spread of *market* and scope of *enterprise* had become too broad to be sustainable, becoming a *trigger* for major financial losses in the late 1970s and early 1980s that brought the organization close to complete collapse.

This in turn became a *trigger* for further fundamental change for the organization. To enable its recovery during the late 1980s and 1990s, Nokia divested its rubber, cable, footwear, and consumer-electronics divisions and refocused itself on the *enterprise* and *market* for telecommunications.

Continuing along that path, Nokia had, by the early 2000s, established itself as probably the leading brand in the global *market* for consumer cellphones and related telecommunications systems. At that time, its website summarized its *enterprise* with the tagline "connecting people"; its stated core values were defined as "Engaging You, Achieving Together, Passion for Innovation, Very Human."

In the 2010s, a new *trigger* for change arose when the market for basic cellphones was decimated by the rise of smartphones from Apple, Samsung, and others. Nokia was forced to reinvent itself yet again, slowly abandoning the consumer-oriented (B2C) cellphone side of its operations, and instead refocusing on the business and government (B2B) *market* for telecommunications infrastructure and related hardware applications such as robotics and internet-of-things. The underlying *technology* for the new enterprise would have been essentially the same as for the old one, though with continual updates and innovations to match the changing needs of that market. On its present website, Nokia summarizes its *enterprise* with the phrase "We create technology that helps the world act together" as its vision statement, followed a summary of its perceived enterprise role as "We are a B2B technology innovation leader in networking, bringing together the world's people, machines, and devices to realize the potential of digital in every industry."

The Nokia history indicates the challenges that can arise when an organization undergoes growth, expansion, and change without an explicit form of enterprise identity to guide choices about what should or should not be included in its structure and story. Without that anchor, as can be seen in the Nokia example during the period from the late 1970s to mid-1980s, the organization's identity and enterprise will begin to fragment over time, causing a loss of clarity and focus, in turn leading to excessive tensions across the entire organization. The break-up of the unstable "conglomerate-consortium" enterprise structure in the late 1980s and 1990s was a necessary foundation for its later growth, because each remaining sub-unit and its market could then be aligned with a more-clearly defined enterprise vision, enabling a "shared-services consortium" enterprise structure.

Interestingly, the one constant *unifying theme* across all of its enterprise reinventions is the location of its home base: the town and municipality of Nokia, in southwestern Finland.

# Into Action

Once your business-transformation project is well on its way, you'll want to engage executives and strategy teams in using ideas from Enterprise Canvas to help them prepare for what might need to happen when the next major change comes through. Use the examples in this chapter and the following questions to help you guide those conversations:

- What major changes do you see in your own organization's history? In each case, what was the *trigger* for the change? What differences in *technology*, *market*, and/or *enterprise* were required by the change, or used to drive the change? How did those differences ripple down through each of the services that underpin the organization and its business?

- How might you use a change in *technology* to trigger a change within your own organization? What implications might that have for your organization's *market* and/or its *enterprise definition* – its vision, values, success criteria, and applicable regulations and standards and the like – or the type of *enterprise structure* required to make the change work?

- How might you use a change in *market* to trigger a change within your own organization? What implications might that have for your organization's *technology* and/or its *enterprise definition* or *enterprise structure*?

- How might you use a change in *enterprise definition* and/or *enterprise structure* to trigger a change within your own organization? What implications might that have for your organization's *technology* and/or its *market*?

- In each case, how would those desired changes affect the design, operation, and governance for each of the organization's internal and external-facing services and products?

# Summary

In this final chapter, we explored how enterprise structure can be used to enable a single organization to serve multiple, disparate markets. To illustrate this, we reviewed five real-world examples where an organization either chose or was forced to reinvent itself via a change in technology, market, and/or enterprise, in each case necessitating a bottom-up or sideways-out re-evaluation of the enterprise vision and values that were used to embed the change into the organization and hold everything together.

# APPENDIX A

# Enterprise Canvas: A Visual Summary

## Organization, Market, and Enterprise

The organization exists within the context of a market, which exists in context of a broader shared enterprise. The same pattern repeats at every level: even a single line of code has its own transactions, market, and broader shared enterprise.

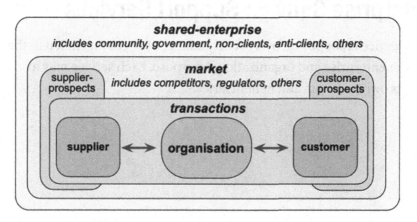

***Figure A-1.*** *The organization and its enterprise context*

© Tom Graves 2023
T. Graves, *Mapping the Enterprise*, https://doi.org/10.1007/978-1-4842-9836-7

# Enterprise Canvas

The enterprise is composed of services, which themselves are composed of services. Products pass between services. Each service has the same conceptual structure of the Enterprise Canvas.

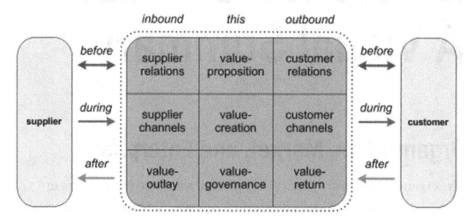

***Figure A-2.*** *Service and its suppliers and customers*

# Enterprise Canvas: Support Services

Each service is supported by a set of guidance services that link it to the broader enterprise and organizational purpose. Each service may also have its own investors and beneficiaries.

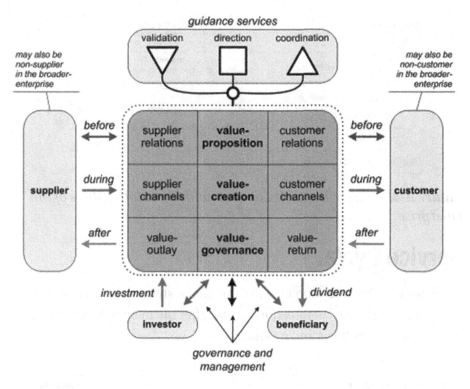

***Figure A-3.*** *A service and its relationships with its support services and other services*

# Enterprise and Service

Value-flow transactions between services are anchored in the market and enterprise. The shared enterprise determines the meaning of value; the market provides governance of value.

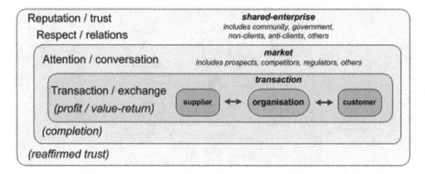

**Figure A-4.**  *The service cycle connects with the relationships of the enterprise*

# Service Cycle

All value flows between services go through the steps of the service cycle. Each step of the cycle, before, during, and after the main transaction, has its own subsidiary flows and products.

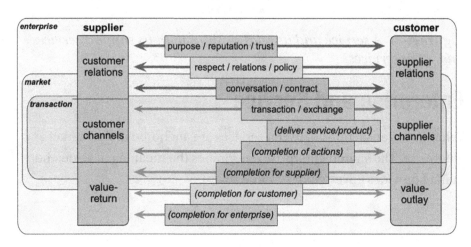

**Figure A-5.**  *The steps of the service cycle*

# Service Layers

The structural content for a service and its products is described in terms of a series of layers of abstraction and realization, from vision to future to present to past, which also specify the type and level of detail for that description.

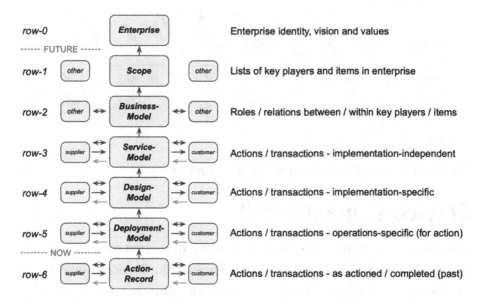

***Figure A-6.*** *Service layers-of-abstraction, adding detail with each layer downward*

# Service Content

The service layers determine how to describe the structural content for services and products.

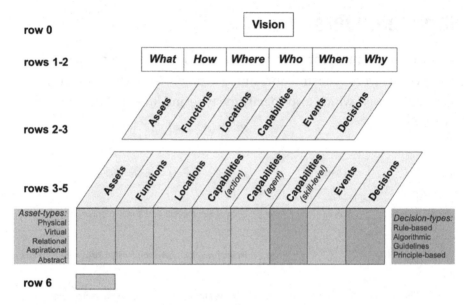

*Figure A-7.*  *Service layers and service content*

# Service-Content Detail

Detail for service content is described in terms of content categories and content types, shown as the columns and rows of the Service-Content model. An actionable service is comprised of a complete set of content categories, with an appropriate mix of content types for each category.

| Asset-types | What | How | Where | | (Who) | | When | Why | Decision/skill-types |
|---|---|---|---|---|---|---|---|---|---|
| Physical | Phys | Phys | Phys | Phys | Phys | Rules | Phys | Rules | Rule-based |
| Virtual | Virtual | Virtual | Virtual | Virtual | Virtual | Algor'm | Virtual | Algor'm | Algorithmic |
| Relational | Reln | Reln | Reln | Reln | Reln | Guideln | Reln | Guideln | Guidelines |
| Aspirational | Aspn | Aspn | Aspn | Aspn | Aspn | Princpl | Aspn | Princpl | Principle-based |
| Abstract | | | Time | | | | | | |

*Figure A-8.*  *Service-Content model*

# Asset Types and Decision Types

The asset-types set summarizes the content types used to describe assets, functions, locations, capability actions, capability agents and events, and also products as assets.

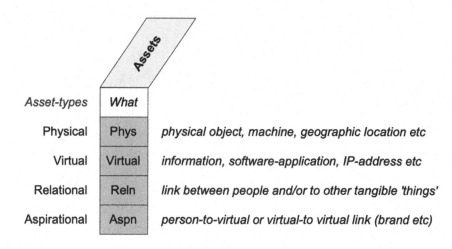

***Figure A-9.*** *Service content: asset types*

The decisions/skill-types set summarizes the content types used to describe decisions and the skill levels for capabilities.

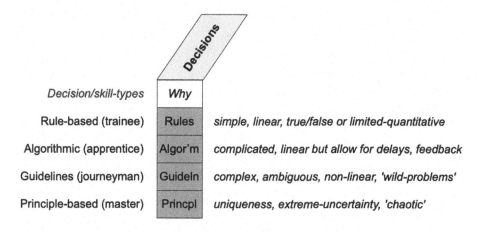

***Figure A-10.*** *Service content: decision types and skill levels*

# APPENDIX B

# Working with Business-Model Canvas

This appendix describes how to transfer a business model from the popular Business-Model Canvas format into a service-style description in Enterprise Canvas format, to identify how to realize the business model in real-world practice.

The **Business Model Canvas** (BMC) is a popular framework for developing business models. It was originally developed by Alex Osterwalder and published in his book *Business Model Generation*. Although mainly intended for developing business models for for-profit organizations, it can also be used for equivalent models for government, not-for-profit, and other types of organizations. It is also the de-rigueur standard in the startup community for defining and shaping the early stages of a startup. The standard version of the Canvas is as shown in Figure B-1.

© Tom Graves 2023
T. Graves, *Mapping the Enterprise*, https://doi.org/10.1007/978-1-4842-9836-7

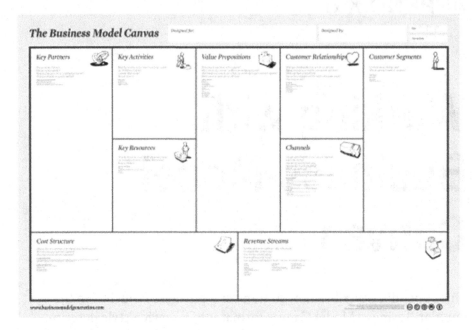

*Figure B-1.*  *Business Model Canvas (CC-BY-SA Alex Osterwalder et al.)*

The BMC is available in the public domain under a Creative Commons "Attribution/Share-Alike" license: it may be used for any purpose, including commercial purposes, with attribution to the author (Alex Osterwalder), and adapted in any way, provided that the adaptation is also released under a similar license.

In essence, it is an organization-centric view into an enterprise supply chain, organized around a business model as the delivery of a value proposition to a set of customer segments. The BMC is largely compatible with Enterprise Canvas, although there are some significant conceptual differences:

- The BMC definition of "value proposition" is viewed only from the organization's perspective – "the bundle of products and services that create value for a specific

284

Customer Segment" – and is not necessarily anchored in the vision and values of any broader shared enterprise.

- The model focuses on only one node in a value web, between a single organization and its customers.

- The model is asymmetric in that it describes the relationships and transactions with customers in detail (Customer Relations, Channels, Revenue Streams), while relationship transactions with suppliers (Key Partners) are not.

- The model describes value primarily in monetary terms (Revenue Streams, Cost Structure).

- In Service-Layers terms, the BMC model sits at the Row-2 to Row-3 level – relationships and abstract attributes – without any direct means to move from abstract model into realizable services and run-time operations in Row-4, Row-5, and Row-6.

Because of these differences, a business model in BMC format will always need some translation and expansion into other model types to make the model realizable in practice.

Overall, it is a frame that makes it easy for most people to grasp what's going on in an organization, at least in terms of those aspects that connect directly with its business model. It aligns well with the underlying core of Enterprise Canvas, because it depicts the business model as a set of relationships between interdependent services. Although the two models have different roles and emphases, Enterprise Canvas was designed to be directly compatible with the BMC, with an intentional similarity of layout to make it easy to translate between them using the following step-by-step guides.

# From Business Model Canvas to Enterprise Canvas

Develop a business model on the Business Model Canvas, using the instructions and guidance in *Business Model Generation*. Then translate from BMC to Enterprise Canvas as follows:

- *Key Partners* [KP] to one or more "Supplier" blocks.

- *Customer Segments* [CS] to one or more "Customer" blocks.

- *Customer Relationships* [CR] to Customer Relations.

- *Channels* [CH] to Customer Channels.

- *Revenue Streams* [R$] to Value Return.

- *Cost Structure* [C$] to Value Outlay.

- *Value Proposition* [VP] to Value Proposition.

- Initially, merge *Key Resources* [KR] and *Key Activities* [KA] into Value Creation, though some aspects are likely to be moved to other cells on detailed analysis.

These translation connections are summarized in visual form in Figure B-2.

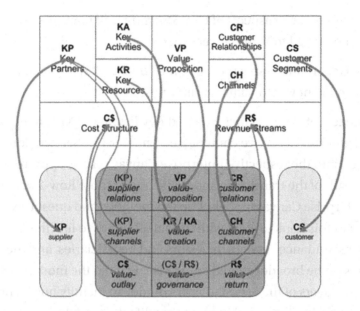

**Figure B-2.** *Mapping Business-Model Canvas to Enterprise Canvas*

Use text descriptions and any other documentation attached to the business model to populate the flows between the core service and its suppliers and customers.

Do a review to check the initial translation. Some aspects may need to be split as follows:

- Some aspects of *Key Partners* [KP] may need to be moved to Supplier Relations and/or Supplier Channels and/or to the respective flows.

- Some aspects of *Cost Structure* [C$] may need to be moved to the supplier-side return channel.

- Some aspects of *Customer Relationships* [CR], *Channels* [CH], and/or *Revenue Streams* [R$] may need to be moved to the respective customer-side flows.

- Governance aspects of *Cost Structure* [C$] may need to be moved to Value Governance.

- Governance aspects of *Revenue Streams* [R$] may need to be moved to Value Governance.

All aspects of *Key Activities* [KA] and *Key Resources* [KR] should be reviewed in terms of service content (see Chapter 13, "Service Content") and moved into the respective Enterprise Canvas cells as appropriate.

The result of the translation should be one or more Row-2 or simplified Row-3 Enterprise Canvas models. Use the methods and questions described in this book to work with the stakeholders to link the business model to its guidance services, investors and beneficiaries, and the vision and values of the broader shared enterprise. Expand the model downward through the layers of the Service-Layers model, to identify how to bring it to real-world implementation and to modify the model as necessary according to real-world opportunities, risks, and constraints.

# From Enterprise Canvas to Business Model Canvas

On occasion it may be useful to translate in the opposite direction, from Enterprise Canvas to Business Model Canvas, such as for a business audience who are known to be familiar with the latter.

In essence the translation is the reverse of that shown in Figure B-1. Start with a simplified Row-3 Enterprise Canvas model. Flows between services, and also between cells within the Enterprise Canvas, should be described as links between cells on the Business-Model Canvas. Note that the translation may not be straightforward in some places, particularly on the supplier-side, because of the inherent asymmetry of the Business-Model Canvas.

Some decisions will be needed to simplify service content into the BMC *Key Resources* [KR] and *Key Activities* [KA] cells. As a guideline:

- Service-content *assets* and *locations* go into *Key Resources* [KR].

- Service-content *functions* go into *Key Activities* [KA].

- Service-content *capabilities* and *decisions* may end up in either cell as appropriate.

- Service-content *events* can be reframed as links between cells.

"Round-tripping" between Enterprise Canvas and Business-Model Canvas can be problematic because information may be lost when translating from Enterprise Canvas – particularly about guidance, investors, and flows. Often the only way to carry this information through to a Business-Model Canvas is via text annotations and hand-drawn links. Hence, although round-tripping is possible here, do be aware of the risks as well as the advantages.

# APPENDIX C

# Enterprise Canvas Notation

What notation should we use for Enterprise Canvas models? Chapter 1, "What Is the Enterprise Canvas?" provides two practical options for this: a simple sketch format that works well for roughing out ideas on paper or a whiteboard, and a more formal style that can be used in diagramming tools such as Visio on Windows, or Omnigraffle for Mac OS.

This appendix describes another option: a notation that can be used within toolsets for service architecture and service design, that is compatible with UML and other UML-derived notations such as BPMN and Archimate. This notation supports formal rigor and model validation and can be implemented directly in many toolsets via a UML profile. Figure C-1 provides a visual summary of this toolset-compatible notation.

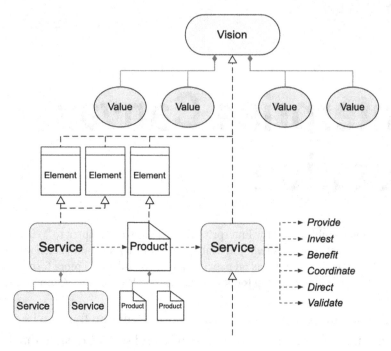

**Figure C-1.** *Summary of toolset-compatible notation for Enterprise Canvas*

This notation is comprised of the following items:

- *Two main entity types*: *Service* and *Product*

- *Three subsidiary entity types*: *Vision, Value,* and *Element*

- *Three relation types*: *Flow, composition,* and *realization*

The three subsidiary entity types are used only in the topmost rows of the Service-Layers model, and are largely optional for most modeling for Enterprise Canvas.

Optionally, UML-style descriptive items such as "Group" or "Annotation" may also be used, and other relation types such as the general-purpose *association* relation, but they are not required, and are not defined as such within the notation syntax.

# Entity Types

The entities most used for modeling with Enterprise Canvas are *Service*, denoting a node of activity, and *Product*, denoting what passes between services. There are also three special-purpose entities: *Vision* and *Value*, used only in the Row-0 Enterprise topmost layer of abstraction; and *Element*, used only in the Row-1 Scope layer.

As described here, there is a recommended default graphic for each entity type; but if the toolset can support such an option, alternative graphics may be used instead. This is often useful to support better understanding of a service model, particularly when applied to *Service* or *Product* entities.

# "*Vision*" and "*Value*" Entity Types

As described in Chapter 4, "Service Vision and Values," the vision and its concomitant values are the ultimate anchors for everything that happens in the shared enterprise. Or, to put it the other way round, every service and product must in some way help toward the realizing of the shared-enterprise vision and its values.

The *Vision* and *Value* entities, as shown in Figure C-2, should appear only in models that describe Row-0 Enterprise and are the only entities that should appear in that layer. For most purposes, only one *Vision* should be used: multiple *Vision* entities should only be used for the special case of assessing clashes between multiple shared enterprises impacting on an organization.

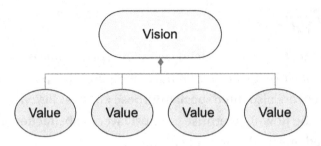

**Figure C-2.**  *"Vision" and "Value" entities*

Any number of *Value* entities may be attached to a *Vision* via *composition* relations.

*Toolset implementation*: For the *Vision* entity, use a rounded-ends lozenge shape or, for compatibility with Archimate, the cloud shape used for the Archimate "Meaning" entity. For the *Value* entity, use an oval shape, for compatibility with the Archimate "Value" entity.

Alternatively, for the *Vision* entity, use the same graphic as for a *Service* entity, because the vision represents the overall service that the shared enterprise provides to the world; and, for a *Value* entity, use the same graphic as for a *Product* entity, because all products are asset types, and a value associated with a vision represents an aspirational type asset.

# "*Element*" Entity Type

As described in Chapter 5, "Service Layers," the service content that arises from the simple interrogatives in Row-1 Scope should be categorized and listed as "elements." These elements are then used as the initial source and cross-checks for service content in Row-2 to Row-6.

The *Element* entity, as shown in Figure C-3, should appear only in models that include Row-1 Scope and are the only entities that should appear in that layer.

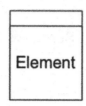

***Figure C-3.*** *"Element" entity*

A Row-1 model may include any number of *Element* entities. Where a Row-0 Enterprise layer is shown in the model, each *Element* entity must be connected via *realization* relations to the *Vision* entity and, optionally, to any number of *Value* entities.

*Toolset implementation*: For the *Element* entity, use a vertically oriented rectangle, or, for compatibility with Archimate, the rectangle-with-horizontal line used for the Archimate "Business-Object" entity.

# *"Service"* Entity Type

As described in Chapter 2, "The Nature of Service," everything within an enterprise either is, represents, or implies a service. In modeling with Enterprise Canvas, anything that *does* something – the service in focus, its "child" services, its suppliers and customers, its investors and beneficiaries, and the services that coordinate, direct and validate it – should all be represented as instances of the *Service* entity type.

The *Service* entity, as shown in Figure C-4, should appear only in models that include Row-2 Business Model, Row-3 Service Model, Row-4 Design Model, and/or Row-5 Deployment Model. *Service* and *Product* are the only entity types that should be present in those layers.

**Service**

***Figure C-4.*** *"Service" entity*

Parameters and parameter values for the internal and structural content for a service represented by a *Service* entity would depend somewhat on the abstraction layer being represented, as described in Chapter 13, "Service Content." Descriptions of the respective service content should be attached to or embedded within that *Service* entity.

A Row-2 to Row-5 model may include any number of *Service* entities. See the "Relation Types" section later in this chapter for the rules that govern how to depict relationships between services and other types of entities.

*Toolset implementation*: For the *Service* entity, use a rounded-rectangle graphic, for compatibility with the Archimate "Business Service" entity and UML or BPMN "Activity" entity.

Include content descriptions for service content and other parameters as required, and as supported by the respective toolset in use; as a minimum, ensure that each *Service* entity has an appropriate "name" parameter as its identifier.

# **"*Product*" Entity Type**

As described in Chapter 9, "Service Flows," a product is or represents anything that is passed between services, or that is used to bridge a gap between services. In modeling with Enterprise Canvas, these are represented as instances of the *Product* entity type.

The *Product* entity, as shown in Figure C-5, should appear only in models that include Row-2 Business Model, Row-3 Service Model, Row-4 Design Model, Row-5 Deployment Model, and/or Row-6 Action Record.

*Product* and *Service* are the only entity types that should be present in the Row-2 to Row-5 layers; *Product* is the only entity type that should be present in the Row-6 layer.

***Figure C-5.*** *"Product" entity*

Parameters and parameter values for the internal and structural content for a product represented by a *Product* entity would depend somewhat on the abstraction layer being represented, as described in Chapter 13, "Service Content." Descriptions of the respective product content should be attached to or embedded within that *Product* entity.

A Row-2 to Row-6 model may include any number of *Product* entities. See the "Relation Types" section later in this chapter for the rules that govern how to depict relationships between products and other types of entities.

*Toolset implementation*: For the *Product* entity, use a "document" image as a default graphic, for compatibility with the UML "Activity Object" ("Document") entity and BPMN "Data Object" entity. Alternatively, use the same nominal entity type, but attach or embed any other graphic or symbol that better represent the asset types and structural content of the respective product: for example, a box for physical objects, a book page for information, a stick figure for relations, or a flash for brands and other aspirational assets.

Include content descriptions for product content and other parameters as required, and as supported by the respective toolset in use; as a minimum, ensure that each *Product* entity has an appropriate "name" parameter as its identifier.

# Relation Types

The notation for Enterprise Canvas uses just three relation types: *flow*, *composition*, and *realization*. Other possible relation types may be considered to be specializations of one or other of these three types.

## "*Flow*" Relation Type

As described in Chapter 9, "Service Flows," services are connected to each other by *flow* relations. Each flow will be associated with one or more products that are either passed along the flow, or indicate how the gap between services will be bridged.

A flow should be represented by a *flow* relation type, a "horizontal" dotted-line connection with an arrow indicating the main direction of flow or relationship, as shown in Figure C-6. For *flow* relations in which there is no emphasized direction of flow, an arrowhead should be shown at both ends of the flowline.

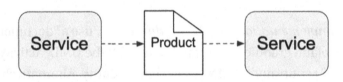

**Figure C-6.**  *"Flow" relation type*

---

For more on how to show a product in an actual flow relationship between services, versus a product that only provides a bridge across a gap between services, see the section "Alternate Modeling for *Product* Entities Within Flows" later in this appendix.

---

A *flow* relation should appear only in models that include Row-2 Business Model, Row-3 Service Model, Row-4 Design Model, and/or Row-5 Deployment Model. They should also link only across *one* Row or layer of abstraction: they cannot and must not be used to link between services and/or products in different layers. Other connection rules for *flow* relations are as follows:

- A *flow* relation may link a *Service* entity to another *Service* entity.

- A *flow* relation may link a *Service* entity to a *Product* entity, or a *Product* entity to a *Service* entity.

In Row-3, Row-4, and Row-5 layers, each *flow* should also take on a distinct role, representing the Enterprise-Canvas inter-service relationships, as follows:

- *Provide*: Simple provision of products and services, used to link with other services in Supplier and Customer relationships to this service (a Supplier is a source for or "provides" a flow; a Customer is a destination for or "consumes" a flow).

- *Invest*: A flow from a service in an Investor relationship to this service.

- *Benefit*: A flow to a service in a Beneficiary relationship to this service.

- *Coordinate*: A flow or exchange with a service in a Coordination guidance relationship to this service.

- *Direct*: A flow or exchange with a service in a Direction guidance relationship to this service.

- *Validate*: A flow or exchange with a service in a Validation guidance relationship to this service.

An open or "unspecified" role should be assigned to all *flow* relations shown in a Row-2 layer and may also be assigned to any *flow* relations in Row-3 to Row-5 layers for the role has not yet been determined.

*Toolset implementation*: For compatibility with Archimate, BPMN, and UML, a *flow* relation should be represented by a dotted-line ending in a solid arrowhead at one end, to indicate the primary direction of the flow, as shown in Figure C-7, or at both ends if the flow is essentially bidirectional.

***Figure C-7.*** *"Flow" line*

Parameters for a *flow* relation may include an identifier for the role (if any), and, optionally, a name for the flow, a description of the triggering events for the flow, a description of flow content (if no *Product* entity is attached), and any other relevant information.

# "*Composition*" Relation Type

As described in Chapter 12, "Service Decomposition," we often need to model the structural composition or make-up of a service or product. For example, in Enterprise Canvas we describe each service as being made up of nine subsidiary "child" services, as its means for tackling the distinct service requirements and flows for a matrix of inbound-facing, self and outbound-facing focus, before, during, and after each main transaction across the service as a whole.

---

Note that those are merely the default partitionings used in Enterprise Canvas, and any appropriate alternate partitioning for a service or product may be used instead.

---

The same principle applies to products, which may be composed or aggregated from any number of "child" products, each with their own mix of underlying asset types. We can then model these composition relationships in two different ways: by connection links, or by "containment," as shown in Figure C-9.

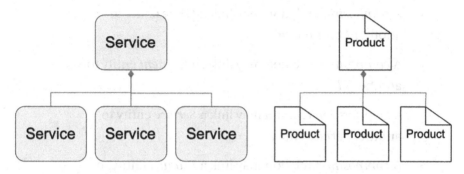

*Figure C-8.* *Composition: "composition"-relation connection links*

To show composition via connection links, use a *composition* relation type, a "vertical" solid arrow with a diamond-shaped head connected to the "parent," as shown in Figure C-8.

A *composition* relation should appear only in models that include Row-2 Business Model, Row-3 Service Model, Row-4 Design Model, Row-5 Deployment Model, and/or Row-6 Action Record. For most purposes, they should link only across *one* Row or layer of abstraction: in general, they cannot and must not be used to link between entities in different layers.

---

The exception to that guideline occurs when modeling a context where some implementation choices have already been made while others remain undecided – for example, some items are in Row-4 while others are still in Row-3. For more detail on how to model that type of situation, see the section "Modeling Implicit Layer Transitions in 'Containment' Views" later in this appendix.

---

With one exception – *Value* as a component of *Vision* – all composition relationships must connect between entities of the same type. The connection rules for *composition* relations are as follows:

- A *composition* relation may link a *Value* entity to a *Vision* entity.

- A *composition* relation may link a *Value* entity to another *Value* entity.

- A *composition* relation may link an *Element* entity to another *Element* entity.

- A *composition* relation may link a *Service* entity to another *Service* entity.

- A *composition* relation may link a *Product* entity to another *Product* entity.

A *composition* relation should always indicate which entity is the "parent" in the relationship, versus the entities that represent the "child" components. The recommended notation for a connection-type *composition* relation, as shown in Figure C-8, is a solid arrow with a diamond head pointing to the "parent."

---

In some cases, it may be useful to annotate a *composition* relation in Row-3 or below as denoting an *aggregation, assignment*, or *uses/used-by* relationship: for these, use the respective Archimate line decoration of open diamond, dot, and line arrow, connected to the "parent." In Enterprise Canvas, though, do note that these are regarded only as variants or sub-types of composition and decomposition; this is not the same as the approach used in Archimate and UML, where these sub-types are all defined as different relation types.

Also, do take especial care when using a *composition* relation to emulate an Archimate "*assigned-to*" or "*uses/used-by*" relationship: those are often used in Archimate as an analogue of a *realization* relation that will link between Archimate's content-based "layers" of Business, Application, and Technology, but at the *same* level of abstraction. For more on potential modeling risks that may arise from this difference in approach, see the section "Problems with Content-Based Layering" later in this appendix.

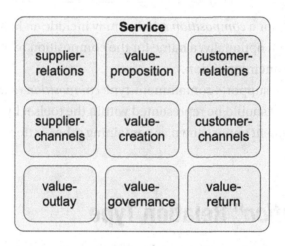

***Figure C-9.*** *Composition: containment*

To show composition by containment, place one or more entities "inside" another entity, as shown in Figure C-9. All entities in a containment relationship *must* be of the same entity type: containment should not be used to depict relationships between a *Vision* entity and its *Value* entities.

*Toolset implementation*: For compatibility with Archimate, BPMN, and UML, a connection-type *composition* relation should be represented by a vertical solid-line arrow ending in a solid diamond-type arrowhead at one end, as shown in Figure C-10, pointing to the "parent in the relationship."

*Figure C-10.* *Composition line*

---

For any usage of the composition subtypes *aggregation, assignment,* or *used-by* ("serving"), use open diamond, solid dot, or line arrow for the respective line decoration.

---

Parameters for a *composition* relation may include an identifier for the role (if any), and, optionally, a name for the composition relationship, and any other relevant information.

If the toolset supports containment-type *composition* relations, the containment should be represented within the toolset by a *Service, Product,* or *Element* entity shown as containing other entities of the same respective type.

# "*Realization*" Relation Type

As described in Chapter 5, "Service Layers" the Service-Layers model describes a set of layers of abstraction that specify the type of content, and level of detail for that content, required for descriptions of service models that represent the respective Row or layer. The layers also connect vertically from big-picture intent to real-world action and outcomes, such that a model in a given layer is described as a "realization" of the respective model in the layer above. For example, a "logical" implementation-independent model in the Row-3 Service-Model layer realizes, or makes more concrete, the support for a business need or business service described in the respective "business-context" model in the Row-2

Business-Model layer; a "physical" implementation-specific design in the Row-4 Design-Model layer realizes a possible implementation for that "logical" service; and so on.

---

Note that a *realization* relation is "vertical" – it links *only* between layers of abstraction. If we're working only within one layer in terms of the Service Layers, we won't need or use any *realization* relations in our model.

Note also that *realization* relations can only link *between* Rows or layers of abstraction: they cannot and must not be used to link between entities in the same layer. To link between entities at the same layer of abstraction, always use a *flow* relation or *composition* relation: a *realization* relation should never be used for this purpose.

---

We also use these realization relationships between models in different layers to denote and map out trails of provenance or "Why," looking "upward" through the layers, and trails of derivation or "How," looking "downward" through the layers. For example, the Row-3 "logical service" is the reason or "Why" for the existence of the Row-4 "physical service"; the Row-2 "business service" is the reason for the existence of the Row-3 "logical service"; and so on, all the way upward to the Row-0 shared-enterprise vision.

A realization relationship between models should be represented by a *realization* relation between the matching entities in the respective layers, in the form of a "vertical" dotted-line connection with an open-triangle arrowhead connecting to the entity in the "upper" (lower-numbered) Row, as shown in Figure C-11.

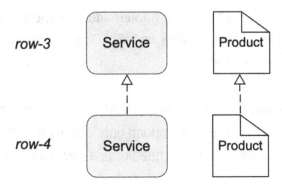

**Figure C-11.** *"Realization" relation*

---

As noted earlier, a realization relationship may also be implied in some cases where containment is used to represent composition relationships. For more detail on this, see the section "Modeling Implicit Layer Transitions in "containment" Views" later in this appendix.

Also, again, take especial care when emulating an Archimate "realization" relation. For more detail on this, see the section "Problems with Content-Based Layering" later in this appendix.

---

A *realization* relation may be used to connect between separate-but-related entities within any pair of layers or Rows, as appropriate. Connection rules for *realization* relations are as follows:

- A *realization* relation may link a *Service, Product,* or *Element* entity "upward" to a *Vision* entity or *Value* entity.

- A *realization* relation may link a *Service* or *Product* entity "upward" to an *Element* entity.

- A *realization* relation may link a *Service* entity "upward" to another *Service* entity.

- A *realization* relation may link a *Product* entity "upward" to another *Product* entity.

There are no sub-types for *realization* relations.

*Toolset implementation*: For compatibility with Archimate, BPMN, and UML, a *realization* relation should be represented by a vertical dotted-line ending in an open-triangle arrowhead at the upper end, as shown in Figure C-12.

*Figure C-12.* *Realization line*

Parameters for a *realization* relation may include an optional name and an optional text description of the context for the realization.

# General Notes on Modeling

Do be aware of the purpose and limits of this toolset-compatible notation for Enterprise Canvas. Much like Archimate for IT architectures, it is primarily intended to support "just enough modeling" to provide architectural overviews and to guide discussions on service design. It is easy to use, and does cover all of the main features of the Canvas, but it is not intended for full-detail design: for example, it does not have any built-in support for modeling the internal content and structure for products and services, as described in Chapter 13, "Service Content." It does allow some degree of support for automated syntax-checking and validation at the entity level, but it does require that more responsibility for correct modeling of underlying detail is passed to the modeler rather than explicit in the notation.

By default, colors for entities and flows are not semantically significant. Use color in any way that suits the meaning best.

Use *flow* and *composition* relations only *within* layers of abstraction (rows); use *realization* relations only *between* rows.

# Alternate Modeling for *Product* Entities Within Flows

The *Product* entities represent whatever will be passed, or act as a bridge, across a *flow*-relation-ship between *Service* entities.

In the standard modeling usage described above, the *Product* is placed between *Service* entities, and the *flow* relation links directly to the *Product* on both the "incoming" and "outgoing" side, as shown in Figure C-13.

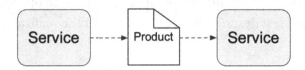

*Figure C-13.* *Inline "Product" entity*

This is probably the best way to model *Product* entities if we want to show actual flows of physical and/or virtual assets, or else if we need to focus on what a service would want produce as its output, and then go looking for other services that might consume that inter-service content.

If we are more interested in modeling relationships between services, particularly those where relational and/or aspirational assets provide the content to bridge the gap between those services, it may be better to attach the respective *Product* entity to the respective *flow* relation, rather than visibly interposing it in the flow, as shown in Figure C-14.

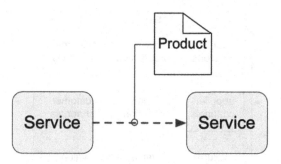

**Figure C-14.** *Attached Product entity*

The disadvantage of the "attached-*Product*" option is that it is not well suited to showing a decomposition split of the *Product* into subsidiary "child"-*Product* items linked to the attached "parent" via *composition* relations: visually it becomes too cluttered, and hard to read. If we need to show composition and decomposition for *Product* entities between services, we should use the in-*flow* format instead.

# Modeling Implicit Layer Transitions in "Containment" Views

As described earlier in the section on the *composition* relation type, containment provides a useful technique to save space in model diagrams and to reduce visual clutter for *composition* relations. An entity can be shown as "containing" other entities of the same type, which then implies that the "child" entities have *composition* relations with the "parent."

In Enterprise Canvas, this type of containment is implied in the subdivision of the core Service entity into nine subsidiary cells, as shown in Figure C-15.

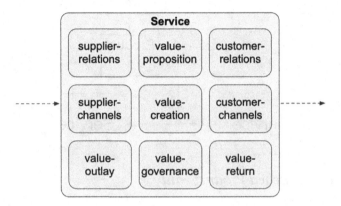

***Figure C-15.*** *A Service contains "child" Services*

It is also implied in the "before/during/after" split of the inter-service flow, as represented by the "wrapper" *Product* entity for the overall supplier-side flow in the model shown in Figure C-16.

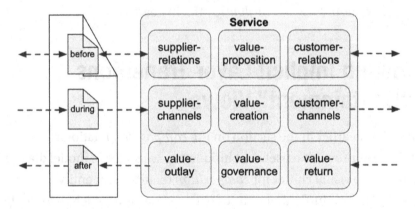

***Figure C-16.*** *Service Product exchanges*

Using a container entity in this way is usually less cluttered and easier to read than modeling the same *Product* flows with *composition* links, as shown in Figure C-17.

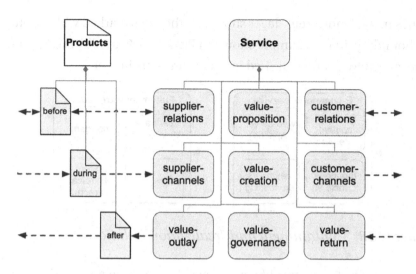

**Figure C-17.** *Unpacked "containment" of "child" Services*

However, do beware that in some cases, an apparent *composition* containment may also need to imply *realization* relationships together with the *composition* relationships. One common example would be where we want to show which decisions have been made regarding implementation of the components for a service – such as a Row-3 *Service* entity containing a set of "child"-*Service* entities that are a mix of Row-3 implementation-undefined and Row-4 implementation-specific. If we want to model use containment to model that context, we need to distinguish between the implied *composition* relations of the containment, versus any *realization* relations needed between the "parent" and any of its "children."

One way to do this would be to use the same dotted-line convention of a *realization* relation to also denote a *realization* relationship within a compositional containment. We use solid-line boundary for a *Service* entity or *Product* entity to denote a "child" that is in the same Row or layer as its "parent"; we use a dotted-line boundary to indicate that the is *not* in the same layer as its parent. The usual recommendation is that entities in the "more-real" layer should be the ones marked with a dotted-line boundary: in the example shown in Figure C-18, a solid-line border represents Row-3, and a dashed border represents Row-4.

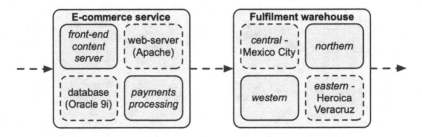

***Figure C-18.*** *Containment and "realization" relations*

Some toolsets may be able to manage this notation automatically, but in almost all cases we should be able to do this manually if required.

# Problems with Content-Based Layering

A reminder may again be needed here that the layers or "rows" in the Service-Layers model for Enterprise Canvas are *layers of abstraction*, not content-based layers such as used in TOGAF, Archimate, and other IT-oriented frameworks and notations.

Content-based layering can be problematic because it can make it almost impossible to model in any consistent way certain essential aspects of enterprise architectures and service design. In particular, this applies to planning for business continuity and disaster recovery, for security-system design, for load-balancing, and for anything else that might require "fungibility" or substitution of some method or content for another that uses a different asset type, decision type, or technology.

For example, Archimate's architecture model defines three content-based layers: "Technology," which describes the physical elements for IT infrastructure; "Application," which describes elements that deal with data, and anything that works on data; and "Business," which provides the context for the technology, applications, and data, and also describes any elements that are not IT-based technology, applications, or data. It then uses a myriad of different entities and relationships in and/or these different content-based layers to denote the differences between Row-3 "logical"-type concepts and their respective Row-4 "physical"-type real-world implementations. In practice, though, we can only get away with that kind of content-based layering *if and only if* our service designs work *only* with IT applications, IT-based data, and IT hardware. There is no way to use it to do consistent modeling *for any other types* of service implementations.

To illustrate why this can be so problematic, consider the following service-design example. In the ZapaMex factory, there is a storage area that contains dangerous chemicals, and by law they must ensure that only authorized people can access that area. In Enterprise Canvas, that requirement would be placed in a Row-3 Service Model; in Archimate, it would be placed in the "Business" layer, probably as a "Business-service" element. All of that would seem straightforward enough at first.

Yet real problems could arise for ZapaMex when they try to model how they might implement that service. For example, they decide that they will fit to the door an electronic lock that could be opened by a fingerprint scanner or RFID tag or, if the power fails, by a physical key; if the lock itself fails, they will assign someone to act as a guard to control access. For Enterprise Canvas, we would model these at Row-4 Design Model, as different implementations or *realizations* of the same Row-3 service and its respective assets, function, location, capability, events, and decisions, all relating to the same service user. But if we try to model this in Archimate, the content-based layering would place the IT-based fingerprint scanner in the Application layer, the physical key in the Technology layer, and the human guard in the Business layer – and there is no means there to show that they are, in fact, just different implementations of the *same* service. These inconsistencies then ripple and multiply across the entire

313

architecture of the enterprise, until it becomes impossible to trace any trails of provenance or interdependence, or what requirement anything serves, or even why anything exists. Content-based layering is *not* the same as layers of abstraction or realization, and it is *essential* not to mix them up.

# Keeping Things Simple

Remember that one of the key aims here is to keep things simple, without ever dropping down into the over-simplistic. Other than the special-case entities for Row-0 and Row-1, there are only main two entity types in the entire notation: *Service*, which does something; and *Product*, which represents something that passes between services. That's it.

There are then only three types of relationship possible between those entities, which in turn follow very simple rules:

- *Composition* relations, showing internal structure of services and products, can only connect *within* a single Row or layer of abstraction.

- *Flow* relations between services can only connect *within* a single Row or layer of abstraction.

- *Realization* relations, from abstract to concrete, can only connect *between* Rows or layers of abstraction.

Again, that's it.

Because the notation is so simple, it allows the true complexity in the context to emerge and surface cleanly through the modeling process. We don't get distracted by arbitrary content-based layering: it's just the enterprise, *as* enterprise.

For many modeling purposes, the only relation type we will need is the *flow* relation. Figure C-19 shows a simple example of the flows, products, and services in a basic supply chain that allows switching between multiple suppliers.

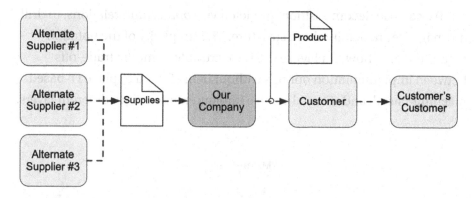

***Figure C-19.*** *Multiple-supplier supply-chain relation*

Figure C-20 shows the flows, products, and services in a business model with multiple client segments, where we use *Product* entities to record the different transactions and transaction content for each client group.

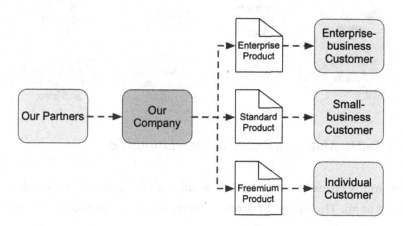

***Figure C-20.*** *Multiple-client supply-chain relation*

315

We can use decomposition, modeled via *composition* relations, to drill down into more details about structure. The simplicity of the notation means that, as shown in Figure C-21, we are able to model trade-offs between implementation options without being forced to place IT-based, machine-based, and manual service implementations into different layers.

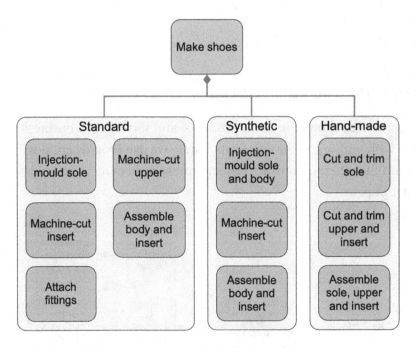

***Figure C-21.*** *Multi-implementation relationships*

For many types of modeling, we would not need to use *realization* relations at all. The only common contexts where we would need to use them are

- Mapping "logical-to-physical" transforms and similar transitions between abstract and concrete.

- Mapping dependencies of "why" and/or "how" between the layers, such as to show how a specific service contributes to the overall aims of the shared enterprise.

Keeping the notation simple in this way makes modeling faster, makes models easier to read, and helps create better understanding of how the enterprise actually works.

# Comparing Notations for Enterprise Canvas

There are three notations for Enterprise Canvas: sketch diagram, formal diagram, and toolset-based modeling. They all share the same underlying principles, such as the enterprise as a shared story, and "everything is a service," and the same underlying concepts, such as *Service*, *Product*, and *flow*, *composition*, and *realization* relations; but they each express those principles and concepts in their own way, and each has their own distinct roles. Understanding the differences and trade-offs between the notations will make it easier to gain the best use from Enterprise Canvas in any given context for service design. We can illustrate this by showing the same "kitchen-sink" model as presented in each notation.

The ***sketch notation***, as shown in Figure C-22, is probably best used for quick, fast-moving whiteboard sessions and live collaborations. By intent, there is no formal rigor, but there *is* just enough structure to keep the modeling worthwhile and meaningful. Lines and elements can be erased and redrawn with ease, items and annotations added and withdrawn, all at breakneck speed, and captured in an instant in photographs or videos, for re-use elsewhere, or used as the basis for a more formal model later on.

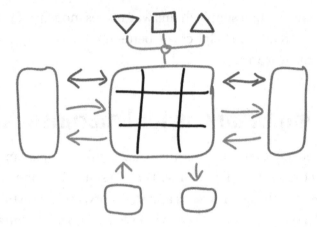

***Figure C-22.*** *Enterprise Canvas "kitchen sink" in hand-sketch format*

The ***formal notation***, as shown in Figure C-23, is probably best suited for presentations, conferences, slidedecks, and training materials. It is not as fast-moving as the sketch notation, and it does not support the automatable formal rigor of the toolset-compatible notation; but it is compact and complete, reasonably easy to produce with common office-diagramming tools, and does provide the right balance for most people's needs.

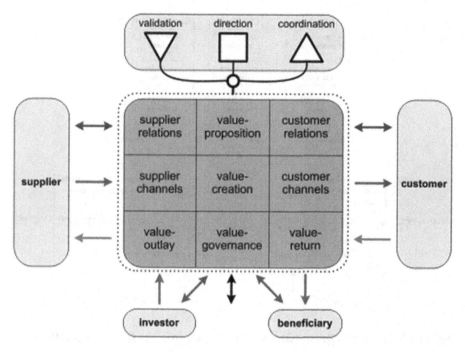

***Figure C-23.*** *Enterprise Canvas "kitchen sink" in formal notation*

The ***toolset-compatible notation***, as shown in Figure C-24, is probably best used when the ideas developed in the sketch notation and formal notation need to be moved forward toward real-world implementation. It is more cumbersome than the other notations, and usually slower to produce, but it does support completeness checks and automated validation and is directly compatible with other existing notations for service design.

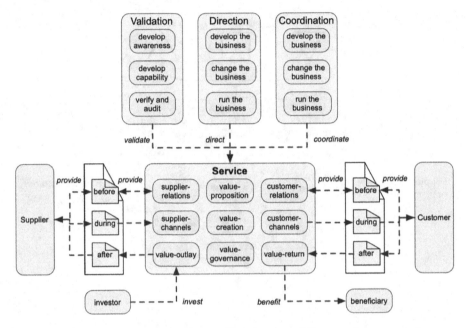

**Figure C-24.** *Enterprise Canvas "kitchen sink" in toolset notation*

The key point, perhaps, is that all these options are there, and available. Switch between notations in whatever way you want, to match the business need.

# APPENDIX D

# Enterprise Canvas and Service Viability

This appendix brings together core concepts and "Into Action" checklists from the main part of the book into a single unified set, to show how to use Enterprise Canvas as a visual checklist to verify completeness and viability of services, in any context within the enterprise.

"Completeness" means that we check that the service has all the connections, support, and flows that it needs, to play its full part in its respective role for the enterprise value network.

"Viability" here is in the sense described in the Viable System Model that the interdependencies that the service needs, both to operate in the "now" and to change appropriately over time, are all in place and in action.

In a service-oriented architecture and service-oriented view of enterprise, *everything* either is, implies, or represents a service. This means that, to ensure completeness and viability, everything in the enterprise will rely on those interlinks and interdependencies between services. As seen in previous chapters, Enterprise Canvas explicitly sets out to model those interdependencies, and hence can be very useful as a means to help identify and verify the required completeness.

© Tom Graves 2023
T. Graves, *Mapping the Enterprise*, https://doi.org/10.1007/978-1-4842-9836-7

# Preparation

For this exercise we will need the overview model of service relationships, as described in the Enterprise Canvas toolset-compatible notation in Appendix C, and as shown in Figure D-1.

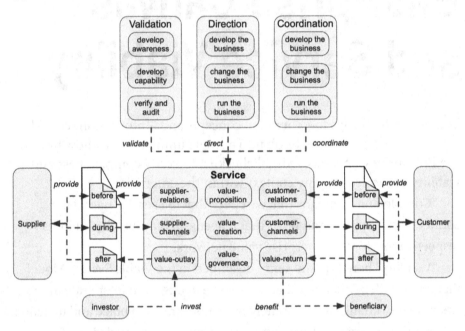

***Figure D-1.*** *Simplified notation: complete Enterprise Canvas*

We will also need the Service-Layers map of layers of abstraction, as described in Chapter 5, "Service Layers," and as shown in Figure D-2.

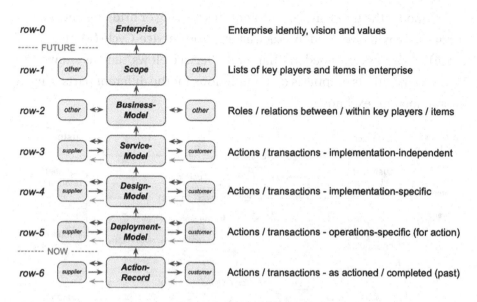

**Figure D-2.** *Service-Layers model – Enterprise Canvas: rows*

We will need the Service-Content model – the "service-content map," as described in Chapter 13, "Service Content," and as shown in Figure D-3.

| Asset-types | Assets | Functions | Locations | Capabilities (action) | Capabilities (agent) | Capabilities (skill-level) | Events | Decisions | Decision/skill-types |
|---|---|---|---|---|---|---|---|---|---|
| | What | How | Where | | (Who) | | When | Why | |
| Physical | Phys | Phys | Phys | Phys | Phys | Rules | Phys | Rules | Rule-based |
| Virtual | Virtual | Virtual | Virtual | Virtual | Virtual | Algor'm | Virtual | Algor'm | Algorithmic |
| Relational | Reln | Reln | Reln | Reln | Reln | Guideln | Reln | Guideln | Guidelines |
| Aspirational | Aspn | Aspn | Aspn | Aspn | Aspn | Princpl | Aspn | Princpl | Principle-based |
| Abstract | | | Time | | | | | | |

**Figure D-3.** *Service-Content model – Enterprise Canvas: service content*

To model the flows and *Product* entities moving or bridging between services, we will also need to check against the Service-Cycle (Market-Cycle) model, as described in Chapter 9, "Service Flows," and as shown in Figure D-4, with its emphasis on completions for the different parts of each interaction and exchange.

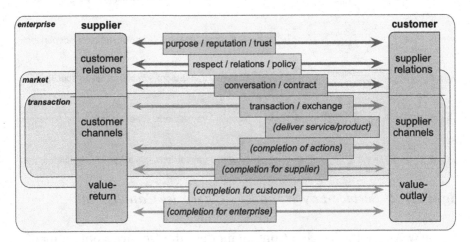

***Figure D-4.***  *Service-Cycle model (service cycle)*

If we want to start from a business model developed on Business-Model Canvas, we will need to first do a cross-map from Business-Model Canvas to Enterprise Canvas, as described in "Appendix B: Working with Business Model Canvas."

To build the model, use either a purpose-built toolset for enterprise architecture or service design, or an office diagramming tool such as Visio, Omnigraffle, or Dia, or else draw the model by hand on paper or on a whiteboard.

# Notes on Process, Layering, and Story

That discipline about *layering* described in Chapter 5, "Service Layers," and "Appendix C: Enterprise Canvas Notation" becomes particularly important when using the checklists here, because our aim is to identify and explore direct interdependencies between services.

Every *flow* relation between services implies an exchange of some kind, even if the exchange consists only of an acknowledgment that a relationship exists – which we would typically document in the model as a relational asset within a *Product* entity. To understand interdependence, we need to identify the content of those exchanges. Hence, this type of modeling demands a discipline about layering that may take some getting used to, but is extremely valuable in practice:

- In general, *flow* relations and *Product* entities should only connect between *Service* entities at the same layer.

- Changes in layer should be indicated by *realization* relations between *Service* entities and/or between *Product* entities.

- Where a *flow* relation must connect directly between *Service* entities at different layers – such as where the actual service for the end-point of that flow is currently unknown – the "different-layer" *Service* must be indicated explicitly by a dotted-line border, as described in the section on "Modeling Implicit Layer Transitions in "Containment" Views" in "Appendix C: Enterprise Canvas Notation."

Most modeling for this viability-checklist process would or should be at a single layer of abstraction – most often Row-3 "Service Model" or Row-4 "Design Model," as described here. For the supply-chain part of the model, this should be straightforward: any changes in layering should usually be self-evident there. However, it can be all too easy to scramble the layering when exploring links with guidance services or with investors and beneficiaries.

For example, if we are using this checklist to focus on a detail-layer web service, there may be a strong temptation to tick off the *Direct::Change* guidance service as "IT Strategy" or the like, and then leave it at that. Yet doing that could be a real missed opportunity: "IT Strategy" is abstract, yet there is real work there that is done by real people, every bit as real as the web service that is our current focus of attention. Hence, it might be useful to ask about what exactly is the chain of responsibilities and connections, and hence *flow* relations and *Products* connecting real-world *Services*, that links between that people-based work and this web service. There are some valuable insights to be gained there about how the enterprise *actually* works, and how it maintains its viability: it is well worth the extra effort around layer discipline in order to obtain them.

Another useful discipline to apply while using this checklist relates to **story**.

So far most of what we have explored in this book has been focused on structure and relationships between structures: services, products, flows, composition, and realization. However, another equally valid way to look at architecture and service design is to explore it in terms of story.

One of the first things we say with Enterprise Canvas is that everything is a service; yet it is equally true to say that everything is a story. Every service is a story, represents a story, has its own story to tell. Every exchange is a story. Every product is a story. Every flow or composition or realization is a story. Every change is a story. The enterprise itself is a story, too. *Everything* is, represents, or implies a story.

An architecture or a service design is all about structure, and dynamics of structure; yet it is *also* all about stories. Stories engage; stories draw people in; stories give people a reason to be involved in whatever it is that the service does and delivers, and how and why and where and with what it does so. It is often in the stories that people tell us that we find the most important clues about what is working or not-working within the enterprise, and what to do to make it work better. In that sense, the stories definitely do matter.

Whenever we look at an architecture or service design, and whenever we look at its structure, we need also to look at, and look for, the stories that underlie and underpin and interweave with that structure. And likewise, whenever we look at the stories, we need to look for the underlying structures that they each imply. Architecture is both structure *and* story.

In that sense, it is useful to see Enterprise Canvas not just as a framework for models of structure, but also as an anchor for stories, about the enterprise, about how everything fits together, or not, within the unified whole that is the organization and its broader enterprise. We need to keep this theme in mind as we work through the viability-checklist process for a service.

# Start with the Service Itself

To get started with the checklist, pick a service – any service, anywhere in the overall enterprise – that happens to be of interest at present. If none comes immediately to mind, start with the organization as a whole, as a service in context of its market and the broader shared enterprise.

Place a *Service* entity in the middle of the model, to represent the chosen "service-in-focus," as shown in Figure D-5. Then follow the instructions below, to see what insights arise as the modeling proceeds.

***Figure D-5.*** *Service*

What *is* this service? We start by assigning it a *name*. If we're doing the modeling within a toolset for enterprise architecture or service design, we should also provide a brief description of the service and its role.

What *layer of abstraction* will we use as the base for modeling this service? This should be one of the following:

- Row-2 "Business Model," to describe the overall context, without much if any description of actual content.

- Row-3 "Service Model," the implementation-independent "logical" layer, where we start to fill in the details of the content of services and the inter-service exchanges.

- Row-4 "Design Model," the implementation-specific "physical" layer.

- Row-5 "Deployment Model," the fine detail intended for use at run time.

Remember that, as described in Chapter 13, "Service Content," if any specific technology or implementation is mentioned, then by definition the description is at Row-4 or below.

Apply a RACI assessment to the service:

- Who is ultimately *responsible* or *accountable* for this service?

- Who *assists* in delivering or running or supporting this service?

- Who needs to be *consulted* about this service, or any changes to this service?

- Who needs to be *informed* about the performance of or changes to this service?

What other responsibilities and accountabilities apply in this context?

# The Core Activities of the Service

As a first step in the functional decomposition of the service – about what it does, and how, and why, as described in Chapter 7, "Service Roles and Relationships" – we should focus attention on the three innermost cells of the Enterprise Canvas view of the service, as shown in Figure D-6.

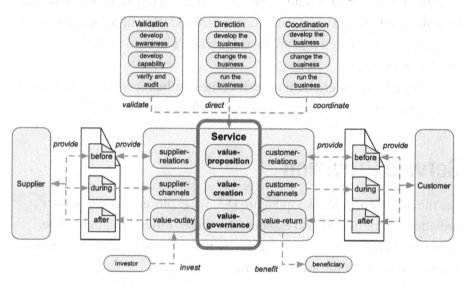

***Figure D-6.*** *Service: core*

What *value* does this service provide – its *Value Proposition*, in terms of the aims and needs and values of the broader extended enterprise? If appropriate, build a trail of linkage up through the layers of abstraction, to connect with the vision and values of the shared enterprise. To model this, link this service to at least one other matching *Service* or *Element* entity in each layer upward to Row-1; then link to one or more *Value* entities in Row-0, and ultimately to the *Vision* entity at that top of the abstraction "tree." We will come back to some of this later when we explore this service's links to its Validation services.

What does this service *do* to create and deliver that value – its *Value Creation* in terms of that Value Proposition? Use the Service-Content model, as described in Chapter 13, "Service Content," to explore and identify the various assets, functions, locations, capabilities, events, and decisions that apply within that value creation. We will come back to some of this later when we explore this service's links to its Coordination services.

What does this service need to *govern* its service delivery – its *Value Governance* to keep the Value Creation on track to the Value Proposition? How does it do this? Under what business rules? We will come back to some of this later when we explore this service's links to its Direct and Validate services.

Apply a RACI assessment to each of these subsidiary "cells" within the service: who is responsible or accountable, for what, and why?

# Service Provision

For the next step, as shown in Figure D-7, we explore what this service provides to others, and also explore who those "others" might be. The connections between services will be as described in Chapter 9, "Service Flows," particularly the section on the Service Cycle.

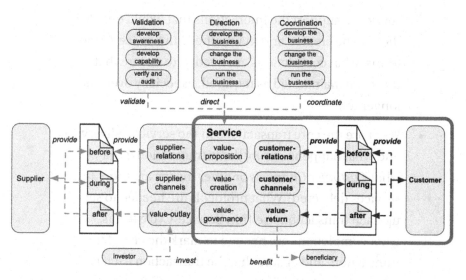

**Figure D-7.** *Service: outgoing*

What does this service *provide* to others – the services or products *consumed* by others?

Using the "Assets" column of the Service-Content map as a guide, what forms does this service provision take, at each stage of the Service Cycle? Model the results of this assessment as one or more *Product* entities, linked via *flow* relations to the right-hand "outgoing" side of the *Service* entity.

Who or what are the customers or consumers of these services? For each distinct customer group, there should be a distinct Service Cycle, usually with at least one distinct *Product* for each stage of that cycle. If necessary, split the overall exchange content into further *Product* entities, each linked to a *Service* entity for each respective customer group.

Review each *Product* in terms of what aspects of the overall exchange and its content take place *before*, *during*, and *after* each main transaction. Use the Service-Cycle model to map these as follows:

- What reputation, trust, relations, and attention need to be in place *before* each main transaction? What *Customer-Relations* subsidiary services exist within the service to support the interactions that would enable these to be created and maintained? In Service-Cycle terms, what completions are needed to ensure that these are maintained as required, especially over the longer term?

- What are the core transactions in the service delivery, and what happens *during* those transactions? Via what *Customer Channels* or other means are the services delivered? What protocols are needed to set up each transaction itself? In Service-Cycle terms, what completions are needed to mark the end of the transaction, and ensure that the transaction itself is closed-off and complete?

- What follow-up interactions need to occur *after* the main transaction – such as payment and the like? What *Value-Return* subsidiary services exist within the service to support these interactions? In Service-Cycle terms, what completions are needed to ensure that everything is complete and all parties are satisfied by or from the transaction?

Define subsidiary *Product* entities as required for each of these *before*, *during*, and *after* flows, and link these via *flow* relations to the respective subsidiary cells of the service.

Optionally, use the Service-Content map to summarize the assets, activities, and other content for each of the subsidiary services and for the products within each of the subsidiary flows.

Apply a RACI assessment to each of these "customer-side" subsidiary services within the service, to identify responsibilities and accountabilities for each aspect of the *Product* transactions and relations with the respective "customer" service.

Given that the *before, during,* and *after* interactions may all occur at different times, through different channels and on different timescales, what mechanisms exist within the service to keep them all in balance, and appropriately linked to the core *Value Proposition, Value Creation,* and *Value Governance* of the service? Who or what is responsible for enacting and governing each of these internal activities and interactions?

## Consuming Other Services

Next, as shown in Figure D-8, we explore the "incoming" side of the service – the services and products provided by and/or consumed from others – and identify who those "others" might be. As in the preceding "Service Provision" section, the connections between services will be as described in Chapter 9, "Service Flows," particularly the section on the Service Cycle.

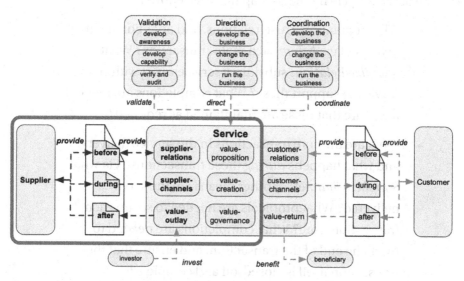

*Figure D-8.*  *Service: incoming*

This is the symmetric opposite of service provision, and hence we should assess and model it in exactly the same way. The "others" in this case are usually described as suppliers or partners.

What does this service *consume* from others – the services or products *provided* by others? What forms does this service provision take? What values, policies, events, content, and trust apply in each service provision to this service? Model the results of this assessment as one or more *Product* entities, linked to the left-hand or "incoming" side of the *Service* entity.

Who or what are the suppliers or partners for each of these services? For each distinct supplier group, there should usually be at least one distinct *Product*; if necessary, split the overall exchange content into further *Product* entities, each linked to a *Service* entity for each respective supplier group.

Review each *Product* in terms of what aspects of the overall exchange and its content take place *before*, *during*, and *after* each main transaction. Use the Service-Cycle model to map these as follows:

- What reputation, trust, relations, and attention need to be in place *before* each main transaction? What *Supplier-Relations* subsidiary services exist within the service to support these? What completions are needed to ensure that these are maintained as required?

- What are the core transactions in the service delivery, and what happens *during* those transactions? Via what *Supplier Channels* or other means are the services delivered? What protocols are needed to set up each transaction itself? What completions are needed to mark the end of the transaction, and ensure that the transaction itself is closed-off and complete?

- What follow-up interactions need to occur *after* the main transaction – such as payment and the like? What *Value-Outlay* subsidiary services exist within the service to support these interactions? What completions are needed to ensure that everything is complete and all parties are satisfied?

Define subsidiary *Product* entities as required for each of these *before*, *during*, and *after* flows, and link these to the respective subsidiary cells of the service.

Optionally, use the Service-Content map to summarize the assets, activities, and other content for each of the subsidiary services.

Apply a RACI assessment to each of these "customer-side" subsidiary services within the service, to identify responsibilities and accountabilities for each aspect of the *Product* transactions and relations with the respective "customer" service.

What mechanisms exist within the service to keep all of the *before*, *during*, and *after* interactions in balance, and appropriately linked to the core *Value Proposition*, *Value Creation*, and *Value Governance* of the service? Who or what is responsible for enacting and governing each of these internal activities and interactions?

Who or what is responsible for the *overall* balance across the whole of the service? (In principle this is a key part of the role of the *Value-Governance* subsidiary services, but may in part be enacted by others: if so, who or what are they, and what mechanisms exist to ensure balance?)

# Guidance Service Relationships

As described in Chapter 10, "Service Guidance," the concept of "guidance services" is adapted from the Viable System Model, with some extensions. These represent the web of service interdependencies that ensure both the *governance* and *viability* of the service – the effectiveness of its operations at run time, and its adaptability and resilience to change, especially over the longer term. These are described under three categories as follows:

- *Direction*: Services that assist in strategy, planning, and day-to-day operations of this service and its clusters of related services.

- *Coordination*: Services that assist in run-time coordination with other services, and with planning and coordination of change.

- *Validation*: Services that help to keep the service on-track with and aligned to the vision, values, and success criteria of the shared enterprise.

These services or functions may be embedded somewhere within the service itself, though also often enacted by separate business functions connected in some way to this service. In a few cases, especially for some aspects of validation services, they may be required by law to be enacted by a completely separate organization. Yet in whatever form they may be implemented in real-world practice, the point is that they must all exist *somewhere*, in *some* form, in an engaged relationship with this specific service, in order to ensure viability of the system as a whole.

# Guidance: Direction

The *direction* services represent the usual "management"-type functions of the enterprise, seen here in relation to the service that is our current focus of attention.

---

Note that, for our purposes here, these "management functions" are viewed here solely as services in relation to other services, with no special priority or importance over anything else. Although business politics may argue otherwise elsewhere, within whole-of-system service design itself, we must view "the management" as just another support service, nothing more nor less than that.

---

As shown in Figure D-9, these direction services can be split into three distinct groups, often referred to as "Develop the Business," "Change the Business," and "Run the Business."

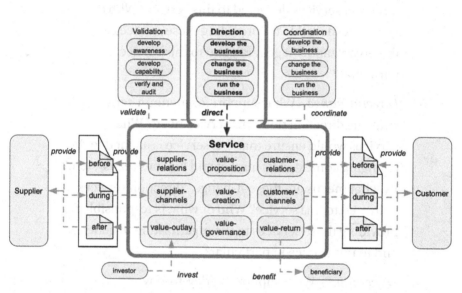

**Figure D-9.**  *Service: direction*

In classic concepts of management, "Develop" and "Change" are primarily viewed as staff functions, whereas "Run" is primarily viewed as a line-management function. There is also a timescale element here: "Develop" tends to have a long time-view, ranging from years to decades, potentially all the way to infinity; "Change" has a medium-term view, from the current quarter out to a few years ahead at most; while "Run" is mostly focused on the day-to-day. Strategy develops out of the intersection between "Develop" and "Change"; tactics from the intersection of "Change" and "Run"; and operations from the intersection between "Run" and this service.

337

Most of these services *must not and cannot be outsourced* to another organization.

Questions to ask here include

- *Direct::Develop* – What support for long-term direction does this service need? What services would ensure that this service is aligned to the overall Vision for the enterprise? By what means are these "Develop" direction services delivered to this service? Who or what is responsible for providing these services to the organization in general, and to this service in particular?

- *Direct::Change* – What support for medium-term strategic direction does this service need? What services would ensure that this service is aligned to the changing context of its market and business ecosystem? By what means are these "Change" direction services delivered to this service? Who or what is responsible for providing these services to the organization in general, and to this service in particular?

- *Direct::Run* – What support for day-to-day management does this service need? What services would ensure that this service has the resources that it needs to do its work in creating value? What performance metrics does this service need to provide to those "Run" direction functions? How are those performance metrics used in providing management services to this service? By what means are these "Run" direction services delivered to this service? Who or what is responsible for these services, and how they apply to this service?

Identify the services and exchanges in each case, typically using the Service-Content map to assess the content of activities of each service. Add the results of this assessment to the model as *Service* entities and *Product* entities, linked to the service-in-focus via *flow* relations. Use either containment (as in the previous diagram) or *composition* relations to link each of these Service entities to the overall Direction *Service*. Annotate each *flow* relation here with a *"direct"* label, to indicate that the flow delivers direction services to the service-in-focus.

---

"Develop the Business" is ultimately a role and responsibility that belongs *solely* to the executive team, on behalf of the organization as a whole in relation to its shared enterprise. Architects and others may provide *decision support* for that role, but *not* the *decision-making*: that distinction is extremely important in practice!

Even so, we do still need to address these issues in the viability checklist, because in some organizations, the distinct tasks of "Develop the Business" may instead be subsumed into "Change the Business" or even "Run the Business." That type of imbalance between the direction services can become a cause of architecturally inadequate support to the organization's overall services and inability to develop and maintain any real strategy, and in turn may lead to organizational failure over the medium to longer term: *it is an extremely important architectural risk for the organization*, and for the enterprise as a whole. In short, if adequate and appropriate direction support is not available, the service will *not* be viable: a key purpose for this part of the checklist is to advise the executive and others of any potential for that type of risk.

---

# Guidance: Coordination

The *coordination* services represent the business functions that coordinate this service with other services.

As shown in Figure D-10, these services can be split into three distinct groups, often referred to as "Develop the Business," "Change the Business," and "Run the Business," in parallel with the matching functions in the Direction services.

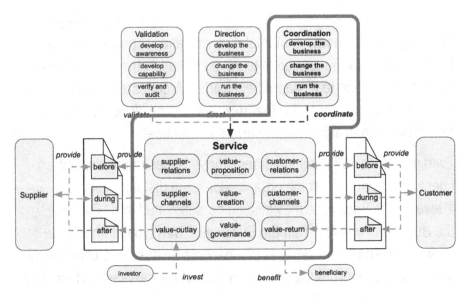

***Figure D-10.*** *Service: coordination*

In classic concepts of management, these services are usually regarded as part of the "management" functions. In practice they will often need to be separate and distinct, not least because in many cases they must somehow bridge *between* management-hierarchy silos. Significant organizational problems can arise from that one fact.

The *Coordinate::Develop* services relate to coordination of strategy and strategic change, and hence will link to both *Direct::Develop* and

*Direct::Change.* It is also often associated with portfolio management and the like.

The *Coordinate::Change* services focus more at the tactical level, and hence link to *Direct::Change* and *Direct::Run.* One classic role for these services is in project management and the Programme Management Office.

The *Coordinate::Run* services would bridge between *Direct::Run* and the actual delivery services.

---

In practice, though, that kind of bridge may risk being interpreted as "insubordination," and hence at the human-coordination level may disappear into a kind of covert "shadow network" via which work is *actually* coordinated and done.

Service designers can sometimes run up against unexpected "political" problems of that kind when doing this part of the modeling work: a certain amount of caution may be advisable here!

---

It is quite common for some aspects of these services to be outsourced to other organizations. If so, additional coordination services would be required, to manage and coordinate the outsourcing process itself.

Questions to ask here include

- *Coordinate::Develop* – What support for long-term strategic change does this service need? What services would ensure that this service is aligned to the overall enterprise strategy? By what means are these "Develop" coordination services delivered to this service? Who or what is responsible for providing these services to the organization in general, and to this service in particular?

- *Coordinate::Change* – What support for medium-term tactical change does this service need? What services would ensure that this service is aligned to and fully supports the changing context of its market and business ecosystem? By what means – such as program- or project-management – are these "Change" coordination services delivered to this service? Who or what is responsible for providing these services to the organization in general, and to this service in particular?

- *Coordinate::Run* – What support does this service need for run-time coordination with other services, and for load-balancing with its sibling services? What services would ensure that this service has the coordination with others that it needs so as to do its work in creating value? What information flows, signaling, or protocols are needed in this coordination support? By what means are these "Run" coordination services delivered to this service? Who or what is responsible for these services, and how they apply to this service?

As before, identify the services and exchanges in each case. Add these to the model as *Service* entities and *Product* entities, linked to the service-in-focus via *flow* relations. Use either containment or *composition* relations to link each of these Service entities to the overall Coordination *Service*. Annotate each *flow* relation here with a "*coordinate*" label, to indicate that the flow delivers coordination services to the service-in-focus.

---

Identifying coordination relationships between services will usually be straightforward, although it can be all too easy to fall into layering mistakes in the modeling process here. A lot of useful insights can be gained here about the interconnectedness of the enterprise, and its dynamics over time. Note, though, that there are also some important architectural risks and opportunities to be identified here: in short, if adequate and appropriate *coordination* support is not available, the service will *not* be viable.

---

# Guidance: Validation

The *validation* services help to enact governance and to keep everything aligned to the enterprise vision and values, whatever those values may be. Note that there should usually be distinct sets of validation services for *each* key value of concern in the enterprise. Typical examples of values in this context would include quality, probity, security, ethics, health and safety, knowledge-sharing, sustainability, waste management, efficiency, effectiveness, and also architecture and service design itself.

A crucial point here is that, unlike strategy, management, coordination, or change, maintaining these values is a *personal* responsibility for *everyone* in the enterprise. There is often a small core group tasked with "holding the flag" for the respective value within the organization, and it's those people – the knowledge-management team, the quality team, the security team, and so on – who we would often regard as the people who deliver such services. In reality, though, it's only the *support* services around each value that most of those teams would deliver: the actual implementation and expression of that value must somehow be embedded and enacted, as activities and checks and the like, within *every* service in the enterprise.

As shown in Figure D-11, these support services for value alignment would be split into three groups: "Develop Awareness" of the value; "Develop Capability" to enact run-time support for the value; and "Verify and Audit," to confirm alignment and compliance to the requirements of the value.

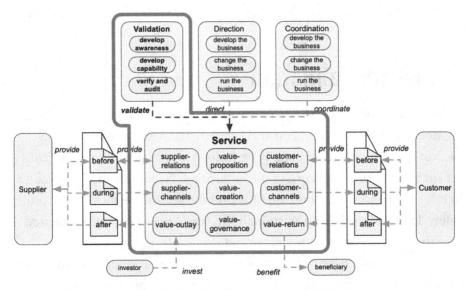

***Figure D-11.*** *Service: validation*

---

In classic concepts of management, these services are often subsumed into the "management" functions, which can often lead to misunderstandings because the managers themselves must be as subject to the values as is everyone else. It is true, though, that in many cases the core support group for each value will be regarded as a "staff" function, often reporting indirectly or even directly to the CEO or overall executive; it's certainly essential for each of these values to have the full backing of the executive, otherwise in practice they end up going nowhere.

---

Although these *validation* services do provide guidance across the enterprise, they are in effect almost orthogonal to the *direction* services such as management, and to *coordination* services such as change management. Some aspects of these services may be outsourced to other organizations, such as training to develop capability, and in many contexts the "Verify and Audit" functions *must* be enacted by an outside organization, either to support certification or as mandated by law. Overall, though, the final *responsibility* for alignment to each of the enterprise values *must* reside within the organization itself: that aspect of these services *cannot* be outsourced.

In effect, these services should represent the nodes of a PDCA (Plan/ Do/Check/Act) continuous-improvement loop for the respective value, starting at the "Act" node.

- *Plan*: "Develop Capability" is crucial to embedding the ability to enact support for the value.

- *Do*: The awareness and capability are applied in practice within each service and service delivery.

- *Check*: "Verify and Audit" confirms compliance, or any deviation from required or intended performance.

- *Act*: "Develop Awareness" is central to taking action toward improving support for the value.

Before any of this modeling work can make sense, there are some essential questions that need to be asked, as described in Chapter 4, "Service Vision and Values":

- What are the enterprise values? Why do these values apply in this enterprise, and in this organization?

- Which of these values are explicitly espoused as matter of personal *choice*, by the executive and/or by others? Which of these values are imposed on the organization from outside, as part of a metaphoric "license to operate" within the industry or broader social milieu?

- What differences – if any – exist between the espoused values and the values actually enacted and upheld within the organization and/or the broader shared enterprise?

As described in "Appendix C: Enterprise Canvas Notation," these values should typically be modeled as *Value* entities in a Row-0 segment of an Enterprise Canvas, attached to the *Vision* entity in the model. Within the model, *Service* entities for all *validation* services should ultimately link back via *realization* relations to one or more Row-0 *Value* entities.

Given that list of enterprise values, questions to ask here *for each enterprise value* include:

- *Validate::Awareness*: What support does this service need to develop and establish awareness of the value and its importance to the organization and enterprise? What services would ensure that this service is aligned to the respective value? By what means are these "Develop Awareness" validation services for this value delivered to this service? Who or what is responsible for providing these services to the organization in general, and to this service in particular?

- *Validate::Capability*: What support does this service need to develop and improve its capability to enact the requirements of the value within the service and its service delivery? What services would ensure that this capability is appropriately developed, and the capability verified prior to action? By what means – such as training programs – are these "Develop Capability" validation services delivered to this service? Who or what is responsible for providing these services to the organisation in general, and to this service in particular?

- *Run-time support within this service*: What functionality and other support exists within *this* service to enact the value within all of its activities and processes? In what ways are the awareness of the value and capabilities to support the value expressed in practice? Since this represents a personal responsibility incumbent on everyone involved, what support exists at run time to ensure that those responsibilities are upheld?

- *Validate::Verify*: What support does this service need so as to verify and audit its actual performance in relation to the respective value? What services would ensure that this service has indeed delivered that performance? What records and other sources are needed in this validation support? By what means are these "Verify and Audit" validation services delivered to this service? By what means are these "Verify and Audit" services themselves verified and audited for alignment to the value? Who or what is responsible for these services, and how they apply to this service?

As before, identify the services and product exchanges in each case. Add these to the model as *Service* entities and *Product* entities, linked to the service-in-focus via *flow* relations. Use either containment or *composition* relations to link each of these Service entities to the overall Validation *Service*. Annotate each *flow* relation here with a "*validate*" label, to indicate that the flow delivers validation services to the service-in-focus.

---

Again, be careful to avoid falling into layering mistakes in the modeling process here. Overall, there are a lot of useful insights to be gained here, about the nature of the enterprise, and about architectural risks and opportunities. The key concern to note, as with the other guidance services, is that the service-in-focus will not be viable – especially over the longer term – unless adequate and appropriate *validation* support is available for *each* value in the context.

# Investors and Beneficiaries

As described in Chapter 11, "Service Investors and Beneficiaries," the Investor and Beneficiary services respectively represent those who contribute value to the service, or to whom value is returned from the service, beyond and outside of the usual transactions of the service's supply chain. The relationships and service roles are as shown in Figure D-12.

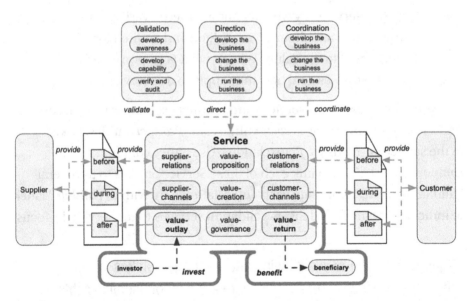

***Figure D-12.*** *Services: investors and beneficiaries*

Note that "value" here has a somewhat different meaning to "values" in the enterprise-values sense referenced by the validation services: the two terms are closely related, but they're not the same.

For our purposes here, "value" is likely to have a much broader meaning than money alone: we may need to track a myriad of different forms of value, and the ways they may be transformed from one type to another within the service itself. For example, in a business-startup context, people may invest time and skill and effort, and hope to receive monetary return, whereas in a non-profit context, people might invest money in the hope of seeing broader social benefit. These same overall principles may apply right down to the level of an individual web service or the like.

Also do be aware that although this is an essential part of the viability checklist, it can sometimes be misunderstood as "political": in commercial organizations in particular, there may be strong pressures to either ignore all non-monetary forms of value, or to try to force all forms of value into monetary terms. For our purposes here, though, we *do* need to model the actual forms of value in each context, *in their own terms, prior to any potential conversion to any other form such as money.* Failing to do so will invariably lead to architectural problems that can have serious impacts on overall viability – particularly via anti-clients and other kurtosis risks.

Questions to ask here include

- *Investor*: Who or what invests value in this service, in order to get it started, or to keep it running? What forms of value are delivered as investment in this service? Via what services, relationships, and exchanges are these investments delivered to this service?

- *Beneficiary*: Who or what receives value as a return from this service? What forms of value delivered by this service as returns to its beneficiaries? Via what services, relationships, and exchanges are these returns delivered by this service?

- *Transformation*: What are the differences, if any, between the forms of value that are invested, and the forms of value that are returned as benefits? By what means do these value transforms take place within this service?

- *Balance*: In what ways and to what extent are the *invest* and *benefit* relationships in balance, both before and after transformations of value within this service? What relationships with other services are needed to monitor that balance, and/or to take action to correct any perceived imbalance? If the two flows do not balance overall, what impact would this have on overall viability, both of this service and of other related services?

As usual, identify the services and product exchanges in each case. Add these to the model as *Service* entities and *Product* entities, linked to the service-in-focus via *flow* relations. If necessary, use either containment or *composition* relations to link each of these Service entities to the overall Investor or Beneficiary *Service*.

Annotate each *flow* relation here with an "*invest*" or "*benefit*" label, to indicate either that the flow delivers investment of some form to the service-in-focus, or that the service delivers benefits to a beneficiary. An "invest" *flow* will typically connect either to the *Service* as a whole, or to the *Value-Outlay* cell, since the latter represents an abstraction of the activities that manage costs and outgoing payments and the like. For much the same reasons, a "benefit" *flow* would typically connect either to the *Service* as a whole, or to its *Value-Return* cell.

---

Once again, do take care to avoid falling into layering mistakes. There are some very important and often enlightening insights to be gained here, again about the nature of the overall enterprise, and about architectural risks and opportunities. The key concern to note is that the service-in-focus may not be or remain viable unless it does have adequate and appropriate investor support, and that, in architectural terms, at least, the balance between investors and beneficiaries is appropriately managed.

---

# Iteration and Recursion

At this point we would have completed the viability checklist for that single service-in-focus – the *Service* entity with which we started. We could now apply the same checklist assessment, recursively and iteratively, to any of the *Service* entities that we have added to the model during this process: everything is, represents, or implies a service, so the same viability principles apply everywhere and at every level.

---

For obvious reasons, don't attempt to apply this to *everything*: by definition, it would take an infinite amount of time to complete the model! Instead, it's wise to hold to the guideline that we *only* create a model in response to an explicit business question, and *only* to the level of detail needed to answer or respond to that question.

---

In the same way, it can often be useful to do a drill-down into the details of a specific service, and apply the same viability assessment at the next level down; or to the next level upward, to a more abstract layer at which redesign and restructure becomes possible. (Or *levels* – again, iteration and recursion would apply in both directions all the way up and down the layers of abstraction.)

In drill-down or drill-up, we do need to be especially careful about the distinctions between layers of granularity and layers of abstraction, because it's very easy to get them confused here. Going up or down in granularity – *composition* relations – is just a change in detail: each "child" – or "parent" – service will handle a subset or superset of the service content and *Product* content of the initial service-in-focus. However, going up or down in abstraction – *realization* relations – involves a change in the *type* of detail that can be described: for example, Row-3 cannot contain descriptions of any specific technology or implementation method, whereas Row-4 can.

Beyond that, though, there are no real restrictions on what we can model in Enterprise Canvas, or why: we are welcome to iterate or recurse to our hearts' content, up and down the layers, and anywhere across the enterprise context.

# APPENDIX E

# Sources and Resources

## Collaborators

I would like to acknowledge and thank the following people (in alphabetical order) who played key roles in the development of core concepts, uses, and business applications for Enterprise Canvas:

- Casimir Artmann (Sweden) tested and applied the "everything is a service" concepts and practices in a major business-transformation project for a large vehicle manufacturer.

- Slade Beard (Australia) tested and refined the use of Enterprise Canvas in large projects in defense and other domains, and also provided the technical review for this book.

- Gavin Beckett (UK) used Enterprise Canvas methods with me to guide the development of a major business-transformation project for a large city in England.

- Shawn Callahan (Australia) helped me to explore how to embed business storytelling into Enterprise Canvas and its methods.

- Joseph Chittenden (UK) worked with me on design and more in our development of the Change-Mapping methods, built around Five Elements and Enterprise Canvas.

- Nate Gerber (Canada) tested live applications of Enterprise Canvas and related tools and methods for business needs in logistics, local government, social service, arts and theatre, and more.

- Milan Guenther (France), Annika Klyver (Sweden), and others at the Intersection Group applied Enterprise Canvas concepts and related methods to industrial design and system design.

- Cynthia Kurtz (USA) provided the core distinction between "order" and "unorder" in the sensemaking aspects of Enterprise Canvas.

- Helen Mills and Peter Tseglakof (Australia) brought me into the world of logistics and whole-enterprise architectures beyond IT, which then provided key parts of the practical basis for Enterprise Canvas.

- Bard Papegaaij (Netherlands) worked with me on linking soft-systems methods and human factors into Enterprise Canvas, and also on development of training courses for applications of Enterprise Canvas and related tools and methods.

- Jose Ramos (Australia) and others on the Strategic Foresight course at Swinburne University in Melbourne introduced me to the futures methods that underlie key aspects of Enterprise Canvas and its related tools.

- Helena Read (Australia) adapted Enterprise Canvas and other methods for use in environmental teaching materials and courses for schoolchildren in Australia, China, and other countries.

- Michael Smith Castillo (Mexico) was one of the key collaborators in the early developments for Enterprise Canvas, also working with me on business applications for the Five Elements model and the "holomap" service-context model, and in testing the work with clients across several industries in Mexico and Guatemala, upon which we built the fictional ZapaMex test case used throughout this book.

- Also my team at Wordsmiths, back in the late 1970s to mid-1980s in southwest England, as we built one of the world's first microcomputer-based typesetting businesses that provided a key precursor for desktop publishing and gave me the first-hand experiences upon which much of my later work on whole-enterprise architectures has been based.

There have been many other collaborators over the years, some of whom I cannot name for reasons of confidentiality and client security, who have worked with me on a diverse range of projects across many different industries around the world. I thank them all.

# Sources

If you're familiar with enterprise architecture or related fields, you will no doubt have recognized a few familiar frames among the various aspects of the Enterprise Canvas – if perhaps in somewhat unfamiliar form at times. Yet this should be no surprise, because a lot of effort has been made to ensure that the Canvas is compatible with other commonly used model types, to simplify translation to and from those models – such as in the example for Business-Model Canvas, as described in Appendix B.

The core idea that "everything is a service" is drawn from my book *The Service Oriented Enterprise*, which in turn draws on principles adapted in part from Stafford Beer's *Viable System Model* (of which more later).

- Tom Graves, *The Service-Oriented Enterprise: Enterprise Architecture and Viable Services* (Apress, 2023)

The concept of vision as an unchanging "guiding star," and the consistent structure for the bridge between that abstract vision and concrete everyday activities, is drawn in part from the ISO–9000:2000 international standard on quality systems.

- ISO–9000:2000: see Wikipedia, en.wikipedia.org/wiki/ISO_9000

The nine-cell structure for the core of the Enterprise Canvas is inspired in part by the Business Model Canvas, developed by Alex Osterwalder and described in the book *Business Model Generation*.

- Business Model Canvas: see Wikipedia, en.wikipedia.org/wiki/Business_Model_Canvas

- Alex Osterwalder, Yves Pigneur et al., *Business Model Generation: a handbook for visionaries, game-changers and challengers* (Wiley, 2011)

The Market Model was in part derived, though much-extended, from the assertion in the *Cluetrain Manifesto* that "markets are conversations." The remainder of the model comes from own work on the *tetradian* dimensions, as described in my book *Doing Enterprise Architecture*.

- Cluetrain Manifesto: see `www.cluetrain.com`

- Tom Graves, *Doing Enterprise Architecture: Process and Practice in the Real Enterprise* (Tetradian Books, 2009)

The layers for the Enterprise Canvas were adapted and extended from the Zachman Framework. Zachman uses five distinct rows or layers of abstraction to describe to sequence of change from future to present; I added one more layer above, and another below, to represent the unchanging future of the vision, and the unchangeable past of actual metrics and records.

- Zachman Framework: see Wikipedia, en.wikipedia. org/wiki/Zachman_Framework

The set of interrogatives – What, How, Where, Who, When, Why – used to identify lists of entities for Row-1 of the Enterprise Canvas was inspired in part from their usage in the Zachman Framework.

- Zachman Framework: as above

The matrix checklist used to in the Service-Content model to identify internal content for services and products is based in part on a much-amended version of the Zachman Framework, and also in part on my own work on the *tetradian* dimensions, as described in my book *Bridging the Silos*.

- Tom Graves, *Bridging the Silos: Enterprise Architecture for IT Architects* (Tetradian Books, 2008)

The method for assessing nodes in the Five Elements cycle within services was adapted in part from the VPEC-T (values, policies, events, content, trust) framework, developed by Nigel Green.

- VPEC-T: see Nigel Green and Carl Bate, *Lost in Translation: A Handbook for Information Systems in the 21st Century* (Evolved Technologist Press, 2007); also Wikipedia, en.wikipedia.org/wiki/VPEC-T

The guidance services for the Enterprise Canvas are adapted and extended from elements of Stafford Beer's Viable System Model (VSM), as originally described in his book *The Brain of the Firm* and used in the groundbreaking Cybersyn system in Chile in 1972. In VSM, the core service ("delivery service") is referred to as System-1, the coordination services as System-2, and the direction services as a collective of three distinct sub-services referred to as System–3, System–4, and System–5. The original for the generic validation services in the Enterprise Canvas was a single function for audit and review in VSM, referred to as System-3*. The extensions to VSM used in the Enterprise Canvas were first described in my book *The Service-Oriented Enterprise*, in which the validation services are referred to as "pervasive services."

- Stafford Beer, *Brain of the Firm* (Allen Lane, The Penguin Press, London, 1972)

- Patrick Hoverstadt, *The Fractal Organization: Creating Sustainable Organizations with the Viable System Model* (Wiley, 2008)

- Tom Graves, *The Service-Oriented Enterprise*: as above

- Viable System Model: see Wikipedia, en.wikipedia.org/wiki/Viable_System_Model

- Project Cybersyn: see Wikipedia, en.wikipedia.org/wiki/Project_Cybersyn

The systems principles referenced in various places throughout the text are derived and adapted from many different sources, such as Stafford Beer's VSM and Peter Senge's *The Fifth Discipline*. The predictability model is derived from an earlier model in my book *Inventing Reality*. The related methods for context-space mapping are derived from and described in my book *Everyday Enterprise Architecture*.

- VSM (Viable System Model): see above

- Peter Senge, *The Fifth Discipline* (Currency, 1990)

- Tom Graves, *Inventing Reality: Towards a Magical Technology* (Gateway Books, 1986 / Grey House, 2007)

- Tom Graves, *Everyday Enterprise Architecture: Sensemaking, Strategy, Structures, and Solutions* (Apress, 2022)

A common underlying theme that surfaces in some aspects of Enterprise Canvas, such as the service-flows model, is based on a Five Elements frame, adapted in part from Bruce Tuckman's "Group Dynamics" project-lifecycle model, together with the *wu xing* five-phase model that underpins much of traditional Chinese philosophy and medicine. Some other present-day business applications of this theme are described in my book *SEMPER and SCORE*.

- Tuckman Group Dynamics: see Wikipedia, en. wikipedia.org/wiki/Forming-storming-norming-performing

- Five Elements (*wu xing*): see Wikipedia, en.wikipedia. org/wiki/Wu_xing

- Tom Graves: *SEMPER and SCORE: enhancing enterprise effectiveness* (Tetradian Books, 2008)

There are probably many other sources for the underlying ideas in the Enterprise Canvas, some of which I have no doubt forgotten, but the preceding are the main examples.

## Other Resources

- Archimate: see Wikipedia, en.wikipedia.org/wiki/ArchiMate; also www.archimate.org and www.opengroup.org/archimate/

- Balanced Scorecard: see Wikipedia, en.wikipedia.org/wiki/Balanced_scorecard

- Blue Ocean Strategy: see Wikipedia, en.wikipedia.org/wiki/Blue_Ocean_Strategy

- Business Motivation Model (BMM): see businessrulesgroup.org/bmm.shtml

- Business Process Modeling Notation (BPMN): see Wikipedia, en.wikipedia.org/wiki/BPMN

- eTOM (Enhanced Telecom Operations Map): see Wikipedia, en.wikipedia.org/wiki/Enhanced_Telecom_Operations_Map

- ITIL (IT Infrastructure Library): see Wikipedia, en.wikipedia.org/wiki/Information_Technology_Infrastructure_Library

- Living organisation: see Arie de Geus, *The Living Company: Habits for Survival in a Turbulent Business Environment* (HBR Press, 2002)

- OODA (observe, orient, decide, act): see Wikipedia, en.wikipedia.org/wiki/OODA_loop

- PDCA (plan, do, check, act): see Wikipedia, en. wikipedia.org/wiki/PDCA

- Porter Five Forces: see Wikipedia: en.wikipedia.org/ wiki/Porter_five_forces_analysis

- Porter Value-Chain: see Wikipedia, en.wikipedia.org/ wiki/Value_chain

- RACI (responsible, assists, consulted, informed): see Wikipedia, en.wikipedia.org/wiki/Responsibility_ assignment_matrix

- Root-cause analysis: see Wikipedia, en.wikipedia.org/ wiki/Root_cause_analysis

- Shell General Business Principles: www.shell. com/sgbp

- Six Sigma: see Wikipedia, en.wikipedia.org/wiki/ Six_Sigma

- Taylorism and "scientific management": see Wikipedia, en.wikipedia.org/wiki/Scientific_management

- TOGAF (The Open Group Architecture Framework): see www.opengroup.org/togaf

- United Breaks Guitars: see Wikipedia, en.wikipedia. org/wiki/United_Breaks_Guitars

- Value-stream mapping: see Wikipedia, en.wikipedia. org/wiki/Value_stream_mapping

- VRMG (vision, role, mission, goal): see www. slideshare.net/tetradian/vision-role-mission- goal-a-framework-for-business-motivation

- Wicked-problems: see en.wikipedia.org/wiki/ Wicked_problem

# Rethinking Vision Bottom-Up: Example Organizations

- Swatch: see www.swatch.com

- MyM&Ms: see www.mms.com; see also the "Design Your Own" configurator at www.mms.com/en-gb/configurat or?customerType=D2C

- Mars Corporation: see www.mars.com

- Play-Doh: see Wikipedia, en.wikipedia.org/wiki/ Play-Doh

- Oceaneering: see www.oceaneering.com

- Nokia: see www.nokia.com

# Index

## A

Actors/entities
  business-transformation
    project, 76
  enterprise vision, 72
  shared enterprise, 71, 76, 77
  ZapaMex's vision, 73–75
Agile-development
  techniques, 18
Archimate, 250

## B

BPMN process-model, 110
Business model, 40
Business Model Canvas (BMC),
  254, 283
  definition, 284
  equivalent models, 283
  instructions, 286, 287
  organization-centric
    view, 284
Business Motivation Model (BRG),
  33, 254, 255, 361
Business Process Modeling
  Notation (BPMN), 10, 110,
  111, 229, 239–241

## C

Content-based layering, 38, 312, 313
Context-space mapping,
  253, 354, 360
"Customer-service" systems,
  25, 121, 141, 152

## D

Decomposition
  child services, 154
  each cell is service, 153
  granularity of services, 153
  real-world services, 151
  service model, 151
  services-within-services, 153
  ZapaMex, 152
Deployment model, 64, 67, 328
Direction services, 121, 124

## E

Enterprise Canvas
  asset-types/decision types, 281
  back-of-the-napkin sketch, 4
  BMC, 288, 289
  business transformation, 12

Printed in the United States
by Baker & Taylor Publisher Services

Printed in the United States
by Baker & Taylor Publisher Services